O MOTHER,
WHERE ART THOU?

BibleWorld

Series Editor: Philip R. Davies, University of Sheffield

BibleWorld shares the fruits of modern (and postmodern) biblical scholarship not only among practitioners and students, but also with anyone interested in what academic study of the Bible means in the twenty-first century. It explores our ever-increasing knowledge and understanding of the social world that produced the biblical texts, but also analyses aspects of the Bible's role in the history of our civilization and the many perspectives – not just religious and theological, but also cultural, political and aesthetic – which drive modern biblical scholarship.

Published:

Sodomy: A History of a Christian Biblical Myth
Michael Carden

Yours Faithfully: Virtual Letters from the Bible
Edited by: Philip R. Davies

Israel's History and the History of Israel
Mario Liverani

The Apostle Paul and His Letters
Edwin D. Freed

The Origins of the 'Second' Temple:
Persian Imperial Policy and the Rebuilding of Jerusalem
Diana Edelman

An Introduction to the Bible (Revised edition)
John Rogerson

The Morality of Paul's Converts
Edwin D. Freed

The Mythic Mind
Essays on Cosmology and Religion in Ugaritic and Old Testament Literature
N. Wyatt

History, Literature and Theology in the Book of Chronicles
Ehud Ben Zvi

Women Healing/Healing Women
The Genderization of Healing in Early Christianity
Elaine M. Wainwright

Symposia: Dialogues Concerning the History of Biblical Interpretation
Roland Boer

Forthcoming:

Linguistic Dating of Biblical Texts: An Introduction to Approaches and Problems
Ian Young and Robert Rezetko

Jonah's World: Social Sciences and the Reading of Prophetic Story
Lowell K. Handy

The Bible Says So!: From Simple Answers to Insightful Understanding
Edwin D. Freed

O MOTHER, WHERE ART THOU?

AN IRIGARAYAN READING OF THE BOOK OF CHRONICLES

JULIE KELSO

LONDON   OAKVILLE

Published by

UK: Equinox Publishing Ltd
Unit 6, The Village,
101 Amies St.,
London, SW11 2JW

US: DBBC,
28 Main Street,
Oakville, CT 06779

www.equinoxpub.com

First published 2007

© Julie Kelso 2007

British Library Cataloguing-in-Publication Data
A catalogue record for this book is available from the British Library.

Library of Congress Cataloging-in-Publication Data
Kelso, Julie, 1970-
  O mother, where art thou? : an Irigarayan reading of the book of
Chronicles / Julie Kelso.
      p. cm. -- (BibleWorld)
  Includes bibliographical references and index.
  ISBN 978-1-84553-323-6 (hb) -- ISBN 978-1-84553-324-3 (pbk.) 1.
Bible. O.T. Chronicles--Feminist criticism. 2. Women in the Bible. 3.
Mothers in the Bible. 4. Irigaray, Luce. I. Title.
  BS1345.6.W7K 2007
                          222'.606082--dc22

ISBN-10   1 84553 323 2   (hardback)
ISBN-10   1 84553 324 0   (paperback)

ISBN-13   978 1 84553 323 6   (hardback)
ISBN-13   978 1 84553 324 3   (paperback)

Typeset by CA Typesetting Ltd, www.sheffieldtypesetting.com
Printed and bound in Great Britain by Lightning Source UK Ltd., Milton Keynes and Lightning Source Inc., La Vergne, TN

For Lillian Alexander

Try to imagine the beginning ahead of you, and the end behind you, and the habitual scene of representation starts to vacillate. Try to imagine it with no way out, and no hidden agenda, in the following scenario: in an eternal present, in the future perfect, in a futurable conditional – not some eternal return of the same – and with absolutely no reappropriation of the beginning in the origin. What vertigo without our reassuring representation of space! What direction do you move in? How do you begin speaking?

What do you say anyway? What meaning can language still have?

(Luce Irigaray, *To Speak Is Never Neutral*)

I have read each page of my mother's voyage.
I have read each page of her mother's voyage.
I have learned their words as they learned Dickens'.
I have swallowed these words like bullets.
But I have forgotten the last guest – terror.

(Anne Sexton, "Crossing the Atlantic")

CONTENTS

Acknowledgments

I cannot remember the reason for my being in the State Library of Queensland some time in 1994. I think I was researching a paper I would never write on an exchange between two art historians and critics – Michael Fried and Linda Nochlan – concerning Courbet. What I do remember is picking up a book (and I have no idea what that book was, only that its author was a feminist critic of something) and becoming utterly engrossed in the author's statements about Margaret Atwood's *The Handmaid's Tale* (Atwood, 1986). I had not read *The Handmaid's Tale* at that stage, but from what this unremembered author told me, I knew I had to do so.

I also knew that something else was building, because I was struck by a particular feature of Atwood's dystopia that my forgotten feminist was telling me: women were not allowed to read the Bible. Why not? I could understand women not being allowed to read philosophy, literature, or law, or just about anything else other than the Bible, which for me was a book (my first error) that told what were pretty much rotten stories about men, war and the Lord (in whom I didn't, and still don't, believe). Actually, in a dystopian future, wouldn't this be the *only* book women *were* allowed to read? It is, after all, the book that has historically and culturally defined our worth and our worthlessness as women. In short, isn't the Bible the locus and guarantee of women's silence? How could I possibly get any ideas from it regarding the future?

Around the same time I began my love affair with the writings of the French philosopher and psychoanalyst, Luce Irigaray. I say "love affair," because back then, at the age of twenty-four, I really had little ability to understand many of the philosophical and theoretical maneuvers Irigaray was asking me to make. But I loved her writing just the same. And I persisted with my love. With Irigaray, and later with the Hebrew Bible, I came to realize that there was and is more to reading than simple comprehension, simple "knowledge," whatever that might mean, past or present. In fact, one of the most seductive aspects of reading, writing, learning, *and living* is the unknowable, which is yet also, the uncanny. Rather than taking flight from the difficulties of living, including the difficulties faced in our intellectual lives, I've learnt the pleasures of an initial *surrender to the unknown*. With Irigaray, this meant letting myself be seduced by a woman writer whose intellect and poetics *refused to let me go*, despite my ignorance. I might say that I never rejected her. But neither did she ever reject me. Between the two of us, the woman philosopher and the woman reader, something akin to love and trust arose. She later taught me the dangers involved, for women at least, when it comes to such an interaction. Together, I think, she has enabled me to thrive.

With the Hebrew Bible, this newfound mode of intellectual engagement and reading meant I could legitimately explore ways of encountering the thoroughly alien literary world without trying to own it, to conquer it, to tame it so that I might feel more comfortable in my own very different world. In short, my intellectual lover/mother taught me how to read and indeed love the foundational texts of my world, without having to "believe" the sacred words I was reading, and without having to own them through a logico-temporal, historical-cultural conquest. That is, through and with Irigaray, I have learnt a mode of reading and critical-analytical thinking that refuses to believe that the (sacred) texts of our cultural past are there simply to be tied down with the weight of a knowledge and an interpretation that has the effect of taming that unknowable "thing" that is the past itself.

But most importantly, Irigaray taught me how to listen. Not, though, as some mute imperialist intent on knowing the meaning of these ancient words and (hi)stories in their own time, as if even possible. And certainly not as an apologist for a belief system I grew up within and which I still inhabit, even if as an atheist. Which brings me to the most difficult question I continue to face: why would a feminist atheist want to read the Hebrew Bible, particularly if she has no interest in ancient history? Why can I not put this material away and pursue other avenues? In time, I began to realize that Irigaray's work was offering me the chance to listen to our foundational texts with both a *future-oriented* politics and an empathy; a charitable mode of reading which enables a therapeutic encounter with the past, *for the purpose of change in the future*. In a way, this thesis is an oblique and perhaps even nebulous answer to this question I find so difficult. And indeed, perhaps this is why Atwood's women in a dystopian future are prohibited from reading biblical texts? Perhaps...

And so, I begin with the end – the book of Chronicles being the final book in the Hebrew canon. Perhaps I should have begun with the beginning, with Genesis. However, certain features of biblical, feminist scholarship led me to the last book of the Hebrew Bible. For Chronicles is the one biblical book that women have failed to engage with in any substantial, feminist-politico-critical manner. When it comes to Chronicles, the relative silence of women in the text is replicated by the relative silence of feminist biblical scholars concerning Chronicles. Furthermore, so far in biblical studies, we have only a few concerted efforts regarding an engagement with the incredibly difficult early work of Luce Irigaray. So apparent is this negligence that I feel it is necessary to draw these two – Luce Irigaray's psychoanalytic reading practice and the book of Chronicles – together. What may come of this? What splendid encounters await us in the future? I humbly begin to engage with this most important question.

*

This book, a revised version of my doctoral thesis, would not have come into the light of day without those people who have withstood me over the last seven years. First, I must thank my associate supervisor Associate Professor Edgar Conrad. A hapless, semi-intelligent individual walked into his "Introduction to Feminist Interpretation of the Bible" course in 1996, with very little idea of her future. Ed Conrad sent her on a career path that both he and she might enjoy, and from which they *both* might learn. Associate Professor Conrad is one of those rare academics – in today's economics-driven, still highly competitive, masculine intellectual climates – who, while in the twilight of his career, has never stopped imagining the possibilities of reading and interpreting the texts that have filled his career life. Ed Conrad is a *true* scholar, whose passion for the Hebrew Bible, and for the students who wish to read it, extends to all modes of reading and interpreting it. He and his wife Dr Linda Conrad have verily laid the foundations for this scholarly life. One could not ask for better intellectual, social, and emotional role models.

Second, is this. Two years into my thesis I was longing for the sharp mind of a feminist mother who would scold her child and direct her *and raise her* (as Maya Angelou [1988] once said). I have used this clause for a reason. In her novel *I Know Why the Caged Bird Sings*, Angelou learns that the successful mother raises her children to know how to live, how to cope with the life they are about to encounter, and how to cope with the living they will have to endure. She raises them *up*. This is something the mother is proud of, and something she insists the child must remember. I think this is what the feminist scholar's successful supervision of a woman student also entails; what the female student must learn. Like Angelou, this is what I have learnt. And this is what I will always remember of, and with ineffable gratitude to, my principal supervisor Dr Michelle Boulous Walker. I never dreamed that the great Australian philosopher Michelle Boulous Walker would spread her wings for me. But she did. So began my journey into *real* self-belief. I owe her so much. She reminds me why I am a feminist, why I've always wanted to be that way, and why it is *good and necessary* to pursue feminist thinking.

Third, in my seven years as a doctoral candidate, I have met people whom I cherish so much, not just for their kindness towards me, but for their intellectual vigor and ethical practices: Marie Porter, Tamara Ditrich, Primos Pecenko, Alexander Pecenko, Jenny Price, Maryanne Dever, Brian Castro, Michael Carden, Patrick Kearney, Marguerite La Caze, Deb Jordan, and Carole Ferrier. These people make me reject that oft-creeping cynicism concerning the institution, for it is people like these who make the institution great, now and in the future. I wish them everything that is good. Thanks must also go to Roland Boer for reading many drafts of the earlier chapters and offering invaluable comments and intellectual support.

Finally, and most importantly, thanks must go to my daughter Lillian. Lillian was eighteen months old when I began. She is now eight and a half years old. She has no memory of a mum who isn't half-mad with a PhD thesis riding her back. Sweet one, of course, this work is dedicated to you.

*

Finally, a note concerning style. All translations of the Hebrew text (copied using the *Bibleworks* programme) are my own, unless otherwise stated. I have chosen to utilize the *Bibleworks* programme for two reasons. Firstly, it meant that I did not have to type the Masoretic text letter by letter (or consonant, vowel, consonant, vowel, etc.), which is very time-consuming and apt for error. Not that "copying and pasting" avoids error. With the *Bibleworks* Hebrew, unless one carefully situates the cursor, one will lose a vowel or two. All efforts have been made to ensure the correct representation of the Masoretes' (digitally reproduced) text. Where I have copied large sections of the Hebrew, I have left all accent marks in place. However, when I copy individual words and phrases and place them within my own discussion, I have removed the accent marks.

However, the major importance of including so much of the Hebrew is that it means that I can ask my reader to encounter the visual text

I encounter when I read. This Hebrew text is exquisitely beautiful, disconcertingly unfamiliar, and utterly seductive. In reading this book, the importance of my utilizing this text will become thoroughly apparent.

Julie Kelso
Toowong
March 2006

INTRODUCTION: A QUESTION OF SILENCE

> So some speak and others are silent
> (Irigaray, 1985a: 257)

Throughout this book I argue that the book of Chronicles silences women in specific ways, most radically through their association with maternity. Drawing upon the earlier, psychoanalytically-inspired work of Luce Irigaray and the more recent work of Michelle Boulous Walker, I argue that we may discern two principal strategies of silencing women in Chronicles: disavowal and repression. In its simplest form, the silencing of women takes place through both an explicit and implicit strategy of excluding them from the central narrative action. Largely banished from the central action, they are hardly able to contribute to the production of Israel's past. On a more complex level, however, women are most effectively silenced through their association with maternity, because the maternal body is both disavowed and repressed in Chronicles. The association of women with maternity, along with the disavowal and the repression of the maternal body as "origin" of the masculine subject, effects and guarantees the silence of the feminine, enabling "man" to imagine himself as sole producer of his world. These strategies of silencing the "feminine" need to be understood in relation to the relative absence of women from the narrative world of Chronicles. This absence, however, has passed by largely unnoticed in Biblical Studies. Chronicles itself is understood as an *inclusive* rather than *exclusive* text. However, I argue that Chronicles depends on the absence and silence of women for its imaginary coherence.

Indeed, this relative silence concerning women extends beyond the biblical text itself into the world of Chronicles scholarship. Chronicles represents a startling absence in feminist studies of the Hebrew Bible. To date, no sustained feminist analysis of Chronicles exists.[1] In fact, it is the only book in the Hebrew Bible that has not warranted a volume in the *Feminist Companion to the Hebrew Bible*, now in its second series. Why, of all the texts in the Hebrew Bible, is Chronicles the only one that does not attract feminist critique or even revision? Within biblical studies in general, Chronicles has always had a rather problematic status, particularly when compared to its apparent sibling, Samuel–Kings, which is valued as both historically more viable a "source," and as a far more "human," yet theologically refined textual body. And, we might add, a textual body that is adorned with more "sexy" narrative apparel. Chronicles, however, excludes most of the salacious stories that Samuel–Kings savours, especially when it comes to the rather unfortunate weaknesses of David and his son Solomon, both of whom are highly idealized in Chronicles. Indeed, it is to a large extent through the absences of Bathsheba, Abishag, and Solomon's foreign wives, that both father and son become rather golden in the eyes of Chronicles, not to mention the reader. And so, if Chronicles is marked by an absence of stories about women, then feminist biblical studies, in its turn, is marked by the absence of Chronicles. This dearth of feminist reading means that there is very little work in Chronicles scholarship with which I can engage on shared feminist ground. It is almost as if the silenced feminine has successfully been transferred to the institutional level. Indeed, what I am suggesting is that the silencing of the "feminine" in Chronicles has been successfully transferred to contemporary biblical scholarship.

And so, here, I begin with a summary of the scholarship that understands Chronicles as a unique, post-exilic text because of its so-called ideology of inclusion, scholarship that ignores what is the obvious absence of many of the stories about women from the alternative history of Israel. Following this, and concluding this Introduction, I provide a brief outline of the chapters to come.

1. *"All Israel" and the "Inclusive Ideology of Identity"*[2] *in Chronicles*

The book of Chronicles is a "sacred" text for which origins or beginnings are a major concern. It provides an alternative, overwhelmingly masculine past, said to constitute the religio-political history of Israel. As Sara Japhet notes, the history of Israel is presented within Chronicles

> from beginning to "beginning," that is, from the inception of human existence with Adam, through the destruction of the first commonwealth during the reign of Zedekiah, to the new commencement with the declaration of Cyrus. It thus constitutes a comprehensive parallel to the earlier biblical historiography from Genesis to Kings – commonly designated the "Deuteronomistic history" – with its conclusion pointing to a new era (Japhet, 1993: 8).

It would seem, then, that Chronicles is a text fascinated with beginnings. While many readers of Chronicles are keen to point out the overt attention paid to institutions such as the monarchy and the temple cult, to my knowledge no reader has attempted an analysis of what seems to be an obsession with institut*ing*. It is not just that Chronicles moves "from beginning to beginning," as Japhet suggests, but that all through Chronicles we witness an obsession with the problem of beginning, of fixing upon who or what constitutes the founding moment for "Israel": Adam? Abraham? Jacob/Israel? Saul? David? And what of Moses? Chronicles does not display much interest in portraying the law-giver as a crucial founding figure. However, one thing is common to all of the possible founding moments espoused by the "Chronicler" – masculinity.

Of course, it can (and should) be argued that the entire body of the sacred text known as the Hebrew Bible presents us with a masculine understanding of the past, present, and future, particularly in relation to origins, their purpose, and their effects. Yet, what is interesting about Chronicles is its manifest concern to "return" to the past in order to effect some change in the present from which it arises (generally presumed within biblical studies to be a post-exilic production). Furthermore, the "present" context of the production of Chronicles is also a present within which it functions as a possible catalyst for future change. The past is something that must be returned to, and reworked, without concern for historical "fact," so that some unimaginable future may unfold from a present that currently forecloses all possibility of doing so. This understanding of origins, and of the past, in relation to the present and the future – as Sara Japhet hints at and Roland Boer (1997) explores in greater theoretical detail – can be read as a *utopian* desire. But, the relationship between origins or beginnings and the past, present, and future in Chronicles, while arguably utopian, participates in a foundational denial. Indeed, as I argue throughout this book, it is the disavowal and repression of corporeal origins, the disavowal and repression of originary maternal space, which *enables* the construction of the socio-political vision of Chronicles. The alternative history given to us here prepares an unimaginable future that enables the progress of the masculine and of men, at the expense of the feminine and of women; a desire readable in the final sentence of Chronicles:

מִי־בָכֶם מִכָּל־עַמּוֹ יְהוָה אֱלֹהָיו עִמּוֹ וְיָעַל׃

Whoever is among you of all his people, may the Lord his god be with *him*. Let *him* go up (2 Chron. 36:23).

According to biblical scholars, the book of Chronicles gives us a rather original picture of Israel. Crucial to the development of this picture is the frequent use of the term "all Israel."[3] While this term appears a number of times in the so-called Deuteronomistic "sources" of Chronicles, it is, as Sara Japhet points out, far more frequent in Chronicles (Japhet, 1997: 270-71). According to Japhet, outside of Chronicles the term "all Israel" has a variety of meanings. It may refer to:

a. the people in its entirety (e.g. Deut. 1:1; 5:1; 11:6);
b. all the people, excluding one named tribe or group (e.g. Judg. 20:1, 34);
c. the northern kingdom alone (e.g. 1 Kgs 14:13, 18; 15:33);
d. an entire segment of the people (e.g. 1 Kgs 15: 27; 16:16); or
e. an assembly of people gathered at one place (e.g. 1 Kgs 8:62, 65).

In Chronicles, too, the term "all Israel" is used inconsistently. It refers to the entire people with all its tribes and components (2 Chron. 29:24; 30:5; 35:3), to the Northern Kingdom alone (2 Chron. 11:13; 13:4, 15; 30:1, 6), and less frequently, to the Southern Kingdom alone (2 Chron. 12:1; 24:8; 28:23). For Japhet, these inconsistencies indicate that the Chronicler employed a broad definition of Israel's identity. And, she notes, this inclusive broadening is somewhat mirrored by the geographical expansion that takes place throughout the period of the divided kingdoms: non-Judean tribes move to Judah during the reign of Rehoboam (2 Chron. 11:13-14, 16), but the boundaries of Judah remain unchanged, restricted to the territory of Judah and Benjamin; during the reign of Asa, the boundaries expand to include a few Ephraimite cities (2 Chron. 15:8), while people from the tribes of Manasseh, Ephraim, and Simeon join forces with Judah (2 Chron. 15:9); during Hezekiah's reign, couriers travel to Ephraim, Manessah and Zebulun to proclaim the forthcoming Passover in Jerusalem (2 Chron. 30:10); and, at the time of Josiah's reforms, the kingdom reaches from Simeon to Naphtali to include "all the lands that belonged to the people of Israel" (2 Chron. 34:33) (Japhet, 1997: 291-98). In other words, Chronicles manifests an effort "to revitalize the concept of 'all Israel' in the widest possible sense" (Japhet, 1997: 299).

Generally speaking, as a post-exilic text, Chronicles is interesting for its somewhat inclusive tendencies when it comes to defining just who constitutes the people of Israel. Of course, as the genealogies make evident, the people belonging to the tribe of Judah especially, because of the Davidic connection, along with the people of the tribes of Benjamin and Levi, are constructed as the most important people. Geographically, narrative emphasis is on the Southern Kingdom of Judah, and more specifically Jerusalem and its religious cult, largely ignoring the Northern Kingdom, and passing over the history of the rival city of Samaria (Ewald, 1867: 174; cf. Dyck, 1998: 28-29). And, in certain narratives there are highly negative references to the Northern Kingdom of

Israel. Most notable is Abijah's speech to Jeroboam (2 Chron. 13:4-12), which insists that the Davidic kingship is god-given and that, because Jeroboam and the Israelites ("all Israel") have rebelled against the Davidic line, and against the Judahites who follow correct cultic procedures, they are doomed to fail in their battle with Judah. In other words, because the northerners are against the Davidic monarchy, they are also against Yahweh.

However, there is an emphasis in Chronicles on the (at least) twelve tribes,[4] represented by the sons of Jacob, as constitutive of Israel as a whole. In the genealogies, Chronicles gives us a fairly literal rendering of this understanding in 1 Chron. 2:1-2, which gives us the sons of Jacob (called "Israel" in 2:1, as he is consistently throughout the book as a whole; see below):

אֵלֶּה בְּנֵי יִשְׂרָאֵל רְאוּבֵן שִׁמְעוֹן לֵוִי וִיהוּדָה יִשָּׂשכָר וּזְבֻלוּן׃

דָּן יוֹסֵף וּבִנְיָמִן נַפְתָּלִי גָּד וְאָשֵׁר׃

These are the sons of Israel: Reuben, Simeon, Levi, Judah, Issachar, Zebulun, Dan, Joseph, Benjamin, Naphtali, Gad, and Asher (1 Chron. 2:1-2).

Thus, Israel is composed of the twelve tribes. That more than the twelve principal tribes appear throughout Chronicles (for example, in the lists of the Levitical cities [1 Chron. 6:39-66] there are fourteen tribes mentioned, and the military list of 1 Chron. 12:23-40 has fourteen, perhaps fifteen tribal components) indicates once again, according to Japhet, the inclusive strategy of the book's author.

Furthermore, unlike its post-exilic siblings, in particular the books of Ezra and Nehemiah, Chronicles does not present a consistently harsh polemic against the people living in the north or against "foreigners."[5] Indeed, along with the many non-Israelite figures mentioned in the genealogies ("foreigners" who thus contribute to the production of Israel's identity in the past), the narrative of the Judahite monarchy includes many intriguingly tolerant references to the people living in the north, particularly during the reigns of Hezekiah and Josiah (2 Chron. 30:1-31 and 2 Chron. 34:33, for example). As Sara Japhet notes, the attitude to the Northern Kingdom in Chronicles is somewhat ambivalent (Japhet, 1997: 318), making it difficult to argue that Chronicles is unequivocally anti-Israel and anti-Samaritan.[6]

For Williamson (1977), as for Japhet, the Chronicler, because he was against the predominant ethnocentricity of his time, was an inclusivist.[7] Williamson describes the inclusivist theme found in Chronicles as an attempt to

> redress the balance with those who, concerned to avoid the dangers of syncretism and assimilation, had allowed the Jerusalem community so to close in on itself as even to exclude some who had a rightful claim to participation. He achieved this by demonstrating from the history of the divided monarchy that a faithful nucleus does not exclude others, but is a representative centre to which all the children of Israel may be welcomed if they will return (Williamson, 1977: 140).

But, given the condemnations against the North in many instances, can we say with any certainty that our author was strictly inclusivist? Japhet argues that these condemnations are not against the people of the North, but against the geographical region, the kingdom itself (Japhet, 1997: 317-18). In post-exilic Judah, Japhet suggests that the inhabitants of Samaria, including the "resident aliens," were considered to be

> descendants of Israelite tribes, the Judeans' brothers and an organic part of the people of Israel. We may say that the Chronicler calls for an end to tension and hatred between segments of the people and summons all Israel to unite in worshipping YHWH in Jerusalem (Japhet, 1997: 334).

This broadening of the definition of Israel's identity extends to non-Israelite groups living in Judah, the "resident aliens" or גרים. According to Japhet, Chronicles ascribes a particular meaning to the word גר, one fairly consistent with a later, post-exilic understanding of the term. The usual biblical meaning of גר is someone who is forced to leave his own village or tribe, whether alone or with his family, because of natural disasters, or a murder accusation, and so forth, and who seeks refuge and residence in a different place, only with diminished social, economic, legal, and religious rights. As such, the term signifies a particular social status. In Second Commonwealth Judaism, however, the term becomes a religious one, referring to those foreigners who have denounced paganism to practice the monotheistic religion of the Israelites (Ezra 6:21; Neh. 10:28-30; Isa. 56:3-8; Tob. 1:8). In Chronicles, the גרים refer to two groups: the remnant of the Canaanites (Amorites, Hittites, Perizzites, Hivites, and Jebusites) living in the land during David's and Solomon's reign (1 Chron. 22:2; 2 Chron. 2:16), and the people who come to Jerusalem from all around to celebrate Hezekiah's Passover (2 Chron. 30:25). According to Japhet, who bases her understanding of the apparent meaning of גר in other post-exilic biblical literature, it is most likely that the גרים in Chronicles are no longer considered to be foreigners in the land:

> At the very minimum, it is possible to understand *"ger"* in the book of Chronicles as we find it in Priestly literature – a sociological term for an alien who could participate in the religious life of the community. However,

> it is more likely that Chronicles already uses the term in its later sense: a *ger* is a member of a foreign people who has joined the people of Israel, adopted their religion, and thus lost his foreign identity... Chronicles describes these members of foreign peoples as "*gerim*" and thereby transforms them into a segment of the Israelite community. As a result of this transformation, there are no longer any foreigners living in the land of Israel (Japhet, 1997: 346).

Japhet also cites the examples of intermarriages within the genealogies of Chronicles (1 Chronicles 1–9) as further evidence that "marrying a member of the people transforms a foreigner, whether man or woman, into an Israelite, and the offspring of that marriage are, unquestionably, Israelites" (Japhet, 1997: 350). Her point is that these examples of intermarriage in the genealogies (1 Chron. 2:3, 17; 2:34-5; 4:17; 7:14) emphasize that Israel's identity must be understood to include a broad range of peoples, especially foreign wives who bear children, now considered to belong within the tribes of Israel (especially Judah and Manasseh).[8] Thus, within the book of Chronicles, foreigners join the people of Israel in two ways: they may marry an Israelite and become an integral part of the tribal system; or, because רג is now understood as someone who, upon taking up the religion of Israel, effectively *is* an Israelite, the tribal framework broadens to incorporate new elements. Japhet insists that both of these examples of the inclusiveness of Chronicles "communicate the ideal of 'all Israel' – the people of Israel at its broadest, perfectly united as one people" (Japhet, 1997: 351).

Jonathan Dyck agrees with the argument of Japhet and Williamson that Chronicles gives us a radically different "picture" and indeed understanding of Israel compared to Ezra–Nehemiah (Dyck, 1998: 77-125). This difference concerning the ideology of identity, Dyck argues, hinges on the differing approaches to the exile and its effects. For Ezra and Nehemiah, exile effects both the depopulation of the land of Israel and a repopulation of the land with foreigners. The exile thus constructs the distinction between the returnees, those who constitute "Israel" for the books of Ezra and Nehemiah, and the rest who are known as either non-Israelites or as "the people of the land." Whereas Ezra–Nehemiah understands Judah and Israel as both exiled, with Judah returning as "Israel," Chronicles refers only to the exile of the North with respect to the Transjordanian tribes (Rueben, Gad, and East Manasseh; 1 Chron. 5:26-27), thus implying that the majority of the northern kingdom remained in the land (Dyck, 1998: 120). Thus, according to Chronicles

> the exile and return does not leave Judah as the sole remnant of Israel on the basis of which it can then claim to be the sole inheritor of the name

> Israel. *It does not establish an inside/outside distinction.* The exile is simply not remembered in the same way as it is in Ezra–Nehemiah. For the Chronicler, the exile is a gap that is overcome, as it is in 2 Chronicles 36, and the bridging of the gap between "pre-exilic" and "post-exilic" has the effect of making the middle term "exile" all but disappear. This blurring of the "then" and the "now" creates a degree of tension in the work which is, I would argue, rooted in a post-exilic struggle to fashion a new ideology of identity: an identity wherein the exile is *both* remembered and overcome (Dyck, 1998: 121; his italics).

As many have noted, Chronicles does not acknowledge the Exodus and conquest traditions (Japhet, 1979; Japhet, 1997: 363-68; Wright, 1997: 157-58). Instead, as the number of geographical references in the genealogies make clear, the image of Israel as a people in relation to the land is one of eternal occupation:

> The genealogies describe Israel as it always was, its inner structure and geographical place. It treats of space not time. There is no contingency, no development, no promise to Abraham, no Moses, no exodus, no Sinai, no conquest, no point at which Israel came into being. *Israel emerged gradually and naturally from Adam, Abraham and Israel.* Israel emerged *autochthonously* in the land of Israel. This is God's order. Israel among the nations. Israel as always in the land (Dyck, 1998: 122; my italics).

Dyck goes on to develop the important argument that identity is inextricably linked, in Chronicles, with both legitimacy and hegemony (on the part of Jerusalem over all the land of Israel), and furthermore that identity and legitimacy are sustained in terms of an understanding of the origins of the theocratic "kingdom of Yahweh" as situated in the Jerusalem temple. However, my interest here is with Dyck's argument that Chronicles eliminates a sense of inside/outside when it comes to the identity of the people of Israel. Obviously this point is a further elaboration of the inclusivist arguments for Chronicles, and as Dyck points out, this idea is tied to an understanding of Israel and her origins in the land. Chronicles presents Israelite identity in terms of both an eternal (because tied directly to Adam, the first man) and *natural* entity, one which emerges "*autochthonously* in the land of Israel." In other words, the Israelites emerge "from the soil," as it were, with the land thus belonging to them because of their status as first inhabitants. From Adam, it seems, Israel simply emerges as a natural entity. There are no real debts to forefathers such as Abraham, Moses, or Joshua, who, according to the so-called Deuteronomist's version of the past, had to fight for the land their god bestowed upon them to enable Israel as a people to emerge and become strong in that land.[9]

This alternative image of "all Israel" as a united Israel embracing all who follow the laws of the monotheistic Jerusalem cult, including non-Israelite peoples (who, the genealogies teach us, participate in the production of Israel's past identity anyway) is, of course, highly idealized. One of the more interesting recent studies of Chronicles is Roland Boer's *Novel Histories* (1997), which argues that this idealization in Chronicles may be read as utopian desire. In other words, we may read Chronicles as if it were utopian fiction, and, indeed, even as if it were the related genre of science fiction:

> Chronicles constructs a world with a smoothly operative deity, a king-ship, people, and a whole range of personnel all devoted to the proper operation of the temple cult. It also constructs a history that is comparable with material found in Genesis to Kings (especially Samuel–Kings), but which differs time and again on historical events and sequences. Or, in Myers [*sic*] words, Chronicles contains "a conception of the saved people, those who had returned from exile, joined by those who had remained in the land and who were ready to accept the returnees' direction and rule, dwelling in the chosen place of the Lord and maintaining their relationship with him in purity and in a kind of magnificent isolation from other peoples" (Myers 1965: lxxxiv). Myers's description might as well be a plot outline for a science fiction novel, set on another planet or perhaps on a post-Holocaust earth (Boer, 1997: 165-66).

I can not, here, go into the intricacies of Boer's highly sophisticated Marxist reading of Chronicles, which operates on a number of inter-related levels. Essentially, however, Boer's argument is that Chronicles presents us with an ideal or utopian Israel, distinct from the dystopian picture provided by the Deuteronomistic History:

> Whereas the latter presents an increasingly apostate people and leader-ship, the former has a much more positive picture of both people and kingship, for whom the exile to Babylon becomes something of an unfor-tunate interlude. In presenting an ideal or utopian past, with the obedience or disobedience of king and people functioning as a trigger for immediate divine favour or disfavour, Chronicles also generates a hope for a future in which such an ideal state will be realized (Boer, 1997: 138).

As Boer points out, this understanding of Chronicles as utopian text is consistent with the vast material that sees messianic, eschatological and theocratic themes dominating and distinguishing the literary world of Chronicles.[10] According to all of these readings, including Boer's, "all Israel" functions as an inclusive ideal, albeit one fraught with contradictions. But, this ideology of inclusivism is one of *ethnic* inclusion. Boundaries may loosen around the concept of ethnic difference, but can we really claim that Chronicles is *gender*-inclusive, in the traditional (though too simplistic) sense of an ideology that willingly advocates the inclusion of women as integral and active – indeed *audible* – members of Israelite society, as it is portrayed in Chronicles?

The picture of the past is overwhelmingly masculine in Chronicles, though there are a handful of female characters and references to women throughout. While a number of female names appear in the genealogies, they hardly hold an equality of presence compared to the overwhelmingly masculine nature of this specific rendering of Israel's history and identity. Furthermore, the narrative of Chronicles almost writes out the presence of women. While there are a number of references to women in general, and a number of formulaic references to the mothers of some of the kings, there are actually only seven cases where female characters appear as integral to the story in some way: Michal, Pharaoh's daughter, the Queen of Sheba, Maacah, Athaliah, Jehoshebeath, and Huldah. All in all, the political, religious, and social past depicted in Chronicles – as what constitutes the "post-exilic" past of "Israel" – is almost exclusively a male affair. Indeed, when we consider the alternative pasts of Israel constructed within the other books of the Hebrew Bible, the relative *silence* of women in Chronicles can – and I think *should* – be read as one of its *constitutive* features.

In direct contrast to my own argument in this book, Labahn and Ben Zvi (2003) claim that the presence of a number of female figures in the genealogies of Chronicles effectively generates a gender-inclusive ideology. They acknowledge that women are largely represented as performing traditional, patriarchal roles such as mother, wife, daughter, and sister (of men), but claim that there are a significant number of women "described as successfully fulfilling roles usually associated within the main (male) discourses of the time" (Labahn and Ben Zvi, 2003: 457-58). For Labahn and Ben Zvi, the "substantial number of instances in which women took upon the roles traditionally carried out by males..." meant that the genealogies "taught its intended and primary readers again and again that gender (and ethnic) boundaries could, were, and by inference can and should be transgressed by the Yehudite community on occasion, with divine blessing, and resulting in divine blessing" (Labahn and Ben Zvi, 2003: 477). I suggest that these females (who actually aren't that substantial in number) and their assigned roles serve to further bolster the importance of male activities, at the expense and devaluation of women's. Furthermore, they even claim that childbirth, as an act only women's bodies are capable of performing in "reality," is represented and acknowledged in the genealogies:

> Needless to say, the male literati responsible for this literature were well aware that only women had the biological ability to give birth to children and therefore to maintain, through the continuous sequence of (female) childbirth, the continuation of a genealogical line and of society as a whole. It is worth stressing that any genealogical list therefore, at least implicitly, acknowledges and communicates the centrality of childbirth and of the females of the society, even if they remain unmentioned in the literary portrait, and if they are excluded from the explicit wording of the text. In fact, these "erasures" of women speak volumes (Labahn and Ben Zvi, 2003: 458-59).

Indeed it does! Labahn and Ben Zvi seem to be suggesting, however, that the very form of genealogy acknowledges women's role in reproduction. Why, then, we need to ask (and I do, in Chapter 3) are male birthing verbs far more substantial than the female birthing verbs? Why is there not a mother mentioned for every son? As I shall argue in this book, the issue of childbirth and the maternal body are directly related to the *silence* of women, *not their acknowledgment or validation*.

It is noteworthy that in Chronicles the stories of David and Solomon largely omit those of the women associated with them elsewhere in the Hebrew Bible. For stories concerning Bathsheba (2 Samuel 11–12; 1 Kings 1:11-31; 2:13-24), Tamar (2 Samuel 13), the woman from Tekoa (2 Samuel 14), Absalom's daughter Tamar (2 Sam. 16:27), David's concubines (2 Sam. 16:20-23; 20:3), the maidservant at En-rogel (2 Sam. 17:17-20), the wise woman of Abel Beth-maacah (2 Sam. 20:16-22), Rizpah and Michal (2 Sam. 21:8ff), Abishag (1 Kgs 1:1-4), the two women who test Solomon's wisdom (1 Kgs 3:16-28), and Solomon's foreign wives (1 Kings 11), we have to go to the other, "Deuteronomistic," history. There are many other female characters from the books of Samuel and Kings missing from Chronicles, not to mention the absences of major female characters from Genesis, such as Eve, Sarah, Leah, and Rachel, in the genealogies of Chronicles. Actually, if we compare the "history" of Israel, from Genesis through to 2 Kings, with that "history" in the book of Chronicles, the number of women (whether characters or names mentioned simply in passing) absent from this alternative history would constitute a very long list indeed. Comparatively speaking, Chronicles is almost entirely about men and their social, political, and religious endeavours. If the task of Chronicles is to retell the past in a certain way, then what are we to make of this absence of women? Throughout this book, I suggest we need to begin thinking about *the complex nature of silence*. Silence can be understood simply as the absence of speech. The relative absence of women and their speech from the textual world of Chronicles is one form of silence. But, as Michelle Boulous Walker (1998) insists, silence needs to be understood in all its complexities. She develops a more radical understanding of silence as "a spoken yet unheard voice" and "a readable absence" (1998: 27). I shall engage in a more detailed fashion with Boulous Walker's important rethinking of silence in Chapter 2.

For now, however, scholarship on the book of Chronicles generally aligns the absence of stories about women in Chronicles with the "author's" lack of interest in matters concerning anything but the Jerusalem cult and the monarchy of Judah.[11] There is no emphasis whatsoever, for example, on Moses and the Exodus tradition. Nor do most of the stories concerning the kings of the Northern Kingdom of Israel appear in Chronicles. Thus, the major foci of scholars has been on the emphasis on the Jerusalem cult, the pro-monarchic equation of kingship with the kingdom of god, an inclusiveness when it comes to other peoples, the themes of election, continuity, and restoration, immediate divine retribution, and the depiction of an ideal Israel under the rule of a male god in a specified geographic setting. Chronicles is thus understood as a distinct, largely idealized or utopian account of Israel's post-exilic past, with an underlying theme of continuity between the people of Israel's past, present, and future. Indeed, the ending of Chronicles presents a far more positive outlook for the future of Yahweh's people than does the Deuteronomistic history. Surely, then, the absence of stories about women needs to be acknowledged within the context of this idealization of the past. My interest is not with dismissing the absence of women on the basis of some speculative, if even probable, authorial intention. Instead, simply put, what I want to suggest is that Chronicles gives us an alternative construction of Israel's past, one that is made up almost entirely of the actions of men, giving us a picture of Israel's past as a world and a history produced largely by men alone. Thus, what needs to be analysed and understood are the various means by which "man" is able to create and sustain this image of himself as self-made and self-sustaining in Chronicles. This is where the earlier work of Luce Irigaray proves to be invaluable.

This book is divided into two parts. In the Part I (Chapters 1 and 2), I introduce the work of Luce Irigaray. The earlier work of Irigaray has never really been discussed in detail in biblical studies. Thus, I have taken the time (and space) to work through the material patiently, presuming my reader to be largely unfamiliar with many of the psychoanalytic concepts necessary for the comprehension of Irigaray's reading project. In essence, I provide a theorized means of reading that helps me, in Part II, to engage with the book of Chronicles in a very specific feminist mode. In Chapter 1, I provide a detailed discussion of Irigaray's earlier writings, especially her critique of psychoanalysis as a discourse concerned with origins. According to Irigaray, psychoanalysis, like all masculine theoretical discourses, "monopolizes the origin." It does this by refusing to hear the possibilities of the origin as not only "paternal," but also "maternal." Irigaray argues that this erasure of maternal origins is the foundation of Western patriarchal culture and social order. I suggest that biblical studies needs to begin contemplating this important argument made by Irigaray because the biblical texts are among those that function as foundation or "origin" in the West. However, I shall also argue that Irigaray's own specific mode of reading is psychoanalytic and that this mode provides me with a viable reading strategy for my feminist-critical engagement with the book of Chronicles. In Chapter 2, I discuss the importance of Irigaray's re-theorization of the psychoanalytic setting (*praticable*) as a mode of reading. Irigaray insists that we listen (psychoanalytically) for the unheard silences of masculine discourses and determine the underlying phantasies that support and sustain those discourses – phantasies that depend upon the silence of women in some important way.

Taking Irigaray's mode of psychoanalytic reading with me to the book of Chronicles (Section 2), I find that there is a discernable – indeed *ideological* – relationship between a phantasy of mono-sexual production and the mother's speech in Chronicles. When maternal women speak there is, each time, a disruption to the orders of language, meaning, and patrilineal socio-political rule. What I wish to suggest is that the relative absence of women from the past as "conceived" by Chronicles should be understood as a *necessary* absence, one which sustains the coherence of this masculine production of the "past," particularly as it pertains to the "present" and "future" possibilities that the text seeks to imagine. And this absence needs to be understood according to the unconscious strategies of silencing the feminine, especially the feminine-maternal, that may be found at work in Chronicles.

"Woman" is not simply absent from the world of Chronicles; more significantly, her meagre presence there is disconcerting. Indeed, as I will show in Chapters 3 and 4, the silencing of the feminine is not reducible simply to the relative absence of women from the world of Chronicles. I argue that women are most effectively silenced in Chronicles through their association with maternity and the maternal body, and this silencing is necessary for a specific reason: it enables the masculine phantasy of mono-sexual production, a phantasy that rejects any notion of the need for women in society. In Chapter 3 I demonstrate that the maternal body is silenced through the "strategy" of disavowal. That is, the maternal body is denied as origin for the masculine subject in the genealogies of Chronicles (1 Chronicles 1–9). In Chapter 4 I show that the maternal body is repressed in the narratives of Chronicles (1 Chronicles 10–2 Chronicles 36). As the repressed of the narratives, the maternal body represents the unthinkable, the unrepresentable, and the inaudible. Thus, when women are associated with maternity (as mothers of sons), they are silenced. I argue (with the assistance of both Luce Irigaray and Michelle Boulous Walker) that we need to comprehend the silence of women as more than just the absence of speech. Following Boulous Walker's re-theorization of silence and Irigaray's particular mode of reading, the other strategies of silencing the feminine at work in Chronicles become readable, and the silence of women becomes audible.

Part I

Feminism, Psychoanalysis, and the Hebrew Bible:
"Introducing" Luce Irigaray

No one method, form of writing, speaking position, mode of argument
can act as representative, model or ideal for feminist theory. Instead of
attempting to establish a new theoretical norm, feminist theory seeks a
new *discursive space*, a space where women can write, read and think *as
women*. This space will encourage a proliferation of voices, instead of a
hierarchical structuring of them, a plurality of perspectives and interests
instead of the monopoly of the one – new kinds of questions and different
kinds of answers (Grosz, 1986: 203-204)

My reading and analysis of the books of Chronicles takes place through
the double lens of feminism and psychoanalysis. While certain feminist
methods across a multitude of disciplines have long been associated
with various psychoanalytic approaches (i.e. Freudian, Lacanian, Klei-
nian Object Relations, etc.), it is acknowledged that feminism and psychoanalysis have a complex and contentious relationship, one, however,
I interpret as ultimately productive.[1] This problematic, yet productive
relationship is radically evident in the work of Luce Irigaray, the feminist philosopher and psychoanalyst[2] with whom I engage in this book.
In the next two chapters, I shall outline those theoretical and methodological aspects of Irigaray's earlier work that I insist are most relevant
to the task of providing a feminist psychoanalytic reading and analysis of
Chronicles.

While biblical studies is relatively familiar with psychoanalytic theory,
particularly Freudian, Jungian, Lacanian, and Kristevan analytic theory,
the work of Luce Irigaray has had very little impact, to date, on studies of
biblical texts, with currently only two introductory discussions provided
by the Postmodern Bible Collective (1995: 217-21, 258-60) and Faith
Kirkham Hawkins (2000). The Bible and Culture Collective includes Irigaray in their discussions of psychoanalysis and feminist criticism, and
Kirkham Hawkins (in the *Handbook of Postmodern Biblical Interpretation*)
provides a brief discussion of Irigaray's theoretical interventions and suggests possible ways of bringing Irigaray to biblical studies. However, no

sustained engagement has yet been attempted with Irigarayan thought by feminist biblical scholars when analysing and interpreting specific biblical texts, her name appearing only occasionally and briefly to augment theoretically related arguments concerning feminist interpretation.[3] Directly related to this lack of dialogue between biblical studies and the work of Irigaray is the fact that, to date, Irigaray's engagement with Hebrew biblical literature is cursorial.[4] That feminist biblical scholars have given her little attention is no doubt due to the perceived paucity of related material. Unlike other recent French thinkers such as Julia Kristeva, Hélène Cixous, and the late Jacques Derrida, Irigaray has not engaged in a necessarily substantial manner with the Hebrew Bible to warrant the same attention from biblical scholars. And yet, the current popularity of European philosophy and literary theory within biblical studies extends beyond those texts concerned explicitly with biblical material to embrace the range of theoretical and methodological implications of European thought (understood largely outside of France as deconstruction, intertextuality, transferential reading, and such like).

So far, it is the theological dimension of Irigaray's work that has proved most enticing for religionists,[5] and has received the most attention in biblical studies. Indeed, within the two most extensive engagements with Irigaray's work within biblical studies mentioned above (Bible and Culture Collective and Kirkham Hawkins), their discussions quickly turn to this theological aspect of her work, with minimal interest given to her distinctive form of psychoanalytic reading. Importantly, as we shall see, for Irigaray it is psychoanalysis that provides feminists with a particular mode of reading and encountering the past that is *radically non-nostalgic*. Thus, such a mode of reading is radically *political* in that the past must be encountered (traumatically) only *for the purpose of change in the present and future*. We really cannot begin to understand Irigaray's theological writings until we understand the politics, and indeed ethics, of her reading practice. Given this, I have decided to leave Irigaray's theological writings to the side, despite the fact that they might seem to be an obvious choice for a feminist reader of the Bible. Instead, I shall focus, in detail, on what it means to read.

Psychoanalytic theory and the biblical story are, of course, intimately related: from Freud's images of himself as Joseph, Moses, even as the slayer of Moses,[6] and his thesis on the "birth" of civilization and religion in *Moses and Monotheism* (1939) to Lacan's "Name of the Father" (1977: 199). As David Jobling (1998: 23) points out, bringing the two together effects a transferential relationship between them, meaning that neither the biblical text nor psychoanalytic theory remain unchanged by the

encounter. As will become clear in the following two chapters, for Irigaray, this mutually dependent (and thus ethical) catharsis is the most
important facet of psychoanalytic reading, but also perhaps the least
practised despite intentions otherwise. As we shall see, Irigaray is scath-
ingly critical of certain analysts (whether professional psychoanalysts or
literary and cultural critics) who perform psychoanalytic *theory* as a universal scientific method upon an "object" of analysis.

Outside of biblical studies there have been three main psychoanalytic
approaches to reading literature: analysing the author using psychoanalytic concepts (a method favoured by Freud himself);[7] analysing the literary characters; and finally, a focus on both the reader and the literary
text as simultaneous players in the psychoanalytic scenario. In contemporary post-structural scholarship, the first approach has largely been
discredited because the idea that a work of literature can be analysed in
place of – and as equivalent to – the author is, arguably, quite naïve in
that it depends on a simplistic theory of the subject of representational
practice (that is, the writing subject) as unproblematically reflective of
the psychic subject in general. The most popular approach has been the
second, where characters are analysed using psychoanalytic concepts, as
if the character is an actual analysand.[8] As Jobling points out, this particular use of psychoanalysis is weak because, while a literary character
resembles a "real" human being, he or she, of course, *is not* a real individual living in the world (Jobling, 1998: 21). Or, as Ilona Rashkow puts it
in relation to the analysis of biblical literary characters:

> biblical characters are both more and less than real persons. This presents
> a problem. While one aspect of narrative characterization is to provide
> a *mimetic* function, that is, to represent human action and motivation,
> another aspect is primarily *textual*, that is, to reveal information to a
> reader or conceal it (Rashkow, 1993: 18).

The third approach is the one most closely related to Irigaray's own
form of psychoanalytic reading. It is also the approach taken by biblical scholars who arguably provide us with some of the best examples
of how fruitful the interpretive and analytical relationship between psychoanalysis and the Bible can be.[9] For David Jobling, Ilona Rashkow, and
(honorary biblical scholar) Mieke Bal, psychoanalytic criticism does not
so much involve the analysis of author or character, where the author or
character functions as the analysand and the critic/reader as the analyst.
Indeed, such an imperialist epistemological model ignores one of the
fundamental innovations of psychoanalysis: the breakdown of distinct
boundaries between subject and object of knowledge. Instead, according

to these advocates of the third approach, psychoanalytic theory must be refused the hegemonic status given to it by the first two approaches. What is argued is that psychoanalytic criticism is more about the unconscious "networks" created in the encounter between two: text and critic/reader.

It is this notion of "transference" that distinguishes these approaches to reading and interpreting biblical literature from the older forms of author or character psychoanalysis, and it is a form of psychoanalytic reading with many debts to feminist scholarship (namely Shoshana Felman, Jane Gallop, and Toril Moi, among others). For Bal, transference

> is the competition between the dramatic and the narrative form. There the analytic subject seeks to play; to repeat the past, rather than to recount it. In this way, the subject of analysis privileges an open subjectivity rather than a deceptive objectification of the narration, a "direct" presentation rather than a past representation, and a dialogue rather than a narrative monologue (Bal, 1991b: 147).

What I want to suggest is that all these elements – the drama of transference and countertransference, the thwarting of diachronic temporality, and the relation "between two" – are fundamental to Irigaray's mode of psychoanalytic reading. I shall explain this in detail in Chapter 2. For Bal, the psychoanalytic notion of transference details the inevitable complicity of the reading/analysing subject with the world of the text, and vice-versa. On the one hand, the reading subject is indeed "created" within the representational frameworks of the text itself, ultimately "finding" him or herself in the text. On the other hand, the reader brings with him or her already established representational frameworks within which meaning arises. It is this interplay "between two" that constitutes transference as part of the drama of interpretation and reading.

This is also David Jobling's understanding of transference. However, I think Jobling's reading practice is far more productively "transferential" than Bal's, which is ultimately at times rigidly structural (she herself admits this). I am referring here to Bal's work on biblical literature (Bal, 1987, 1988, 1989). Her later work, especially *Reading Rembrandt* (Bal, 1991a), foregrounds transference more so than the earlier works. With respect to her work in biblical studies, Bal's interests as a narratologist lean towards the development of a *model* of analysis produced by the productive encounter between narratology and psychoanalysis.[10] Her insistence on psychoanalytic criticism as an analogue or model (based on her admiration for the Habermasian position of psychoanalysis as a science which has managed to incorporate self-reflection; Bal, 1991b: 35ff) is a position entirely rejected by Irigaray. The incorporation of psychoanalysis as a *method* or *model* of interpretation and reading is, according to Irigaray, problematic indeed. I discuss this aspect of Irigaray's critique of psychoanalysis as interpretive practice at length in Chapter 2.

For both Jobling and Rashkow, however, their status as both subject and object of representation is never concealed in the process of interpretive readings.[11] For example, in his commentary on 1 Samuel, Jobling sets up his discussion by outlining his development as a biblical scholar (Jobling, 1998: 4-24). More importantly, in the final chapter of his book he focuses on the question of why certain stories or verses (in his case 1 Sam. 26:19) resonate with different readers, almost re-presenting for the reader their own story:

> We need to take such experiences seriously. Those of us who are brought up with the Bible (and this includes everyone who is a product of Western culture) are *enmeshed* in it in ways that are often unconscious or semi-conscious. We need to find ways of examining these strange associations, these "hauntings" – ways of bringing them to the surface. One reason why we need to come to terms with them in our scholarly work is that they operate at a level far deeper than our intentional scholarship. They *inhabit* our scholarship, so that we may be playing out internalized biblical scenarios just when we think we are being most objective... If for Freud dreams are the "royal road" to the individual unconscious, for me transference is the royal road to the "biblical unconscious." So deeply is the Bible inscribed within us that the processes by which we read it are simply the rehearsal at another level of what we find in it (Jobling, 1998: 283).

The "mirage" of one's own history or theoretical-methodological activity at work, impossibly, in an ancient text alerts us to a different process that arises as an effect of the reader-text coupling. In the case of Chronicles (and preempting my discussion of the psychoanalytic process to come in this part), the very project of Chronicles seems to be to return to (even confront) "the past" and re-narrate that (traumatic) past in terms that allow for the possibility of a better future. This is precisely what psychoanalysis as a therapeutic process is said to enable. Is it simply that the logic of psychoanalysis is equivalent to that of Chronicles? Hardly. What transference enables is the silences ("these 'hauntings'") of the text "to speak." In other words, the main benefit of transferential reading is the disclosure of certain aspects of the text that remain silenced or concealed by the so-called rational, scientific, objective methodologies. And, importantly, this "speech" is produced "between two," analyst and analysand, text and reader, confronting and disabling the pretence of a subject of representation who has no debts to or dependence on the other for "his" status as subject.

Ilona Raskow also maintains that the psychoanalytic notion of trans-ference provides us with a particular "theory" of reading, analysis, and interpretation, one which, along with "intertextuality" can account for the differences in readers' responses to the text:

> According to the psychoanalytic account of transference, the structures of the unconscious are revealed by the analyst's encounters with the analysand's discourse. The analyst, in effect, repeats the experience described by the analysand and thereby gains particular insight into the analysand's psychical life. Thus transference is a repetition linking the analyst to the analysand. Similarly, reading is a repetition of the text it seeks to analyse. Prior readings, particularly those which have narrative similarity, are not errors to be discarded, but revealing recurrences of textual structures. It is through transference, then, that the analysand tries to force or coax the analyst to play out a scene he or she has in mind. As a result, this self-reflexiveness does not produce or induce a closure in which the text is the thing it describes, but rather leads to a multiplicity of representations, a plurality of meanings, but rather that the text cannot be reduced to *a* meaning (Rashkow, 1993: 36).

What I think Rashkow implies is that "meaning" is always open-ended, and somewhat elusive. It is never cemented in the text, awaiting excavation by any anonymous, objective, and unaffected reader. And this is a crucial point.

It is important to note that, despite their different approaches, Jobling, Rashkow, and Bal all bring a feminist political position to bear on psychoanalytic theory. Their practice, as readers and interpreters of biblical literature, is guided by both feminist critical theory and psychoanalytic theory. However, Irigaray's psychoanalytic reading practice needs to be understood differently. In this first part, I shall argue that Irigaray's specific psychoanalytic reading practice needs to be understood as a mode of reading specifically *for women*. Now, I think that this is where Irigaray's own brand of psychoanalytic reading potentially contributes the most to feminist biblical studies. This is not to dismiss the important contributions of male scholars such as Jobling, who has been one of the main advocates of feminist interpretation within biblical studies. However, as I show in the following two chapters, the truly radical nature of Irigarayan reading comes out of her resolute insistence that the sexuate status of the reader's body needs to be foregrounded rather than neutralized in any reading practice. This approach to reading, based on psychoanalytic *practice* rather than *theory*, is, according to Irigaray, a politically progressive act in itself, one consistent with a feminist politics. I go to great lengths in Chapters 1 and 2 to explain the importance of this practice for women who wish to encounter texts of origins such as the Hebrew Bible.

What shall be clear by the end of Part I is that by advocating psycho-analysis as a mode (and not method) of reading, writing, thinking, and speaking "as woman," my development of Irigaray's early critique of psy-choanalytic theory, along with her own form of psychoanalytic reading practice, offers women a productive new mode of interpretive encounter with the Hebrew Bible, one which depends crucially on a different feature of transference. Irigaray's re-thinking of transference is directly related to her critique of the concept of "origin" and the sexuate subject's relation-ship to it. Thus, in Chapter 1, I discuss Irigaray's important critique of psychoanalytic theory as a discourse on "origins." Essentially, this critique of psychoanalytic theory is crucial for the development of her own spe-cific mode of reading, one that utilizes the tools of psychoanalysis, but which more importantly foregrounds the setting itself. Following this, in Chapter 2, I provide a detailed outline of Irigaray's re-thinking of the psy-choanalytic setting and what I believe to be its potential for enabling us to hear the silences of ancient biblical literature (and, indeed, the means by which women have been silenced), for the purpose of radical change in the future.

Chapter 1

"The Monopoly of the Origin" and the Mute Foundation of Psychoanalysis: The Theoretical Interventions of Luce Irigaray

The culture, the language, the imaginary and the mythology in which we live at the moment... I say to myself...let's have a look...this edifice that looks so clean and subtle...let's see what ground it is built on. Is it all that acceptable?

The substratum is the woman who reproduces the social order, who is made this order's infrastructure: the whole of our western culture is based upon the murder of the mother. The man-god-father killed the mother in order to take power. And isn't there a fluidity, some flood, that could shake this social order? And if we make the foundations of the social order shift, then everything will shift. That is why they are so careful to keep us on a leash... (Irigaray, 1991a: 47).[1]

1. *Introduction*

In this chapter, my focus is on Irigaray's claim that all Western theoretical models function through an unacknowledged silencing of women, thus perpetuating what she considers to be the foundation of Western culture: the murder of the mother. Specifically, my interest here is with Irigaray's critique of psychoanalysis as a discourse of origins. According to Irigaray, this fascination with beginnings in the West, be they cultural or individual beginnings, has been monopolized by masculine thought and experience, at the expense of women. In particular, psychoanalytic theory perpetuates this silence through its own masculine configurations of individual and cultural genesis.

For Irigaray, this "monopoly of the origin" (Irigaray, 1985b: 102) equates to a "murder" of the mother, and this is the main theoretical issue that I intend to deal with in this chapter. I shall, with Irigaray, argue that the extrication or "forgetting" of the mother from the original or primal scene serves man (and men) rather well in that it enables him to perceive himself as self-made, or at least in debt only to the father who bears an uncanny resemblance to himself. In later chapters, I will show that this "forgetting" is the principal feature of Chronicles, what constitutes and organizes the "reality" of this particular masculine (re)production of the past. This symbolic matricide is ultimately, for Irigaray, a symptom of the failure of sexual difference to be incorporated within Western systems of thought. Crucially, an effect of this matricide is that the genealogy of women has necessarily been suppressed in order to enable the paternal line to have a monopoly on symbolic value:

> In some way, the vertical dimension is always being taken away from female becoming. The bond between mother and daughter, daughter and mother, has to be broken for the daughter to become a woman. Female genealogy has to be suppressed, on behalf of the son-father relationship, and the idealization of the father and husband as patriarchs (Irigaray, 1993b: 108).

In this chapter, I intend to read this repression of maternal origination and female genealogy as a constitutive feature of patriarchal discourses, as the necessary absence that guarantees or shores up meaning, and not simply as that which lies outside the radar of male systems of thought. I shall argue that the texts of our cultural heritage, be they philosophical, scientific, religious, legal, etcetera, bear the traces of this forgetting in their drive for totality or closure, and must therefore be analysed with this insight in mind.

For Irigaray, this brutal erasure of the *other* line, the mother line, means that the mother-daughter relationship remains largely unsymbolized in our culture. By unsymbolized, Irigaray means that in the West "there is an absence of linguistic, social, semiotic, structural, cultural, iconic, theoretical, mythical, religious or any other representations of that relationship. There is no maternal genealogy" (Whitford, 1991: 76). Much of the so-called first phase of feminist inquiry has focused on exhuming the presence of women from the dark shadows or crypts of history to construct something of a female genealogy, and Irigaray's own work on mythology is certainly of this ilk.[2] But the majority of Irigaray's early critical analyses search for the traces of this erasure, whether female characters or figures are present or not. Irigaray's approach to reading the texts of our cultural past is more than just a revisionist exercise. It seeks to build a feminist mode for articulating the desire for origin, beyond a nostalgia for the past.

Interestingly, when it comes to the reading and interpretation of sacred texts, Irigaray is critical of what she considers to be little more than nostalgic encounters with the texts held up as sacred in our culture, approaches that fail to look for "what remains to be discovered, especially the future in the past":

> The myths and stories, the sacred texts are analyzed, sometimes with
> nostalgia but rarely with a mind to change the social order. The texts are
> merely consumed or reconsumed, in a way. The darkness of our imaginary
> or symbolic horizon is analyzed more or less adequately, but not with the
> goal of founding a new ethics. The techniques of reading, translating, and
> explaining take over the domain of the sacred, the religious, the mythical,
> but they fail to reveal a world that measures up to the material they are
> consuming or consummating (Irigaray, 1993a: 86).

Clearly Irigaray advocates a particular reading strategy, especially with
respect to our "sacred" texts, and it is a strategy that is concerned less
with "knowing" the past than it is with "founding a new ethics." Given that
female genealogy has suffered symbolic erasure, this means that current
analytic and interpretive methods, which are necessarily complicit with
given intellectual frameworks, only allow for the daughter-critic to relate
to a *paternal* origin (or discourse), without offering the means for articulating a relationship to the maternal.

The crucial question that Irigaray raises throughout her work is how to
articulate a relation to and desire for maternal origin if, as a woman, you
are theoretically prohibited from doing so. Irigaray is adamant that it is
psychoanalysis that unwittingly reveals how discourses of truth (religion,
theory, philosophy, etc.) rely upon the prohibition against women articulating a relation to origins outside of the (nostalgic) phallic or Oedipal
daughter-father model. There is a certain irony here because, while psychoanalysis is arguably itself a patriarchal discourse of truth, it is also a
practice that makes possible a critical, feminist analysis of the "father's
story."

Margaret Whitford has suggested that we cannot begin to comprehend the work of Irigaray without fully taking on board the importance
of Freudian and Lacanian psychoanalysis for her thinking, particularly
with her earlier work, and I think this is an important point. Irigaray is
certainly not a "dutiful daughter" taking up and continuing the work of
the "father" without questioning it in any way. However, and this provides something of a tension, Irigaray is an analyst herself, and most of
her work from the 1970s and 1980s is dependent – in complex ways – on
psychoanalytic concepts. Irigaray's intellectual practice is, in the first
instance, philosophy, and one can really only comprehend her work when
one appreciates this fact. However, as I have suggested, she also borrows
heavily from psychoanalytic practice, though her approach is far from
orthodox. Irigaray is critical of the narratives of origins that psychoanalytic theory offers. And yet, her critique of psychoanalysis is in many ways

indebted to Freud and Lacan. So, while she makes use of the psychoan-alyst's interpretive tools, looking for the unconscious phantasies of texts and the defense mechanisms (repressions, foreclosures, displacements, etc.) underpinning representational systems (including psychoanalysis itself), it is important to note that she does so while simultaneously chal-lenging the universal nature of the fundamental tenets of psychoanalysis (Grosz, 1989: 104).

In light of the complex relationship that exists between Irigaray and psychoanalysis, I shall structure my discussion in the following way. First of all, I shall discuss Irigaray's claim that Western philosophical dis-course, within which we must include psychoanalysis, has consistently relied upon the mute status of women. "Woman," or the "feminine," is man's mute, self-reflecting other, the guarantee of his status as the ratio-nal master of all that he surveys. I shall explore Irigaray's analysis of Plato's myth of the cave here as a preface to her related critique of the psychoanalytic narratives of origins. I will demonstrate in the following chapter that, in universalizing its own theoretical concepts and struc-tures, psychoanalysis disavows its own culturally and historically deter-mined status. For Irigaray, Plato's story of the philosopher's escape from the cave in the pursuit of truth provides the model of repression that similarly underpins both Freudian and Lacanian theory.

Secondly, I shall provide a detailed overview of Lacan's theoretical for-mulation of the genesis of subjectivity through the mirror-stage, along with Irigaray's principal criticism that the Lacanian mirror effectively erases any sense of maternal debt or autonomous feminine sexuality. After this, I shall turn to Irigaray's famous critique of Freud's theory concern-ing the origins of female sexuality. Crucially, for Irigaray, the principal problem that Freud (unwittingly) reveals is the (patriarchally prescribed) inability of women to articulate a relation to and desire for origin (to the mother) outside current phallocentric models of knowledge, models that arguably afford women no subjective status. I wish to contend that it is this aspect of Irigaray's critique that warrants serious attention in feminist biblical studies, given the location of the Hebrew and Greek Bibles as "origins" of western culture. I intend to use Irigaray's work as a starting point in order to question the ways that we traditionally engage with these crucial foundational texts in the West. As I shall explain in the following chapter, I intend to mimic Irigaray's psychoanalytic mode (as distinct from method) in my engagement with the book of Chronicles, itself a text concerned with the (re)construction of origins and the past.

Returning to this chapter, my discussion of Irigaray and Lacan pre-cedes my discussion of Irigaray and Freud because of the importance of Lacan's concepts of the Imaginary and the Symbolic (notably as they appear in his story of the "mirror-stage") for Irigaray's own interpretation of Freud's discourses on femininity – and for her interpretation of Western thought in general. Irigaray's charge against Freud is that his discourse on origins, while providing an insightful description of the status of women within modern patriarchy, fails to analyse its own imaginary structure. For Irigaray, this imaginary structure has been present since Plato, and is implicated in the ongoing repression of sexual difference from Western thought. Given the significance of this imaginary structure I need first to provide a summary of the Lacanian concepts, especially the Imaginary and the Symbolic, which Irigaray strategically both utilizes and criticizes.

Irigaray's own project, as Whitford famously points out, can be characterized as "a sort of 'psychoanalysis' of western culture and metaphysics, seeking what underpins its fragile rationality, looking for the 'repressed' or unconscious of culture" (Whitford, 1991: 31). Irigaray's claim is that the Lacanian "Symbolic" – the universal condition of subjectivity – is the *male* imaginary "transformed into order, social order too," and is a socially sanctioned support for a "strict cultural endogamy among males" (Irigaray, 2002a: 218). Her analyses of western theoretical discourses – those that "pretend" to truth – can be understood as an analysis of the means by which this Imaginary is given support and coherence through the historically and culturally determined symbolic structures presumed to be universal in Lacanian thought.

Finally, I discuss Irigaray's refutation of Freud's myth of an originary parricide at the base of Western civilization. For Irigaray, certain myths of ancient Greece, notably the *Oresteia* by Aeschylus, reveal a different story concerning the origins of patriarchy and history "proper," namely that it is founded on matricide rather than a parricide, as well as on the sundering of female genealogies. What Freud (and Western culture) forgets, by privileging the Oedipal scenario, is that the mother-woman has *always already* been silenced prior to the murder of the father, thus enabling the struggle between father and son over her to take place without any consideration of her own desire. "Mother" has already been silenced. Thus, parricide and the Oedipal myth present a sham origin of patriarchy because woman and her "genre" have already been positioned within culture and the symbolic order as its *very mute foundation*. Indeed, Irigaray's fundamental interpretive task, be it with psychoanalytic, philosophical, religious, scientific, political, or mythological texts, is to give voice to the silent traces of the *historical* process of this erasure. Irigaray suggests that by refusing the universal status of theoretical conceptions of (paternal) origins we can return to origins and rework them without continuing to be "accomplices in the murder of the mother" (Irigaray, 1991d: 44).

2. *The Specularization of Woman-Mother in Philosophy*

I want you to go on to picture the enlightenment or ignorance of our human condition somewhat as follows. Imagine an underground chamber like a cave, with a long entrance open to the daylight and as wide as the cave. In this chamber are men who have been prisoners there since they were children, their legs and necks being so fastened that they can only look straight ahead of them and cannot turn their heads (Plato, 1974: 317).

Plato's famous allegory of the cave, related by Socrates in Book VII of *The Republic*, tells of how ordinary men are shackled in what we might (prematurely) refer to as the womb-like space of a cave, with their backs turned to the cave's entrance. Unable to move, they can stare only at the back wall of the cave which functions as a screen for the shadows of other figures passing behind the prisoners. Their shadows are cast by a fire situated between the prisoners and the entrance to the cave. According to Socrates, the philosopher is the man who is able to unbind himself from these shackles (but only with the assistance of the pedagogue-philosopher: Socrates, himself), turn around and leave the cave, walking out into the light of day, never to return to the darkness of that original and inferior representational scene. Only with the sun, a far superior source of light according to Plato's allegory, can man encounter Truth through reason and logic; a rational mode of thinking thus depends on shunning the dark and (painfully) heading for the light.

I shall first summarize Irigaray's main argument in "Plato's Hystera," the final chapter of *Speculum of the Other Woman* (Irigaray, 1985a), before moving to a more detailed discussion of her reading of the allegory. According to Irigaray, woman is the mute foundation and unacknowledged resource of philosophical speculation. Woman is not simply silenced through her exclusion from philosophical discourse, but is also incorporated *within* that discourse as "the silent, unacknowledged *place* of philosophy, its empty/subjectless interiority" (Boulous Walker, 1998: 12). She is both the theatrical space of representation from which the philosopher must break free and the representative of nature/corporeality upon which he is utterly dependent, without acknowledging that dependence, in his transcendental quest for Truth. Furthermore, her mute status within philosophy carries over into the social. The order of both is patriarchal, and the muteness of woman beyond her relation to the masculine standard guarantees the stability of that order. She is never afforded the status of sexual "other," independent of any relation to the mono-standard (i.e. the masculine). She is only ever the "other of the Same" guaranteeing that she always falls short of that standard, always appears as "the weaker of the two" sexes (Plato, 1974: 235). If anything, she is the mediating object that sustains the desire of men for each other.

More specifically, in "Plato's *Hystera*," Irigaray provides a close reading of Plato's allegory of the cave.[3] Her work provides an extremely complex analysis of Plato's story of the philosopher's painful liberation from intellectual immaturity through the discernment of Truth, a myth that Whitford characterizes as "a working of the themes of loss of origin, identity, and death" (Whitford, 1991: 105).[4] Irigaray pays great attention to what are usually considered to be minor details in Plato's analogy, the props of Plato's theatre (e.g. the cave itself, the screen, fire, and the neck of the cave). As Whitford points out, this attention to detail manifests the psychoanalytically inspired nature of Irigaray's interpretive project (Whitford, 1991: 105-106). Accordingly, Irigaray analyses Plato's division of his stage or theatre of representation into three distinct regions (the cave, the world, and the Forms) wherein his myth unfolds through analogical progression. Her argument is not simply that the cave represents the womb, and that the pursuit of truth is a movement away from the realm of the senses, aligned here with the maternal (with Socrates starring as midwife in the rebirth into knowledge, the reunion of the soul and knowledge), but more significantly that the whole economy of truth, dependent on the metaphysics of presence, ocularcentrism, and heliotropism, relies upon the non-representation of the maternal role in procreation. It is not a womb that the prisoners are trapped in, but already a cave. Already the womb has been displaced through metaphor. If woman is present at all, it is only silently as the phantasized container or receptacle of the inchoate:

> Already the prisoner was no longer in a womb but in a cave – an attempt to provide a figure, a system of metaphor for the uterine cavity. He was held in a place that was, that meant to express, that had the sense of being *like* a womb. We must *suppose* that the womb is reproduced, reproducible, and reproductive by means of projection. That it is already subject to the laws of symmetry and analogy which, theoretically, would have given it the *form* of a grotto, would have transformed it into a cave. By/for representations. The farthest wall of that den would serve both as a horizon-limit and as a backcloth for projection (Irigaray, 1985a: 279).

The glorious birth into knowledge takes place only through the obstetrically enforced tergiversation from the back wall of the cave/womb.

Irigaray insists on revealing the prop status of this cave, placed into the scene as both the material support upon which only inferior copies are produced, and as the space that imprisons those who have forgotten the soul's intimate knowledge of the truth of the Form. The soul is weighed down by the materiality of the body, and as such, cannot conceive of or envision anything beyond the resemblances or copies of the Idea.

According to Plato, it is only upon escape from the cave that the child-like man can attain wisdom. The process, however, is physically very painful, especially given the power of the sun and the weakness of his eyes:

> "And if," I went on, "he were forcibly dragged up the steep and rugged ascent and not let go till he had been dragged out into the sunlight, the process would be a painful one, to which he would much object, and when he emerged into the light his eyes would be so dazzled by the glare of it that he wouldn't be able to see a single one of the things he was now told were real" (Plato, 1974: 318).

Here, in the second scene – the world above the cavern – the reflections in the water and shadows cast by bodies are said to be more "real" because of the "natural" status of the screens and reflectors (water, bodies, etc.). No suggestion is made that God is like the "magicians" (to use Irigaray's term) below, orchestrating the necessary conditions of presence. As Whitford points out, according to Plato's analogy, the world should belong to the realm of appearance or semblance (Whitford, 1991: 111). And yet, the reflections and shadows are more real than the images found on the wall of the cave. For Irigaray, this higher value accorded to the reflections, whose source is the Sun/Father, naturalizes the scene, making it more authentic because already belonging to "the realm of the proper" (Irigaray, 1985a: 297), that is, of property and the proper name. In both the scene of the cavern and the scene of the world,

> what has happened is a surreptitious incorporation of the body or nature (the maternal) which at the same time obliterates the traces of the maternal role in reproduction. In the process, the maternal genealogy is written out of the scene of representation, leaving only the paternal line. Thus the pure Idea/Intelligible has no need of a vehicle or receptacle (Whitford, 1991: 111).

In other words, the newborn philosopher has left the cave behind because of its inferiority to the other scenes of representation beyond it, realms which depend upon and belong to the Father-Sun. The original space is belittled and replaced by the glorious light as source of all representation and being:

> "Later on he would come to the conclusion that it is the sun that produces
> the changing seasons and years and controls everything in the visible
> world, and is in a sense responsible for everything that he and his fellow
> prisoners used to see... And when he thought of his first home and what
> passed for wisdom there, and of his fellow-prisoners, don't you think he
> would congratulate himself on his good fortune and be sorry for them?"
> (Plato, 1974: 319).

In opposition to the scene of the cave, where only artificial copies are conceivable, the world of Ideas is, for Plato, a world of pure self-presence. Thus, the condition of Truth is the absence of any reflection (Whitford, 1991: 109). What could be further, then, from the contemplation of Truth than the realm of the cave with its naïve subjects contemplating semblances and believing them to be real? Furthermore, he who is finally able to "see" the truth does so without any material support. The material condition of vision, in the encounter with Truth, is unnecessary in Plato's account, with "seeing" finally attributed to the soul. For Irigaray, the complete denial of bodily or material support within this economy of Truth[5] – the splitting of the Sensible from the Transcendental – is equivalent to the valuing of the paternal procreative role over the maternal. Only the Father/Sun/Idea produces that which is authentic or "real," while the Mother/cave produces the "more or less good copies of reality" (Irigaray, 1985a: 300). So, in the economy of truth upheld by philosophy, woman/mother can only represent the sensible; she stands for what must be shunned in the pursuit of truth. To be born again into the resplendent realm of truth (the Intelligible), man must extract himself from the grips of the material or corporeal (the Sensible) which shackles him to the semblances, the inferior copies of the "original" for which he strives.

Crucially, Irigaray reads Plato's myth as an imaginary primal scene (i.e. the phantasmatic representation of the copulative act between the parents) which has attempted, paradoxically, to extricate the mother from the picture altogether. In other words, what underlies the economy of truth is both the elision of the mother's role in procreation, and the appropriation of her bodily power by the paternal "source," enabling man to see only himself reflected everywhere, guaranteeing his status as eternal begetter, never begotten. As Whitford explains, "Truth becomes linked to the paternal metaphor, the Idea/Father engendering copies and reflections without apparent need for the other partner normally required in processes of reproduction" (Whitford, 1991: 110).

The economy of truth has only one standard by which everything must be measured. Given the paternal status of this standard, woman can only ever appear as inferior copy. Because her role is removed from the scene of the discovery of Truth – reduced only to the container and screen within and upon which the philosopher orchestrates the production of poor copies, the cave realm later forgotten in the blinding contemplation of Truth – women can only ever enter the scene of representation if they can assimilate to masculinity as closely as possible. And in the broader context of Plato's *Republic*, a utopian envisioning of the ideal community, women are only able to participate if they too can play the roles assigned to and defined by men, bringing nothing that is unique to women into the administration of the polis ("And can you use any animal for the same purpose as another," I asked, "unless you bring it up and train it in the same way?" [Plato, 1974: 229]). And, according to Irigaray, within the genealogy of Platonic thought, psychoanalysis is heir apparent. Given this, I want to turn now to Lacan's story of the birth of the subject of language to discuss Irigaray's critique that, in a manner not dissimilar to Plato's subjects, the Lacanian subject must forgo any acknowledgment of debt to the materiality of women's bodies and value only the disembodied paternal contribution.

3. *The Lacanian Universe*

Lacan's "mirror-stage" is a feature of his famous reconstruction of the Freudian thesis concerning the genesis of the ego in terms of signifying systems rather than biology. Lacan theorizes that three orders – Imaginary, Symbolic, and Real – exist out of which the narcissistic ego[6] of the infant is formed, establishing a relationship between it and its reality. The function of the mirror stage is "to establish a relation between the organism and its reality" (Lacan, 1977: 4) established through the recognition of lack, or of a gap between the seeing-perceiving organism and its image located elsewhere, in a mirror and in another being.

There are three distinct theories of the mirror-stage developed by Lacan between the 1930s and 1980 (Ragland-Sullivan, 1992: 173-76). However, because Irigaray's critique relates to the earlier elaboration, notably as it appears in "The Mirror Stage as Formative of the Function of the I" and "Aggressivity in Psychoanalysis" (Lacan, 1977: 1-7, 8-29), and as he developed it in his first seminar (1953–1954) under the heading "The Topic of the Imaginary" (Lacan, 1991: 71-159), I shall limit my discussion to this first phase.

In his 1949 *Écrits*, Lacan argues that the basis of the mirror stage is the "real *specific prematurity of birth* in man" (Lacan, 1977: 4). Unlike other animals, humans are born without the benefits of a mature physical development which would enable independence (from the mother) from an early age. The body of the infant is completely uncoordinated, and without a sense of itself as total and integrated. Furthermore, the human infant lacks the ability to distinguish itself from its surrounding world, not yet having a sense of itself as separate from its immediate objects, especially the maternal body:

> In the beginning we assume there to be all the ids, objects, instincts, desires, tendencies, etc. That is reality pure and simple then, which is not delimited by anything, which cannot yet be the object of any definition, which is neither good, nor bad, but is all at the same time chaotic and absolute, primal (Lacan, 1991: 79).

As such, the child exists in a state of plenitude characterized by the absence of lack, the inability to register absence of any kind. In Lacanian terms, the human child is born into the Real. Elizabeth Grosz explains:

> The Real is the order preceding the ego and the organization of the drives. It is an anatomical, "natural" order (nature in the sense of resistance rather than positive substance), a pure plenitude or fullness. The Real cannot be experienced as such: it is capable of representation or conceptualization only through the reconstructive or inferential work of the imaginary and symbolic orders... Our distance from the Real is the measure of our socio-psychical development. The Real has no boundaries, borders, divisions, or oppositions; it is a continuum of "raw materials." The Real is not however the same as reality; reality is lived as and known through imaginary and symbolic representations (Grosz, 1990: 34).

It is only with the inauguration of the mirror-stage that the ego begins to be built through the internalization of the image of bodily coherence and the organization of the child's bodily pleasure zones. Images or representations of the human form (in the mirror and eventually the actual corporeal presence of another being) as unified and coherent feeds the ego with the promise of what will be.

Taking his lead from comparative psychology, Lacan notes that at a certain age (as early as six months and usually culminating at eighteen months) a child whose motor skills are less advanced than a chimpanzee's can still, remarkably, recognize his own image in a mirror held before him.[7] Unlike the chimp, which develops an instrumental relationship with the mirror once it realizes that the image is not a "real" chimp, the child develops a fascination with the spectral form itself:

> Unable as yet to walk, or even stand up, and held tightly as he is by some support, human or artificial (what, in France, we call a "*trotte-bébé*"), he nevertheless overcomes, in a flutter of jubilant activity, the obstructions of his support and, fixing his attitude in a slightly leaning-forward position,

> in order to hold it in his gaze, brings back an instantaneous aspect of the image... This jubilant assumption of his specular image by the child at the *infans* stage, still sunk in his motor incapacity and nursling dependence, would seem to exhibit in an exemplary situation the symbolic matrix in which the *I* is precipitated in primordial form, before it is objectified in the dialectic of identification with the other, and before language restores to it, in the universal, its function as subject (Lacan, 1977: 2).

The infant is gradually able to imagize itself as a complete unity, in direct contrast to its still uncoordinated and fragmented experience of its own body. And what is perceived there in the mirror, in the form of a unified image, is the ideal ego (*Idealich*). The jubilation that is expressed by the child in misrecognizing itself as a complete being through narcissistic identification with the image is an *anticipatory* pleasure of what "I" will be. The image or *Gestalt* holds the (false) promise of the future totality of being, now constituted in relation to space. This identification with the image of another reassures the subject, falsely, that it is a stable and unified subject:

> That is what I insist upon in my theory of the mirror-stage – the sight alone of the whole form of the human body gives the subject an imaginary mastery over his body, one which is premature in relation to a real mastery. This formation is separated from the specific process of maturation and is not confused with it. The subject anticipates on the achievement of psychological mastery, and this anticipation will leave its mark on every subsequent exercise of effective motor mastery. This is the original adventure through which man, for the first time, has the experience of seeing himself, of reflecting on himself and conceiving of himself as other than he is – an essential dimension of the human, which entirely structures his fantasy life (Lacan, 1991: 79).

This "whole human body" or *Gestalt*, which gives the illusion of mastery, is not, however, a sexed body. The recognition of sexual difference is only possible for the subject of the Symbolic, a subject of language. It is simply the recognition of a form that the nascent ego somehow recognizes as like unto its own species. Interestingly, Lacan uses the case of the female pigeon to make this point: "...it is a necessary condition for the maturation of the gonad of the female pigeon that it should see another member of its species" (Lacan, 1977: 3). Lacan is not suggesting that human sexuality develops the same way as the biological sexual development of pigeons, or any other animals, but that the Imaginary relation (the only order within which non-human animals seem to operate) provides the foundation for the development of sexuation upon entry into the Symbolic.

It is this dualistic specular relation, between self and other, which constitutes the Imaginary Order (the order of images and representations). Prior to the mirror-stage the child exists in a symbiotic relationship with the maternal body, and as such cannot recognize absence or lack. For example, sucking can satisfy the child even when milk is absent (Freud, 1911: 219; Grosz, 1990: 34). It is through the mirror-stage that the child is able slowly to distinguish himself from his mother and from the rest of the world. And as such, he comes to realize that he is not in a state of completeness, that he is not "one" with the world. But because the mirror-stage is a process involving the self and the other (the child and mother) as inextricably implicated, and because the child only ever encounters his image as a future possibility, the mirror-stage paradoxically posits a subject who is both distinct from the other and a subject utterly determined by the other, a subject caught by the *illusion* of its own autonomy.

Nevertheless, the mirror-stage introduces a lack, a gap between the Real and the being himself. The Imaginary order is the first representational structure which enables the child to reflect upon himself as a being in the world, a being in relation to the Real. It constitutes the origins of distinction between inside and out, self and other, and subject and object, and these structural distinctions remain into adulthood (Grosz, 1990: 35). Hence, and this is important, the Imaginary is not a process that gets left behind with entry into language (into the Symbolic), but is, rather, an order that enables the adult subject to conceal the lack that constitutes his subjectivity through appropriative specular identifications. As Slavoj Žižek puts it, the imaginary enables "the illusion of the self as the autonomous agent which is present from the very beginning as the origin of its acts: this imaginary self-experience is for the subject the way to misrecognize his radical dependence on the big Other, on the symbolic order as his decentred cause" (Žižek, 1989: 104). The subject will henceforth accept those images that return to himself a satisfying image of himself, though always rightly suspecting that something of his being is lacking in images or representations, including his social environment.[8]

Because the self is now recognized from an (internalized) exterior position, the mirror-stage can be said to effect the splitting of the subject into both subject who sees and object seen. As Lacan will later put it, "I see only from one point, but in my existence I am looked at from all sides" (Lacan, 1998: 72). So, while the image generates a jubilant response through its symbolization of "the mental permanence of the *I*," it also prefigures the alienated status of the subject to come (Lacan, 1977: 2). Thus, the internalization of the image (of the self constituted in relation to an other) which libidinally invests the narcissistic ego, is also perceived as somehow lacking due to the fact that the being is not in the place where he sees himself, but only in the place from which he misrecognizes himself in the other.

As the child experiences discord between his lived experience of the body, still uncoordinated, and his external image (or the image of himself he obtains from others, usually the mother) as unified, Lacan argues that the ego at this point is characterized by two opposing experiences: jubilation or enjoyment, and frustration and aggression. The latter experience is said to be the result of the paranoic knowledge produced by the splitting of the subject: the subject who misrecognizes himself in the place of the other. Lacan argues that it is the recognition of alienation, of the subject split off from his being, that underlies aggressive behaviour. Having invested everything in the image (which is and is not himself), and internalized it, the child takes the image for himself. And yet, being outside himself, he cannot fully control it. As Grosz puts it, the subject

> takes as its own an image which is other, an image which remains out of the ego's control. The subject, in other words, recognizes itself at the moment it loses itself in/as the other. This other is the foundation and support of its identity, as well as what destabilizes or annihilates it. The subject's "identity" is based on a (false) recognition of an other as the same (Grosz, 1990: 41).

Unable to distinguish fully between self and other (between himself and his mother), the child still held within the imaginary relations supported by the mirror-stage displays all the jealous and aggressive behaviours of transitivism:

> The child who strikes another says that he has been struck; the child who sees another fall, cries... There is a sort of structural crossroads here to which we must accommodate our thinking if we are to understand the nature of aggressivity in man and its relation with the formalism of his ego and his objects. It is in this erotic relation, in which the human individual fixes upon himself an image that alienates him from himself, that are to be found the energy and the form on which this organization of the passions that he will call his ego is based (Lacan, 1977: 19).

The frustration felt by the child over his lack of coordination and fragmentary experience of his body is directed precisely where he misrecognizes himself as other. For Lacan, representative of this aggression is the retroactively constructed relation between man and the archaic fragmentary units of the body, the *"imagos of the fragmented body"* (Lacan, 1977: 11):

> Among these *imagos* are some that represent the elective vectors of aggres-
> sive intentions, which they provide with an efficacity that might be called
> magical. These are the images of castration, mutilation, dismemberment,
> dislocation, evisceration, devouring, bursting open of the body... One
> only has to listen to children aged between two and five playing, alone
> or together, to know that the pulling off of the head and the ripping open
> of the belly are themes that occur spontaneously to their imagination,
> and that this is corroborated by the experience of the doll torn to pieces
> (Lacan, 1977: 11).

Lacan is alluding to the pleasure and pain associated with the Imaginary
state of being, be it by the child playing with a doll or the various adult
representational fascinations with the grotesque body in bits and pieces.
Whenever these images appear, it is the pre-oedipal, imaginary body that
is being retroactively posited.

For Lacan, the Imaginary, ordered by dual relations wherein the subject and his (m)other are mutually defined as the illusory fulfillment of
desire for and in each other, constitutes the condition of transference.
That is, the Imaginary order is the realm of transference, understood as
"a drama where narcissism and aggression, love and hate, play themselves
out" (Ragland-Sullivan, 1992: 174). Because desire in the Imaginary is
pre-Symbolic, it is assumed to be fully present in relation to the other.
The mother is believed to be the bearer of the phallus (Freud's "phallic
mother"), while the child believes himself also to bear the phallus that
can satisfy the maternal desire.

The image satisfies the child as a fully adequate representation of
himself. The other is not conceived of as completely separate, but as the
internalized condition of the subject's identity. That is, "[b]efore desire
learns to recognize itself – let us say the word – through the symbol, it
is seen solely in the other" (Lacan, 1991: 170). This is what Lacan means
when he states that "*man's desire is the desire of the other*," and the alienation of desire in the Imaginary is considered to be the "original, specular
foundation of the relation to the other" (Lacan, 1991: 176). And the only
outcome possible for such relations, wherein desire "exists solely in the
single plane of the imaginary relation of the specular stage, projected,
alienated in the other" is the "destruction of the other" (Lacan, 1991:
170). So, according to Lacan, the crucial structure of the subject on the
imaginary plane is "to destroy the person who is the site of alienation"
(Lacan, 1991: 172). Imaginary mastery always involves an annihilation of
the (m)other.

The subject within the Imaginary order, whose entire understanding
of external reality is represented by the other (the body of the mother),

is hardly capable of being a subject of culture. Like Freud's pre-oedipal child, the imaginary subject is aggressive, sadistic, and in constant pursuit of incestuous pleasure. Lacan famously rereads Freud's oedipal cleaving of this dyadic relationship, through the intervention of the father's threat of castration, in terms of language. What is lacking in the imaginary is the mediating function of the symbol, of language. For Lacan, in order for the child to take his place in language and society, this incestuous satisfaction of desire needs to be mediated by a signifier of desire, short-circuiting this anti-social and aggressive relation. Desire must give way to a demand, that is, to the "no" (*non*) of the law. And in the familial con-structs of patriarchal order, it is the father who symbolizes this regulatory function of the law. For Lacan, within patriarchal order it is the father's name (*nom*) and prohibition (*non*) against the desire of the mother, in both senses of the genitive, that carves out a symbolic place for both the male and female child.

While the Imaginary order functions according to the dual relation between the ego and its (m)other, the Symbolic order functions accord-ing to three fields of exchange – the subject, the other, and the Other. While "other" specifies the relationship with a specular other, the "Other," broadly speaking, refers to the order of language and speech. It is the nec-essary structural locale for the individual subject (only in the Other can the subject find its signifying place; Lacan, 1977: 285). Because the Law/name of the father forbids the maternal body and its desire, any desire for her and the anti-social plenitude generated by the Imaginary order must be repressed. This primary repression of desire is what founds the unconscious.

For Lacan, whose linguistic theory is indebted to Saussure and Jakob-son, the mechanics of desire and language are homologous. Desire, like language, can never be fully satisfying or present to itself. Desire is never satisfied, its mechanics understood as the movement from one object to another in endless frustration. And like desire, words are never the things themselves, but mark the place of their absence. Meaning will only ever be the effect of the endless movement from signifier to signi-fier. Because the unconscious is founded on the repression of desire, its content will be structured like language. After the entry into the Symbolic through acceptance of the paternal metaphor (whose symbol is the Phallus), it is only in the unconscious that maternal desire is present. Without accepting the paternal metaphor (the father's name and law), the subject cannot take his place in the Symbolic, remaining trapped instead in the immanence of the mother's bodily pleasure and desire, effecting a psychotic subject.

Because the child is born into "a world of others who speak," eventually he must take his place within the a priori order of language structures and social laws, the Symbolic order, as an "I." The axis of the Symbolic is one of desire or lack as the child becomes separated from its first love-object/mother, to hold a now distinct position in the network of established symbolic and social structures, beyond the immediacy of the maternal body. In developing language, the child learns that a word stands in the place of the thing desired, now present in its absence. As a consequence, desire is constituted in the Symbolic by lack. Split off from his being, the child now desires the impossible reunion with the "lost object" or *objet petit a*, that part of himself given up (castrated) upon entry into the realm of law, language, and culture. The subject of the Symbolic is necessarily a subject of lack, a *desiring* subject. The "Phallus" is the Lacanian term for the signifier of desire, that is, the signifier of the lack that constitutes the subject of language as a subject of desire (Lacan, 1977: 281-91). As such, it is a "signifier without signified," "the signifier intended to designate as a whole the effects of the signified, in that the signifier conditions them by its presence as a signifier" (Lacan, 1977: 285).

The formation of the subject, in Lacan's theory, is the formation of a logical subject, a subject of language and its laws, rather than the formation of a biological subject (Ragland-Sullivan, 1992: 205). Unlike Freud, for whom the recognition of castration by the child is a recognition of biological fact, Lacan insists that what the child (male and female) perceives is the mother's subordination to the law of the father, and her desire for him. In punishing or denying the child, mother is relying upon the law or language of the absent father. In desiring him, father is seen to be the one who *has* the desired power, the phallus. And yet, because the father desires the mother, she is imagined to be the one who *is* the phallus, the object of desire. Her relation to the phallus is one of being, not having. And so, in recognizing that the mother does not have the phallus, and repressing the desire for her (maternal phallus) that prevents him from taking a place in the wider social network (thus instituting the unconscious, and the establishment of the superego which regulates enjoyment), the child also becomes a sexed being. *He* is now given a place within the Symbolic, and in compensation for the ban on the mother (the father's woman), his position in the Symbolic as upholder of the father's law guarantees him the promise of a woman of his own. His anticipatory pleasure is now that of the future proprietor of the phallus.

For the girl child, however, things are not quite as simple or as beneficial. In response to her rejection of maternal desire and her assumption of the paternal metaphor, the father's name and his law, she will henceforth take her place in the Symbolic as a speaking being, an "I." But she is only ever a mimic of the masculine subject because, like her mother, she is the one who *is* the phallus (the object of a desire that is understood as masculine), never the rightful owner. She is positioned at the place of lack, as castrated, as that which is desired but never desires in her own right. What she does desire is to be desired, and in so desiring erases the possibility of any desire specific to her as woman:

> Paradoxical as this formulation may seem, I am saying that it is in order to be the phallus, that is to say, the signifier of the desire of the Other, that a woman will reject an essential part of femininity, namely, all her attributes in the masquerade. It is for that which she is not that she wishes to be desired as well as loved. But she finds the signifier of her own desire in the body of him to whom she addresses her demand for love (Lacan, 1977: 289-90).[9]

As many have noted, while Lacan is adamant that the phallus is not the penis,[10] the privileging of the masculine here is undeniable. As Elizabeth Grosz points out, "(t)he phallus cannot be regarded simply as a neutral term which positions both sexes within the extra-familial social field, for the effects of such positioning are very different, and the narcissistic 'wound' to the woman's body depicted by the castration fantasy is the unspoken cost of men's positions of social and sexual primacy" (Grosz, 1990: 322). Irigaray asserts that the Lacanian phallus, despite its logical rather than biological function, presents no challenge to patriarchal order:

> In this perspective, we might suspect the *phallus* (Phallus) of being the *contemporary figure of a god jealous of his prerogatives*; we might suspect it of claiming, on this basis, to be the ultimate meaning of all discourse, the standard of truth and propriety, in particular as regards sex, the signifier and/or the ultimate signified of all desire, in addition to continuing, as emblem and agent of the patriarchal system, to shore up the name of the father (Father) (Irigaray, 1985b: 67).

However, it is important to note that Irigaray is not advocating an anti-castration position that would entail the rejection of the paternal metaphor, for such a rejection inevitably produces the psychotic subject. Instead, as Whitford rightly points out, Irigaray is arguing that it is the *non-symbolization* (a foreclosure, in psychoanalytic terms) of the maternal and the relation to the maternal body as specifically feminine (i.e. non-phallic) that constantly *threatens* women with psychosis (Whitford, 1991: 86). While the non-symbolization of the maternal body ensures the sanity of the son, it threatens the daughter with madness. Without the means to represent the original loss (the necessary separation or "castration" that must occur for a subjective position to be assumed within the Symbolic), women find themselves in a Symbolic and social order that affords them no subjective position outside phallic terms. Explicitly, the only valid place for woman in the Symbolic is the *place* of the mother (Lacan, 1999: 91). For Irigaray, this Symbolic place not only ensures the mono-sexual and auto-generative logic of Western thought (the philosophical imaginary) by representing woman only as maternal *function* for man, reproducer of his name, but it also prevents women from having any ideal image of themselves and their bodies outside of this function (the narcissistic "wound"). There is no sexually specific ideal image for women within the Symbolic. I discuss this aspect of Irigaray's thought, particularly with respect to maternal genealogy, in the next two sections dealing with Freud.

Before moving to a more thorough discussion of Irigaray's critique of Lacan's mirror-stage, it is first necessary to understand the dialectical relations between the Imaginary, the Symbolic, and the Real. Neither the Imaginary nor the Real is capable of articulation outside of Symbolic operations. And yet, both the Imaginary and the Real participate in the Symbolic in constitutive ways. The Real is what is unrepresentable, even disruptive of Symbolic order. In Žižek's terms, the Real is "the 'hard,' traumatic reality which resists symbolization" (Žižek, 1997: 175). And yet, it is this repressed trauma that not only enables our construction of reality through phantasy formations[11] – "the impossible-real kernel around which symbolization turns" (Žižek, 1997: 95) – but it is also what disrupts any symbolic identity for the subject. In simpler terms, the unrepresentable Real both guarantees the necessary functioning of the Symbolic for the subject, and thwarts the full representation of the subject to himself within the Symbolic. The subject feels that there is always something more to him, something lost or absent from Symbolic representations because of this impossible-real kernel of his being sacrificed upon entry into language.

As outlined above, the Imaginary is the first representational structure that enables the child to reflect upon himself as a being in the world, introducing a gap between himself and the Real. And yet, Imaginary relations themselves are only articluated retrospectively from within the given Symbolic framework or structure. That is, it is only through language that we can theorize Imaginary relations. The Imaginary, like the Real, is both constitutive of and constituted by the Symbolic.

Returning now to Irigaray, her interest in Lacan's theory of the birth of the subject concerns the familiar relationship between the specular and knowledge, cast in masculine thought as the universal condition of all human beings. Irigaray argues that this psychoanalytic subject of specul(ariz)ation is an implicit male subject, and that Lacan fails to acknowledge that his own theoretical formulation of the genesis of the ego is fully consistent with a philosophical imaginary that erases feminine specificity or autonomy. The mirror that reflects the future possibilities for the nascent ego is a mirror capable of seeing only one sex, despite Lacan's disclaimer that the sex of the other in the specular economy of the Imaginary is of no consequence. For Irigaray, that Lacan's ego-in-process is jubilant before a specular image of himself[12] that excludes recognition of sex (i.e. a non-sexed body) signals that the economy of the Imaginary is an economy of the Same where the male sex is masked by neutrality.

The Lacanian mirror is flat, according to Irigaray (who is reading Lacan literally, taking him at his word), for reasons that Lacan seems either unaware of or unwilling to acknowledge in the earlier stages of his work. That is, the flat mirror that Lacan utilizes sustains the construction of a particular subject in relation to origins that is at the heart of western philosophy, a unified *male* subject able to disavow any debt to the maternal. This may seem to be an erroneous criticism given Lacan's somewhat anti-Cartesian philosophy,[13] not to mention the presence of the mother in the mirror stage. However, Irigaray argues that the presence of the mother at the formative stages of the infant's development serves only as a support or prop for the production of a nascent subject able to misperceive himself as a unified, co-ordinated and coherent being, identifying "with the visual *Gestalt* of his own body" (Lacan, 1977: 18). While the mother supports the child as he reflects upon his reflection, she herself is invisible. He comes to see only himself in the place that she occupies *for him*:

> Now, if this ego is to be valuable, some "mirror" is needed to reassure it and re-insure it of its value. Woman will be the foundation for this specular duplication, giving man back "his" image and repeating it as the "same." If an *other* image, an *other* mirror were to intervene, this inevitably would entail the risk of mortal crisis. Woman will therefore be this sameness – or at least its mirror image – and, in her role of mother, she will facilitate the repetition of the same, in contempt for her difference. Her own sexual difference (Irigaray, 1985a: 54).

Irigaray's claim is that Lacan's insistence that the sexual specificity of the other is insignificant in the Imaginary betrays the inability to think sexual difference *within* the Symbolic. By retroactively positing the non-sexed body or *Gestalt* as constitutive of subjectivity, Lacan perpetuates the dominant philosophical blindspot of woman's sexual specificity. Irigaray argues that the non-sexed body is, in fact, paradoxically a non-sexed male body:

It behooves us, then, to look into the status of the "exteriority" of this form that is "constitutent (more than constituted)" for the subject, into the way it serves as screen to another outside (a body other than this "total form")... And *so far as the organism is concerned, what happens if the mirror provides nothing to see?* No sex, for example? So it is with the girl. And when he says that in the constituent effects of the mirror image, the sex of one's like(ness) does not matter ("it is a necessary condition for the maturation of the gonad of the female pigeon that it should see another member of its species, of either sex" [p. 3]) and also that "the mirror-image would seem to be the threshold of the visible world" (ibid.) isn't this a way of stressing that the feminine sex will be excluded from it? And that it is a sexualized, or unsexualized, male body that will determine the features of that *Gestalt,* matrix irreducible to/from the introduction of the subject in the social order (Irigaray, 1985b: 117-18).

With no sexually specific reflection of her own, woman will thus serve to assure man that his illusion of mastery and totality is a reality. Even if this coherence is a misrecognition, it still provides the male ego with enough sustenance and fortification to serve it well enough in the social and symbolic spheres into which it will eventually fit as a subject. However, because the Symbolic offers no value to the female sex beyond its function in the phallic economy of desire, no such ego sustenance is available to "woman" who, upon entry into the Symbolic, will take on the very place of lack. If the entry into the Symbolic realms of language and culture involves a cost for the subject (the lost relation to the Real), there is, in the case of the female child, a far greater cost. While man is afforded a place within a structure that does value *his* body, specifically his sexed body (with the Phallus of Lacanian theory perpetuating the phantasy of valuable masculine-paternal origins and negligible or unrepresentable feminine-maternal origins), no such place or structure exists for woman.

Furthermore, Irigaray finds in Lacan's revised oedipal narrative of origins the Platonic logic of metaphoric erasure, the concealment of the process of movement from one field to the next – "the forgotten transition" – the "other or like act of forgetting, the foundation it rises out of" (Irigaray, 1985a: 247). It is only upon realizing that the mother is castrated, in Freud's terms, or does not possess what symbolizes the signifier of desire – the Phallus – in Lacan's terms, that the child will renounce and repress his desire for the mother. In taking up the name of the father, the child (male or female) enters the order of metaphor and substitution, and forgets that he has forgotten any debt to the mother. Consistent with the intellectual traditions and social orders of the West, in Lacanian theory, corporeal maternal origin is effaced and replaced by the Phallus. And the effect of such a coherent intellectual and social ordering, for women, is the prohibition against articulating a relationship to origins:

> ...woman's symbolization of her beginning, of the specificity of her relationship to the origin, has always already been erased, or is it repressed? by the economy that man seeks to put in place in order to resolve the problem of his primary cause. A problem to be solved by putting the Phallus at the beginning, and at the end (Irigaray, 1985a: 60).

In place of the flat mirror, Irigaray posits another mirror, the speculum, the mirror whose curved surface may be capable of seeing and articulating something *other* than what is reflected on the flat surface of the Lacanian/Platonic mirror. It is a mirror which is capable of destroying the illusion that all that is not readily visible to the naked eye does not, in fact, exist. The speculum arguably makes visible the concealed maternal support of the subject before the flat mirror. And this something "other" is of course the "other woman" of the title *Speculum of the Other Woman*. The figure of the concave mirror allows for the possibility of articulating the sex of woman as *different* to man, rather than appearing as the lack or "nothing to see" which the flat mirror can only provide. Crucially, the speculum figures a new mode of encounter in the desire for knowledge and its relation to subjectivity through the alternative means it offers for representing original loss, particularly for women. It is a prop capable of disturbing the scene of representation constructed by man to serve him well in his relation with reality:

> Thus it was necessary both to reexamine the domination of the specular and the speculative over history and also – since the specular is one of the irreducible dimensions of the speaking animal – to put into place a mode of specularization that allows for the relation of woman to "herself" and to her like. Which presupposes *a curved mirror*, but also one that is *folded back on itself*, with its impossible reappropriation "on the inside" of the mind, of thought, of subjectivity. Whence the *intervention of the speculum and of the concave mirror*, which disturb the staging of representation according to too-exclusively masculine parameters. For these latter exclude women from participation of transactions among men (Irigaray, 1985b: 154-55).

In summary, Irigaray's main criticism of the Lacanian mirror-stage is that this flat mirror is the prop that allows Lacan to re-stage the origins of a masculine subject in relation to *his* world, without admitting the masculine sexualization of the scene he sets, and the matricide that this scene depends upon for its consistency. The specular is "one of the irreducible dimensions of the speaking animal" (Irigaray, 1985b: 154), and the mirror-stage is "the original adventure through which man, for the first time, has the experience of seeing himself, of reflecting on himself and conceiving of himself as other than he is – an essential dimension of the human, which entirely structures his fantasy life" (Lacan, 1991: 79). Irigaray wants to insist that such a conceptual framework for articulating a relation to origins must be understood within the context of philosophical thought as an effect of the dialectical relations between a sexually specific, not universal, masculine Imaginary and Symbolic. And in this representational economy, woman can only ever function as "a *hole* in men's signifying economy. A nothing that might cause the ultimate destruction, the splintering, the break in their systems of 'presence', of 're-presentation' and 'representation' " (Irigaray, 1985a: 50). The invisibility of mother-matter in the flat mirror guarantees man that his only debts belong to the father and not the mother. Again, Lacan's mirror stage may be read as a "primal scene" that attempts to extricate the mother from the originary, (pro)creative moment.

Thus, Irigaray's fundamental criticism is that despite the disruptive aspect of Lacan's theory of subjectivity with respect to the stable subject of western philosophy up until Freud (i.e. the ego is precariously dependent on others for its coherence, and a subject is only ever a subject constituted by lack), the logic of the Lacanian mirror stage, like Freud's Oedipal complex, is fully dependent on the privileged status of the visible. Like all patriarchal modes of knowledge, as Irigaray claims in *Speculum of the Other Woman*, psychoanalysis is blind to anything that is not fully visible and therefore knowable. Here, at the eroticized conjunction between knowledge and ocularcentrism, woman only ever appears as lack itself. "Woman" is that which is made to bear the lack that man himself cannot acknowledge. Indeed, this is arguably what Lacan means when he says "woman is a symptom of man" (Ragland-Sullivan, 1992: 175).

According to Irigaray, Lacan's insistence that the sexual specificity of the other is irrelevant in the Imaginary guarantees the silence of the feminine in the Symbolic. And crucially, for Irigaray, this exclusion has dire effects for women in the Social. While "woman" may be excluded from the Symbolic (or rather, included as that which is necessarily silenced, its mute foundation), women themselves are in fact not absent from the social. Without social and Symbolic structures that acknowledge women outside of phallic imaginary relations (as man's self-reflecting other), women are left with a relation to their bodies and to other women that is constituted by detritus or debris, the unnecessary remainders of culture. So, it is crucial to understand that Irigaray is challenging Lacan's move to *universalize* the mirror-stage, not the theory itself. She is not offering an alternative psychoanalytic theory, but is rather analysing the phallic structuration of the theory itself. Lacan's tale of the birth of the ego presents clearly the familiar relation of the male subject to origins (mother – son, or rather, father's producer – son), but forecloses any possibility of articulating another relation pertaining to the feminine (woman-mother – daughter). This, Irigaray claims, is consistent with the philosophical denial and erasure of mother-matter from the representative original scene of epistemology (exemplified by Plato's myth of the cave), guaranteeing only paternal origination as that which is valued, thus also guaranteeing one line of descent at the expense of the other.

Having given a detailed outline of Lacan's rereading of Freud's theories concerning the origins of the human subject, along with Irigaray's critique of Lacan, I now want to return to Freud himself. The discussion of Lacan's Imaginary, Symbolic, and Real is a necessary prelude to Irigaray's criticisms of Freud because it is these three concepts, most especially the Imaginary, that provide her with the critical tools to analyse the discourse of the father of psychoanalysis. Irigaray's concern with Freud's discourse on femininity is to analyse the phantasmatics of his own Imaginary economy, the corporeal images and scenarios that enable Freudian speculation and conceptualization adequately to re-present the origins of subjectivity to himself and his (male) psychoanalytic colleagues. Her claim is that Freud's science (and Lacan's reformulation of it) is structured according to an anal-sadistic model of desire, a model that participates within and perpetuates the phantasized auto-productive homo-logic of Western metaphysics.

4. *Psychoanalysis, the Economy of the Same, and the Monopoly of the Origin*

According to Freud, female sexuality is the "dark continent" of psychoanalytic discourse. In her readings of Freud's texts concerned with the question of female sexuality, particularly his late (fictive) lecture "On Femininity," Irigaray contends that Freud cannot allow for the possibility of female sexual development that works according to a different economy than that of the male model he develops, namely the Oedipus Complex. Freud is "blind" to sexual difference, allowing only one genital configuration – that of the male sex. When he looks at woman's sex, there is either only the insufficient clitoris/penis or there is "nothing to see." Woman is, therefore, a "lesser" man than man himself, and crucial to her "normal" sexual development is her realization of this "fact of castration."

According to Irigaray, psychoanalysis is incapable of approaching female sexuality in terms other than those modeled on masculine identity and subjectivity because of its unacknowledged and unchallenged

adherence to the western philosophic order. Freud most radically transforms the belief in the rational and unified subject of western philosophical idealism through his theorizing of the unconscious as simultaneously
constitutive of and threatening for subjectivity. And yet, when it comes
to female sexuality, he constantly falls back upon and within the economy
of the logos, where reason and truth are accorded transcendental and
eternal status:

> For example, Freud undermines a certain way of conceptualizing the
> "present," "presence," by stressing deferred action, overdetermination, the
> repetition compulsion, the death drive, and so on, or by indicating, in his
> theory or his practice, the impact of so-called unconscious mechanisms on
> the language of the "subject." But himself a prisoner of a certain economy of
> the logos, he defines sexual difference by giving *a priori* value to Sameness,
> shoring up his demonstration by falling back upon time-honored devices
> such as analogy, comparison, symmetry, dichotomous oppositions, and so
> on. Heir to an "ideology" that he does not call into question, Freud asserts
> that the "masculine" is the sexual model, that no representation of desire
> can fail to take it as the standard, can fail to submit to it (Irigaray, 1985b:
> 72; see also Irigaray, 1985a: 28).

And yet, through this failure to call into question the very ideology that
supports the phantasy of the mono-sexual and the desire for the same,
Freud inadvertently reveals what has been at stake all along in discourses
of truth: sexual *indifference*:

> Psychoanalytic discourse on female sexuality is the discourse of truth.
> A discourse that tells the truth about the logic of truth: namely, that *the
> feminine occurs only within models and laws devised by male subjects*. Which
> implies that there are not really two sexes, but only one. A single prac-
> tice and representation of the sexual. With its history, its requirements,
> reverses, lacks, negative(s)...of which the female sex is the mainstay.
>
> This model, a *phallic* one, shares the values promulgated by patriarchal
> society and culture, values inscribed in the philosophical corpus: property,
> production, order, form, unity, visibility...and erection (Irigaray, 1985b: 86).

Thus, for Irigaray, Freud "strikes at least *two blows* at the scene of representation": the breakdown of the notion of the unified essence of the
subject of speech and the unveiling of the monosexual nature of metaphysical discourse:

> The other blow, blinder and less direct, occurs when – himself a prisoner of
> a certain economy of the logos, of a certain logic, notably of "desire," whose
> link to classical philosophy he fails to see – he defines sexual difference
> as a function of the a priori of the same, having recourse, to support this
> demonstration, to the age-old processes: analogy, comparison, symmetry,

dichotomic oppositions, and so on. When, as a card-carrying member of an "ideology" that he never questions, he insists that the sexual pleasure known as masculine is the paradigm for all sexual pleasure, to which all representations of pleasure can but defer in reference, support, and submission. In order to remain effective, all this certainly needed at the very least to remain hidden! By exhibiting this "symptom," this crisis point in metaphysics where we find exposed that sexual "indifference" that had assured metaphysical coherence and "closure," Freud offers it up for our analysis. With his text offering itself to be understood, to be read, as doubtless the most relevant remark of an ancient dream of self...one that had never been interpreted (Irigaray, 1985a: 28).

As we know, Freud argues that the pregenital or pre-oedipal phases of sexual development (oral, anal, phallic)[14] are the same for both the boy child and the girl child. This symmetry is ensured by Freud's insistence that libido is "invariably and necessarily of a masculine nature" (Freud, 1905: 219). Thus, the little girl is psychically, despite her physical difference, a little boy who must *become* a girl, and ultimately a *feminine* woman. As Irigaray points out, this path to "normal" femininity, fraught with troubled twists and turns that the boy child never has to negotiate because he never has to *become* masculine (i.e. the changes in both erotogenic zones and object choice are features of the girl's maturation only), is in fact the path to an asexual *maternity*. According to Freud, femininity is characterized as "giving preference to *passive aims*," which he differentiates from passivity through the assertion that passive aims may require a large amount of activity. Furthermore, because her sexual life ("...her share in the *sexual function*") is the behavioural model for her social life, women thus find themselves carrying a preference for "passive behaviour and passive aims" (Freud, 1932a: 115-16). Irigaray points out that what Freud is actually referring to when he speaks of the sexual function is not women's desires or pleasures, but her role in the *reproductive* function:

> The reproductive function is not explicitly named, but passages before and after, as well as references to other texts, indicate clearly that when it comes to sexual function and its model-value, the reproductive function alone is being referred to. The point being that man is *the* procreator, that sexual *production-reproduction* is referable to his "activity" alone, to his "pro-ject" alone. Woman is nothing but the receptacle that passively receives his *product*, even if sometimes, by the display of her passively aimed instincts, she has pleaded, facilitated, even demanded that it be placed within her. Matrix – womb, earth, factory, bank – to which the seed capital is entrusted so that it may germinate, produce, grow fruitful, without woman being able to lay claim to either capital or interest since she has only submitted "passively" to reproduction. Herself held in receivership as a certified means of (re)production (Irigaray, 1985a: 18).

Freud's "blindspot" is female sexuality, the "dark continent." Neither the girl child nor the "normal" woman is imagined as having a sex of her own, but only a sex or sexual (re-productive) function in relation to man. This path to adult sexuality is, for the woman, the very theft of her sexuality that is necessary for man and his social, cultural, and theoretical configurations. Freud's theory of female sexuality is clearly heir to the Platonic augmentation of the paternal over the maternal, a particular "imaginary" feature that Irigaray insists is constitutive of speculation in the West. Furthermore, given Irigaray's insistence that Freud's own theorization of female sexual development is consistent with the logic of anality as theorized by Freud himself, and thus that his theoretical model betrays his entrapment within an "anal imaginary," I should outline, briefly, what Freud means by anal eroticism before moving on to a discussion of his work on female sexual development.

Following the first or oral phase of libidinal organization, where oral pleasure is gained through suckling, is what Freud calls the *"sadistic-anal* organization" (Freud, 1905: 198-99). Where the sexual aim of the oral phase consists in the incorporation of the object (first food, then other objects such as the thumb, etc.), the anal phase concerns the pleasure afforded by the mastery of fecal production, both expulsion and retention. This is said to be sadistic on two counts: pleasure is gained through expulsion and rejection, and through mastery of the muscular contractions. As such, two currents, active and passive, which will be present throughout all sexual life, begin at this stage: the active mastery of the somatic musculature, and the passive pleasure of the anal mucous membrane upon expulsion. As Freud puts it, "the organ which, more than any other, represents the *passive* sexual aim is the erotogenic mucous membrane of the anus" (Freud, 1905: 198). At this stage of erotogenic organization, there is no recognition of sexual difference. Nor in Freud's phallic phase does sexual difference exist. While the active-passive antithesis dominates the sadistic-anal, it is the split between uncastrated phallic and castrated phallic that dominates the phallic stage. Only with puberty, according to Freud, does "the sexual polarity coincide with *male* and *female*" (Freud, 1923: 145). And, in a philosophically familiar move, the active-passive antithesis present in the sadistic-anal stage of the individual is later split into two, redistributed according to males/masculinity (active, aggressive, productive) and females/femininity (passive, compliant, receptive).

Freud is adamant, however, that the two antitheses are not to be confused, calling such a confusion "the error of superimposition" (Freud, 1932a: 115). But as Jane Gallop has shown, despite his insistence for over twenty years that these oppositions must remain distinct, his own theories consistently fail to do so (Gallop, 1982: 67-70). And for Irigaray, the principal symptom of Freud's entrapment within an anal-phallic phase[15] dominated by an anal logic (of anal-logical reasoning), is his constant superimposition of masculine sexuality upon the feminine. In other words, while Freud believes he is theorizing sexual difference, comprehending the development of two distinct sexes, he does in fact theorize only one sexual pole.

For Freud, the disappearance of certain pregenital trends present in the girl are the "natural" outcome of her realization, in the phallic phaze, that she bears an inferior sexual tool (Freud, 1924: 179). The girl child's activity in all three phases is understood as masculine, especially where the clitoral activity in the phallic stage is commensurate with the masturbatory activity of the boy with his penis. That is, the clitoris is a small penis. Recognition of this equivalence is something that will devastate the little girl when she eventually realises her sexual "equipment" to be inferior, leading her to blame her equally poorly-equipped mother for their inferiority. Furthermore, she will spend the rest of her life envying and desiring to have this valued sexual apparatus (and guarantee of value itself) in various forms. This early recognition of the "fact of castration," leads the girl to hate her mother, turn away from her towards the father who possesses the longed for signifier of power. Where the castration complex supposedly instigates the *end* of the oedipal complex for the boy (who recognizes that his mother does not have a penis, and that the father who does have it threatens to castrate the boy if he persists with his desire for the mother),[16] for the girl child it is the knowledge of castration that propels her *into* the oedipal structure of desire for the father. The three possible lines of development for the girl are sexual inhibition or neurosis, a masculinity complex, or "normal" femininity (Freud, 1932a: 126). The path to "normal" sexuality is successful if, upon rejecting her mother but ultimately realizing she cannot have the father, she thus returns to identify with (the place of) her mother. This initial rejection of the mother by the daughter is necessary if the girl is to grow into a normally functioning woman who desires man, and more importantly, desires to reproduce for him. And it is necessary if she is to grow up to be a "normal" woman whose fate is forever to desire to be (like) a man. Which is another way of saying to desire like man.

Crucially, the little girl's development is not complete until her desire to have a penis, her initial "penis envy," is replaced by the desire for a child, especially a boy child. Through this equivalence of baby-penis, Freud assures, "the ancient masculine wish for the possession of a penis is still faintly visible through the femininity now achieved" (Freud, 1932a: 128). Freud's emphasis on the product of sexual relations, the child, indicates strongly, for Irigaray, that Freud is describing not female sexuality, but her place within an anal-masculine economy of sexuality (Irigaray, 1985a: 73-76).

Within this economy, woman's sexual specificity ("femininity") is absorbed into an asexual maternity. Woman only wants the penis for its procreative power, rather than for any corporeal pleasures it may afford, so that all her attentions may be focused onto the product of copulation, the child-penis. And of course, it is the boy child, the one who actually has the penis, who is truly desired. Irigaray points out that the boy child, who appears as both penis-substitute and penis-product (Irigaray, 1985a: 74), effectively negates any contribution on the part of the mother. Her body is merely the vessel for the father's seed to reproduce itself, and the boy "is the sign of the seed's immortality, of the fact that the properties of the sperm have won out over those of the ovum. Thus he guarantees the father's power to reproduce and represent himself, and to perpetuate his gender and his species" (Irigaray, 1985a: 74). Finally, this substitutive equivalence of penis-child derives from, and indicates, the primacy of anal eroticism over genital sexuality. The faeces, once believed to be a gift-child produced for and with the mother, are substituted, in the case of the girl child, first by the penis and then by the child:

> "The concepts *faeces* (money, gift), *baby* and *penis* (Freud's italics) are ill-distinguished from one another and are easily interchangeable." The vagina – and even the womb? Of which, paradoxically, no mention is made in this context – functions like the anus, rectum, and intestines. In fact "interest in the vagina, which awakens later, is also essentially of anal-erotic origin." This is not to be wondered at, for the vagina itself, to borrow an apt phrase from Lou Andreas Salome (1916) is "taken on lease" from the rectum (Irigaray, 1985a: 74).[17]

The governing phantasy of Freud's theories of sexuality is the body able to produce a child without needing a womb or vagina to do so. According to such a phantasy, woman, with her specific bodily organization, is not required. Indeed, the standard of value within this economy seems to be the fecal mass, with the penis itself representing the fecal column. In this phantasy, woman is nothing but "the receptacle for the sperm (gift) injected by the penis (stool) and forces the child (feces) out through the vagina (rectum)" (Irigaray, 1985a: 75). What underlies and underwrites Freud's theoretical body concerning "origins" is the predominant phantasy of the sadistic-anal phase: the productive male body capable of birthing through the anus. Again, it is a phantasy that elides the creative power of women's bodies. And in the place of the erased maternal origin stands the phallus/fecal column.

For Freud, the little girl (who is a little boy) loves the *phallic* mother.[18] Upon realizing her mother's "lack," and her own, she turns towards the father and proceeds down the path to femininity, having finally left the phallic phase of sexualization and entered into the Oedipal complex (with the active/phallic clitoral production of pleasure cast aside in favour of the more "passive" vaginal longing). The feminine is not something that is ever produced and recognized by a mother and her daughter. According to Freud, when a girl plays with a doll and acts out the mother-daughter relationship (the girl representing the mother and the doll representing the child herself), this is not an attempt at expressing her femininity, her status as like the mother, though separate from her. It is not a means of representing her own specific separation from a body that resembles her own. It is *phallic* in that she is acting out the desire to identify with her mother "with the intention of substituting activity for passivity. *She* was playing the part of her mother and the doll was herself: now she could do with the baby everything that her mother used to do with her" (Freud, 1932a: 128). The girl child only identifies with the misrecognized phallus in the mother, accounting for her activity. On the other hand, when the girl's doll game manifests a desire for the penis, for the father's child, only then is the game considered "feminine." In taking the place of the mother and desiring to produce a child with or for the father, the girl child begins to take her place in this economy of desire as "feminine." And within this economy, mother and daughter can never share the same space in any way except competitively. "Feminine" activity is character-ized by the problematically sadistic-symbolic obliteration of the mother by the daughter.

The implications of all this, for women, are dire. Desiring the father (the opposite sex) only takes place through the rejection of the mother (and women in general, i.e. those hated for not having the penis), and woman's relation to origin, including her desire for origin, is unrepre-sentable in terms other than those imposed by the masculine model:

> The girl, let us repeat, has no right to play in any manner whatever with any representation of her beginning, no specific mimicry of origin is available to her: she must inscribe herself in the masculine, phallic way of relating to origin, that involves repetition, representation, reproduction (Irigaray, 1985a: 78).

For Irigaray, the "fact of castration" that woman is said to encounter in the bodies of herself, her mother, and all women, "has to be understood as a definitive prohibition against establishing one's own economy of the desire for origin":

> In fact this desire for re-presentation, for re-presenting oneself, and for representing oneself in desire is in some ways *taken away from woman at the outset* as a result of the radical devalorization of her "beginning" that she is inculcated with, subjected to – and which she subjects herself: is she not born of a castrated mother who could only give birth to a castrated child, even though she prefers (to herself) those who bear the penis? This shameful beginning must be forgotten, "repressed"... Therefore the girl shuns or is cast out of a *primary metaphorization* of her desire as a woman, and she becomes inscribed into the phallic metaphors of the small male (Irigaray, 1985a: 83-84).

In place of the absence or "taking leave" that constitutes the place of origin for the girl, according to Freud, is the desire for the phallus-penis. Freud's insistence that the penis (and eventually, all things going to plan, the [boy] child) will be the only means by which the girl will come to be accorded any value whatsoever, is interpreted by Irigaray as the appropriation of the relation to origin that consistently guarantees phallocentric thought. The phallus is understood as the "(e)mblem of man's appropriative relation to origin," as "an appropriation of the relation to origin and the desire for and as origin" (Irigaray, 1985a: 42, 33). Disavowing any relation to origins other than the Oedipal, where woman avails man of his fear of castration/death, Freud effectively castrates woman's sexual specificity to ensure the continued valuation of the phallus-penis and the paternal as source of all that is knowable and representable. This means that, for women, "*the beginning was the end of her story*, and that from now on she will have one dictated to her; by the man-father" (Irigaray, 1985a: 43).

Without the means of articulating her own loss with respect to origins, woman's best option is to assume her place within this economy of desire as either a mimic of men (though always falling short because of this "fact of castration") or the successfully "feminized" reproducer of the same: "mother."

> She is left with a *void*, a lack of all representation, re-presentation, and even strictly speaking of all mimesis of her desire for origin. That desire will henceforth pass through the discourse-desire-law of man's desire. "You will be my woman-mother, my wife, if you would, and (like) my mother, if you could," is a statement equivalent to: "You will be for me the possibility of repeating-representing-appropriating the/my relation to the origin." Now this operation – and we quote Freud's own words against him here – in no way constitutes a *displacement* of the origin – desire of the little girl, of the woman. It is more in the nature of an exile, an extradition, an exmatriation, from this/her economy of desire (Irigaray, 1985a: 42-43).

As representative of origin (for man), woman can have no relationship with "it"; there can be no "other side" of the representation of origin. Woman cannot turn it into her project of return or turning back (Irigaray, 1985a: 41). She is in a state of "exile" or "dereliction." In fact, Irigaray points out, if we take Freud's theoretical discourse of feminine sexuality at its word, the little girl's libidinal economy after the recognition of the "fact of castration" (explicitly, her mother's) bears a close resemblance to melancholia.[19]

The symptoms of melancholia, according to Freud, are "a profoundly painful dejection, cessation of interest in the outside world, loss of the capacity to love, inhibition of all activity, and a lowering of the self-regarding feelings to a degree that finds utterance in self-reproaches and self-revilings, and culminates in a delusional expectation of punishment" (Freud, 1917a: 244). He explains the complex process by which melancholia takes place as follows:

> An object-choice, an attachment of the libido to a particular person, had at one time existed; then owing to a real slight or disappointment coming from this loved person, the object-relationship was shattered. The result was not the normal one of a withdrawal of the libido from this object and a displacement of it on to a new one, but something different, for whose coming-about various conditions seem to be necessary. The object-cathexis proved to have little power of resistance and was brought to an end. But the free libido was not displaced on to another object; it was withdrawn into the ego. There, however, it was not employed in any specific way, but served to establish an *identification* of the ego with the abandoned object. Thus the shadow of the object fell upon the ego, and the latter could henceforth be judged by a special agency, as though it were an object, the forsaken object. In this way an object-loss was transformed into an ego loss and the conflict between the ego and the loved person into a cleavage between the critical activity of the ego and the ego as altered by identification.

> One or two things may be directly inferred with regard to the preconditions and effects of a process such as this. On the one hand, a strong fixation to the loved object must have been present; on the other hand, in contradiction to this, the object cathexis must have had little power of resistance (Freud, 1917a: 248-49).

Irigaray sees in this description the very same process that the little girl undergoes, according to Freud, when faced with the "fact of castration." The ambivalent feelings felt by the melancholic/little girl towards the lost object/mother, namely both love and hate ("the one seeks to detach the libido from the object, the other to maintain this position of the libido against the assault"; Freud, 1917a: 256), prevent the work of mourning taking place, the work required for the subject to move on from the lost object through a series of displacements. Irigaray places next to the symptoms of melancholia certain statements made by Freud developed from his "empirical" studies on women to show how melancholia is an apt diagnosis for women within phallocentric culture (loss of libidinal activity and loss of interest in masturbation when the previously loved object and organ are devalued; lack of interest in and contribution to society; the "desire" for the father being driven not by love but by greed, envy, and jealousy; the so-called passive nature of women; and the mortification of her self-love when comparison is made with the boy's far more impressive sexual equipment; Irigaray, 1985a: 66-67).[20] Given Freud's insistence that the narcissistic ego is derived from bodily sensations, and may be "regarded as a mental projection of the surface of the body" (Freud, 1914: 84), the realization of the "fact of castration" means that the girl introjects her own (and her mother's) shortcomings. In acknowledging her own flaw, she also acknowledges her inferiority to the far superior male.

Interestingly, Freud distinguishes melancholia from mourning by the inability of the melancholic to see clearly that which has been lost: "This would suggest that melancholia is in some way related to an object-loss which is withdrawn from consciousness, in contradistinction to mourning, in which there is nothing about the loss that is unconscious" (Freud, 1917a: 245). Without the ability to at least name the lost object of love, the work of mourning can not take place. Irigaray draws together Freud's theses concerning female sexuality and melancholia to extrapolate that, for the little girl, separation from her mother and from her *own* sex cannot be worked out through mourning (Irigaray, 1985a: 67) because there is no *symbolic* representation or value afforded to her own sex, no symbolic representation of what it is that has been lost. The relationship to the lost object (the relationship to origin) is marked by conflict and ambivalence that remain unconscious, without recourse to a language or system of representation that can replace or assist this conflict:

> *...the "loss" suffered by the little girl also affects the "ego."* As in melancholia. The little boy is narcissized, ego-ized by his penis – since the penis is valued on the sexual market and is overrated culturally because it can be seen, specularized, and fetishized – but this is not true for the little girl's sex organ(s). What is more, mother, whom the little girl is identifying with and using to build her ego, suffers from the same misfortune. Thus, in the ordeal of castration as "accomplished fact," the little girl's ego suffers, helplessly, a defeat, a wound, whose effects are to be made out in the broad outlines of melancholia (Irigaray, 1985a: 68-69).

Man is not only able to recreate his relationship to origin through his relationships with other women, but there is also an isomorphism between his sexuality and symbolic structures. For women, no such relationship can exist because she is not "a" sex – "The 'no sex' that has been assigned to the woman can mean that she does not have 'a' sex and that her sex is not visible nor identifiable or representable in a definite form" (Irigaray, 1977: 64; cited in Grosz, 1989: 111). As Elizabeth Grosz explains, Irigaray's positing of an isomorphism is not a naïve biological determinism or essentialism,[21] nor is she suggesting that language merely reflects, in a neutral or unmediated fashion, the anatomy of the male body. Irigaray is not speaking of anatomy but *morphology*, the construction of the body and its experiences through language:

> Bodies are not conceived by Irigaray as biologically or anatomically given, inert, brute objects, fixed by nature once and for all. She sees them as the bearers of meaning and social values, the products of social inscriptions, always inherently social... Her emphasis on morphology in place of anatomy indicates that she has stepped from the register of nature into that of social signification (Grosz, 1989: 112).

So, without the means to articulate her loss, without knowing what exactly has been lost in the movement into a symbolically situated subjectivity (the alienating effects of the entry into the symbolic, taking up the "I" of discourse, as Lacan will later rework the Freudian idea of castration), woman can have "no *consciousness* of her sexual impulses, of her libidinal economy and, more particularly, of her original desire and her desire for origin" (Irigaray, 1985a: 68). The relationship between mother and daughter remains buried in the unconscious.[22]

The problem that psychoanalysis diagnoses is the apparent struggle faced by women to remain separate and distinct from the maternal figure (and each other), with this failure being constitutive of melancholia (and hysteria) in women.[23] For Irigaray, however, this diagnosis of lack of individuation is itself a symptom of women's exclusion from the symbolic, beyond the maternal function.[24] As I mentioned above, Irigaray is arguing that a feminine relationship to origins that does not obliterate the mother, the first love-object with whom a separation must take place, is necessary if women are to avoid the various forms of madness that currently afflict them. It is not simply a case of extricating the introjected mother, "the maternal Thing," (Kristeva, 1989), but of creating a symbolic space for women distinct from the maternal function (the son's mother), so that the articulation of their distinction can take place. In other words, naming the problem on an individual level, without questioning the historically and culturally-determined features of this problem, can only orchestrate the successful return of the melancholic or hysteric into an unchanged patriarchal social order. Having been "fixed," the woman can assume her feminine role as it is prescribed by society and reinforced by psychoanalytic discourse.

In this section I have outlined Irigaray's main analysis of Freud's theoretical discourse concerning the origins of sexualized subjectivity, especially of female sexual development, as dependent upon an unacknowledged phantasmatic arrangement that she calls the anal imaginary. According to such a specul(ariz)ation, woman has no specific role in childbirth and her body can only ever appear as a flawed version of the male body. As bearer of lack, of the nothing to see, she comes to represent the "hole" of representation itself. She is the "dark continent," unknowable and invisible. Such a symbolic bodily construct ensures that she never threatens man's specular arrangements wherein he is able to imagine himself to be responsible for all production (of knowledge). Being invisible, she functions as the mirror (or the tain of the mirror) reflecting back to man only himself as possessor of all that is valuable and valued. However, such an imaginary obliteration of maternal power, the predominant imaginary of Western thought and social order, has dire effects for women. The daughter is prohibited from offering any re-presentation of her original relationship with the body of her mother. This ban threatens women with psychosis because of the failure to articulate something of the loss that must be incurred upon entry into language and society, particularly given the complicity of Western symbolic and social systems in this "burial" of the non-phallic feminine.

And so, finally, I turn now to Irigaray's challenge to Freud's other narrative of origins, specifically concerning civilization and religion, characterized by primal parricide. For Irigaray, certain myths of ancient Greece (and I limit my discussion here mainly to the Orestes legend and briefly to the Demeter-Persephone couple) contain traces of the matricide and the sundering of the mother-daughter bond at the base of recorded history in the West. By re-entering such mythologies into cultural and intellectual circulation, Irigaray is attempting to offer alternative possibilities for women in relation to origins. And she is also showing how the prohibition against the mother has, for a very long time in our cultural history, serviced masculine identity and subjectivity at the expense of the feminine, especially when it comes to relationships among women.

5. *The Murder of the Mother and the Forgetting of Female Ancestries*

In a lecture given in Montreal in 1980, titled "Le Corps-à-corps avec la mère,"[25] Irigaray asserts that western culture and civilization is founded on matricide, not the parricide that Freud famously postulates in *Totem and Taboo*. Prior to any murder and consumption of the father by the primal horde is an originary matricide that effects a social order. This "original sin" is unspeakable and must necessarily remain concealed if civilization is to sustain its semblance of order. As Elizabeth Grosz explains, for Irigaray, Freud's parricide is not the first cultural act, but the first recognized, symbolized, or recorded act. The privileged position of the father as controller of both women and sons is only enabled through a prior "murder" of the mother, that is, the cutting of the umbilical link between mother and child (Grosz, 1989: 163).

For Irigaray, it is the murdered body of the woman-mother that haunts the religious, scientific, psychoanalytic, and philosophical traditions held dear in the west. Irigaray's work, from *Speculum* onwards, approaches major philosophical thinkers such as Plato, Descartes, Spinoza, Hegel, Nietzsche, Heidegger, Merleau-Ponty, and Levinas. While the tone of her work alternates from the scathing critical irony (and at times sarcasm) of *Speculum* and *This Sex Which Is Not One* to the lamentation-like love discourses or "letters" of *The Forgetting of Air in Martin Heidegger* and *Marine Lover of Friedrich Nietzsche*, all of her readings of the philosophers seek out the buried mother within their discourse. Using a psychoanalytic framework, Irigaray searches for the symptomatic presence of this originary matricide within the philosophical unconscious. This "murder" is the complete repression and denial of any debt to the mother, which Irigaray interprets as the principal feature of the philosophic-psychoanalytic imaginary, as I have already discussed. Certain phantasies persist in truth discourses of the west that Irigaray traces back to this alternative "beginning." The sophistication of philosophical thought relies "upon an unacknowledged foundation, the unsymbolized maternal-feminine" (Whitford, 1991: 75). Man, as a social and thinking being, perceives himself (misrecognizes himself as) entirely responsible for his own creations: his social world, his language, his abstract categories, and himself. Man is, according to Irigaray, caught in the phantasy of being always self-made. Elizabeth Grosz puts it this way:

> ...the son is unable to accept the debt of life, body, nourishment and social existence he owes the mother. An entire history of Western thought is intent on substituting for this debt an image of the self-made, self-created man. One could go even further and suggest that the idea of God itself is nothing but an elaborate if unconscious strategy for alleviating man's consciousness of and guilt about this debt. As man's self-reflecting Other, God usurps women's creativity and their place as the source of the terrestial. God (and through Him, man) becomes the creator or mother of the mother.

> Born of woman's body, man devises religion, philosophy and true
> knowledges not simply as sublimations of his desire, but as forms of dis-
> avowal of this maternal debt. (Grosz, 1989: 120-21)

Psychoanalysis locates the Oedipal myth as *the* myth of the origin of
civilization, of social order under paternal rule. However, Irigaray insists
upon reading other myths so as to construct a different model of beginnings, one that incorporates the erasure of maternal power and genealogy
(the mother-daughter bond) into the story of the origin of civilization.
For Irigaray, one of the founding myths of patriarchal social order is the
Oresteia. Irigaray claims the *Oresteia* indicates that, contra Freud, there is
an unacknowledged matricide prior to any parricide that institutes social
order. Furthermore, the principal elements of the *Oresteia* – the murder
of the mother, the madness of the daughter who participates in her mother's murder with her brother, the saving of the murderous brother from
madness so as to establish patriarchal order, etcetera – are all still with us
today.

This facet of Irigaray's research is inextricable from her criticism that
while psychoanalysis can acknowledge the debt to the father (for language,
culture, order, etc.), it has very little, if anything, to say about maternal
debt (for blood, life, and the body) (Irigaray, 2002a: 219). And concerning mother-daughter love, psychoanalytic *theory* struggles to contribute.
Psychoanalysis, as a discourse of the West, arises out of and perpetuates a particular social order that has, since ancient times, attempted to
erase the maternal body, beyond its container-like procreative role for
men, from its field of vision. For Irigaray, this "murder" of the woman-
mother is certainly present in philosophy, from Plato to the present day,
and in psychoanalysis, a discourse that guards the "subject" from the
desire of the mother, from her all-consuming body and the madness that
it represents.

Like Freud, Irigaray has turned to the myths of Classical Greece to find
this moment of renunciation of the mother at the heart of our cultural
origins, a moment that seems to be submerged almost entirely within the
Hebrew creation myths. In the myths of ancient Greece, she argues, we
find evidence of the epochal shift that occurs when men begin to dominate and control women, suggesting that patriarchal rule has a history and
that we can begin to imagine a time when men do not dominate women.
In Freud's narrative of social origins, this epochal shift from matriarchy
to patriarchy takes place after a certain period of time (and as a result of
certain cultural "advances") *after* the murder of the father, the deed that
institutes the first epochal shift. Mother rule (or rather, mother-son rule)

arises after the removal of the despotic father, but gives way eventually
when the ambivalent emotional responses held by the sons to the original
"deed" bring about a return of the rule of the father.

For Irigaray, this "historic" shift is readable through the figure of the
murdered maternal body and the erasure of maternal genealogy within
the myths themselves. In a sense, Irigaray is following Freud's own suggestion in *Moses and Monotheism* that the *Oresteia* contains an echo of
the revolutionary moment that effected this shift (Freud, 1939: 113-14).
For Freud (following Bachofen), this revolution came in the form of "a
triumph of intellectuality over sensuality or, strictly speaking, an instinctual renunciation, with all its necessary psychological consequences"
(Freud, 1913: 113). Where maternal origins are always visibly verifiable,
that is verifiable through the senses,[26] paternity is "a hypothesis, based
on an inference and a premises (*sic*)" (Freud, 1939: 114). And so, Freud
suggests, this triumphant shift from sensuality to intellectuality, or from
the mother to the father, was a momentous step that leads, of course, to
our present situation.

Now, in Freud's mythic narrative of the origin of civilization, originally argued in *Totem and Taboo* and reiterated in *Moses and Monotheism*, matriarchy itself comes about after the murder of the primal father.[27]
Freud follows Darwin's thesis that humans originally lived in hordes
that were dominated by an older male who insisted upon having all the
women for himself (Darwin, 1871). Drawing also upon Atkinson's suggestion that patriarchy ends due to an uprising by the younger males against
the father (Atkinson, 1903), who then kill and eat him, and Robertson
Smith's work on totemic systems (Smith, 1894), Freud suggests that the
murder of the father consequently gave way to the totemic brother clan.
This brother clan, out of guilt for the crime, renounced the women for
whom they murdered their father. This instituted a matriarchal familial
structure. Matriarchy itself gives way to a return, though with diminished
power, to father rule due to an evolutionary progression from the totemic
animal who represents the father to the anthropomophic representation,
and eventually to the one father god that still persists today.

So, once again, in positing an originary matricide, Irigaray refutes
Freud's thesis that the first murder was that of the father, suggesting
instead that the parricide conceals the unspeakable prior murder of the
mother:

> When Freud describes and theorizes, notably in *Totem and Taboo*, the
> murder of the father as founding the primal horde, he forgets a more
> archaic murder, that of the mother, necessitated by the establishment of a
> certain order in the polis (Irigaray, 1991d: 36).

> And when Freud speaks of the father being torn to pieces by the sons of the primal horde, doesn't he forget, in a complete misrecognition and disavowal, the woman who was torn apart between son and father, between sons? (Irigaray, 1991d: 38).

The dramatic treatments of the Orestes legend, by Aeschylus, Sophocles and Euripides, reveal what the Oedipal myths, and Freud himself, forget: the murder of the mother, the concealment of the crime, and the institution of an order designed by and for men. The phantasy of the threatening and polluting mother, Irigaray suggests, can only make sense after the fact of this "matricide." Aeschylus' *Oresteia*, on the other hand, gives mythic representation to the expulsion of the mother from culture and from the Symbolic order (Hirsch, 1989: 30). The murder of Clytemnestra reveals the violence, metaphoric and real, of women's exclusion from the realms of law, language, and society in general. For Irigaray, this matricide and ensuing madness of the murderous daughter, speak to the very contemporary pathologies still endured by women (the narcissistic wound) because of this sundering of maternal genealogy in favour of the father's line and the place of the father over the mother. Psychoanalysis is heir to this tradition in that it fails to conceive of the mother-daughter relationship in terms other than those that sustain the patriarchal order.

In the *Oresteia*, Clytemnestra murders her husband Agamemnon because he sacrificed Iphigenia their daughter for military purposes – "He killed her for a charm to stop the Thracian wind!"[28] Clytemnestra's murder of Agamemnon, read as an act of jealousy or fear, is also interpreted by Irigaray as a response to his sacrificing of their daughter to the conflicts of men, "a motive which is often forgotten by the tragedians" (Irigaray, 1991d: 37). Clytemnestra's murderous act is one of vengeance against the sacrifice of her daughter for the good of the state. But where Clytemnestra's crime is punishable, her own murder by her son Orestes, who follows the oracle of Zeus' son Apollo, and by her daughter Electra, is left unpunished. And the final argument delivered by Apollo in defense of Orestes, puts forth the reason for the acquittal of matricide:

> The mother is not the true parent of the child
> Which is called hers. She is a nurse who tends the growth
> Of young seed planted by its true parent, the male.
> So, if Fate spares the child, she keeps it, as one might
> Keep for some friend a growing plant. And of this truth,
> That father without mother may beget, we have
> Present, as proof, the daughter of Olympian Zeus:
> One never nursed in the dark cradle of the womb;
> Yet such a being no god will beget again (Aeschylus, 1959: 169-70).

The maternal body and its power is here diminished to that of "nurse," while the true creative power is given over to the father and his seed. And the very proof of this superior creator of life is Athena, the motherless daughter, who springs fully formed out of the head of Zeus.[29] Athena, product of the father's procreative power, is behind Apollo's justification of matricide, and indeed casts the final vote that saves Orestes from punishment.

Electra, however, though also the father's daughter, has gone mad. While Orestes is saved from his madness through the legitimization of his act as one of allegiance to the state, Electra becomes the site of "the burial of the madness of women – and the burial of women in madness" (Irigaray, 1991d: 37). The son can have his madness (represented by the Furies whom Orestes calls "avenging hounds incensed by a mother's blood") lifted, indeed buried, through allegiance to the father. But while the daughter who plots with her brother to murder her mother is left in silence in Aeschylus' account, never appearing in the story after the plot is set, her madness takes center stage in the reworkings by Sophocles and Euripides.

This madness of the daughter who blindly loves the father and shuns any association with the mother is a madness that psychoanalysis has had trouble addressing because this rejection of the mother for the father is, in fact, the very definition of normal sexual development for the girl-child. According to Irigaray, the psychoanalytic adherence to the Oedipal myth – with its dramatization of desire for the mother and the ultimate submission to the law of the father and rejection of the mother – as the founding myth of how we become "subjects" in and of the world, maintains the sanity of man at the expense of woman and her relationships with other women, most especially her mother. In psychoanalysis, as with all discourses concerned with the "subject," it is male desire *only* that pre-determines and regulates our understanding of subjectivity in universal terms.

Irigaray has named this particular organization and ordering of culture and society "hom(m)o-sexual."[30] She claims that patriarchal social order and the exchange relations it creates and regulates are hom(m)o-sexual, and women function merely as the conduits for relations between men and (their) meaning: "The law that orders our society is the exclusive valorization of men's needs/desires, of exchanges among men. What the anthropologist calls the passage from nature to culture thus amounts to the institution of the reign of hom(m)o-sexuality" (Irigaray, 1985b: 171). This social order relies upon the repression of the maternal body and the denial of the desire of the mother. And buried beneath this precious corpse is the "dark continent of the dark continent," the fully repressed narrative of mother-daughter love.

In "The Forgotten Mystery of Female Ancestry" (Irigaray, 1994: 89-113) it is the various versions of the Demeter-Persephone/Kore myth that Irigaray pursues. In these stories, she argues, we can still see what once was a powerful bond between women, a bond that has its own history. Demeter is the mother of a daughter, and she is a mother who only "agrees to be fertile *with her daughter*" (Irigaray, 1993a: 79). The various Demeter-Persephone myths give us insight into the crucial dependence of patriarchal social order on the separation of women, a dependence that is at the very heart of psychoanalytic theories of origins.

For Irigaray, this brutal erasure of the *other* line, the mother line, means that the mother-daughter relationship remains unsymbolized in our culture. Irigaray's return to Greek myths, particularly the mother-daughter pairings (especially Clytemnestra – Iphegenia/Electra, Demeter – Persephone, Jocasta – Antigone) is a strategic return to reread within these myths the very *historical* process of this erasure. Irigaray is not attempting to recover some "original," authentic, woman-centered or matriarchal past obliterated through patriarchal control of cultural production. Her purpose in engaging with Greek myths is to reread and reinvent them, to take back what has been stolen from the feminine (Haigh, 1994). By rereading and creatively reinterpreting myths that include the mother-daughter relationship as visibly in the process of disintegration, Irigaray is re-entering these myths into the realm of philosophical circulation, a realm that has for too long privileged the Oedipal myth above all else. Needless to say, when it comes to the Hebrew Bible, it cannot be a matter of simply exhuming stories that include mothers and daughters because such stories are few and far between.[31] But this absence itself must be read as one of the organizing features of patriarchal storytelling, mythmaking, and historiography.

One of the most recurring and insistent themes from *Speculum of the Other Woman* (Irigaray, 1985a) onwards is that the mother-daughter relationship is the least thought relationship in western male-dominated culture and history, and necessarily so. As Freud makes explicit, the mother-daughter tie must be severed so that woman can enter into desire for the man-father, to take the place of the mother while never having a relationship with her in that place, *ensuring the repetition of the social order*. This "taking the place of the mother" is a symbolic repetition of the originary matricide. Thus, Irigaray says:

> The culture, the language, the imaginary and the mythology in which we live at the moment...let's see what ground it is built on... The substratum is the woman who reproduces the social order, who is made this order's infrastructure; the whole of western culture is based upon the murder of the mother... The man-god-father killed the mother in order to take power (Irigaray, 1991a: 47).

When Irigaray asserts that western culture is founded by the (forgotten, repressed, denied) murder of the mother, she means the symbolic murder of the flesh and blood woman, the sexuate being refused access to the spheres of religion, culture, law, etcetera. As such, women can have no valuable identity within the symbolic order other than as the site of the maternal function. For the mother and the daughter, there is no possibility for the sharing of space together. And the consequence of this is the inability of women to have a productive relationship with each other, and the inability to represent their relationship to origins. This thus "prevents them from constituting any real threat to the order of western metaphysics," described by Irigaray as a metaphysics of the Same. They remain "residual," "defective men," "objects of exchange," and so on (Whitford 1991: 79).

Thus, the mother-daughter relationship constitutes a real threat to this social order that requires both the separation of the mother and the daughter, and their lack of subjective distinction as prisoners of the maternal site within the symbolic:[32] "In our societies, the mother/daughter, daughter/mother relationship constitutes a highly explosive nucleus. Thinking it, and changing it, is equivalent to shaking the foundations of the patriarchal order" (Irigaray 1991a: 50). So, to ensure the continuation of a social order that values only the masculine, at the expense of the feminine through the exploitation of natural (re)production, it is necessary to ensure that woman remains imprisoned in her maternal function, the site of her silence (cf. Boulous Walker, 1998). This ensures that all relationships among women – the vertical mother-daughter relationship and the horizontal axis of women-amongst-themselves – are excluded from the symbolic and are marked by a poverty of existence that Irigaray calls *dééreliction*. As Margaret Whitford explains, this term of Irigaray's refers to the lack of symbolization available to women, but also connotes the state of being abandoned by God, or like Ariadne, "abandoned on Naxos, left without hope, without help, without refuge" (Whitford, 1991: 78). As prisoners of their symbolic mandate as "mothers," that is, as holders of the place of the mother or the maternal function, women can only relate to each other aggressively.

Furthermore, this sundering of female genealogies enables the main-tenance of the "maternal" as the mother of a *son*. Social order is ruled by the oedipalized son's relation to the maternal, never the daughter's. For Irigaray, the moment the mother-daughter relationship is symbolized and valued, a social order that relies upon the exchange of women and the exploitation of their bodies begins to collapse, as "woman" begins to exist.

Rather than reading Irigaray's insistence that civilization is instituted through an original murder of the mother as a single act from which all history unfolds, we need to remember the importance of the work of Heidegger for Irigaray. As Joanna Hodge points out, the Heideggar-ian "originary event" stands against this notion of one original source generating a logical sequence. Instead, Hodge explains, "(a)n originary event articulates itself as an omnipresent and recurrently affirmed set of parameters that open up certain lines of possibility while closing off others" (Hodge, 1994: 192). In other words, an originary event is what is continually reinscribed within various systems of representation or discursive frameworks as origin. For Freud, it is parricide that "returns" time and again in the texts of our past and present, suggesting that par-ricide lies at the origin of civilization, as the trauma that, through its repression, institutes a certain order. For Irigaray, however, this parricide that is inscribed as the first moment of history "proper," of civilization, and indeed, psychoanalysis itself, conceals the more archaic deed, "the mother who was sacrificed to the origins of our culture" (Irigaray, 1991d: 43); the unpunished matricide.

In summary, Irigaray's insistence that an unacknowledged matricide lies at the base of western culture and thought directly challenges the psychoanalytic narrative of origins, particularly Freud's parricide. For Irigaray, Freud's parricide reiterates the phallic appropriation of origins readable in his and Lacan's psychoanalytic construction of origins without maternal debt. Through her readings of certain Greek myths, particularly the Orestes Legend, she endeavours to remind Freud, and us, of the prior expulsion and exclusion of women from the social realms of culture, lan-guage, and law, the Symbolic murder of the mother.

Importantly, however, Irigaray's rereadings are psychoanalytic undertakings. Just as she claims that her process of interpretive reread-ing the philosophers "has always been a *psychoanalytic undertaking* as well" (Irigaray, 1985b: 75), so too her engagements with myths. Indeed, Irigaray finds in Demeter and Persephone's reunion a possible model for a feminist psychoanalytic return to the past:

Mother and daughter are happily reunited. Demeter asks Persephone to tell her everything that has happened to her. She does so, beginning at the end. In a way, she goes back in time, as must any woman today who is trying to find the traces of her estrangement from her mother. That is what the psychoanalytical process should do: find the thread of her entry into the Underworld, and, if possible, of her way out (Irigaray, 1994: 107).

So, according to Irigaray, the most important and most difficult objective for women as daughters is to conceive the means of representing/symbolizing the woman effaced by the masculine-maternal, the woman behind the "mother" from whom she has been separated for the good of man's social order. And crucial to this project is the return to those points of "origin," in her case Greek mythology, wherein we may discern the traces of this historical process of matricide and the rupture of female genealogy.

6. Conclusion

In this chapter, I have provided a detailed overview of Irigaray's criticisms of the theoretical narratives of origins offered by Freud and Lacan. For Irigaray, these conceptualizations of the origins of subjectivity and civilization must be understood within the context and genealogy of Western philosophy, a system of thought underwritten by the mute status of women. In particular, it is the maternal body that functions as the mute foundation and unacknowledged resource of philosophical speculation.

Irigaray finds in Plato's myth of the cave a theoretical narrative model for the psychoanalytic representation of a relationship to origins. All of these "stories" need to be understood as a discursively masculine relation to origins (a "monopoly of the origin") which, Irigaray insists, works according to a sadistic-anal logic wherein the recognition of debts to the mother have been obliterated. Only paternal debts can be acknowledged, enabling the predominant phantasies of philosophy – the decorporealized, male subject of speculation who has extricated himself from the grips of maternal materiality to contemplate and participate in the higher orders of language and culture, and the phantasy of mono-production, or self-birthing – to remain unchallenged. In this particular specular or imaginary configuration, woman functions as a mirror for man, with no image of her own. As the mother-mirror or reduplicator of the Same, woman perpetuates this image man has constructed of and for himself, to the detriment of her own identity and subjectivity, with especially dire consequences for her relationships with other women. Most devastating of all is the prohibition against the daughter representing her own specific relation to the maternal-feminine body, and to the necessary separation that must take place for her to become a fully functioning and valued subject of society. Instead, both mother and daughter are abandoned to a state of non-distinction within the male imaginary and symbolic, a state that generates an ambivalent aggression between the two. The psychoanalytic theories of origins maintain the sanity of men, and leave women buried in a madness that it struggles to recognize outside of phallic relations.

For Irigaray, the indistinguishability of mother and daughter is the direct consequence of the separation of mothers and daughters and the Symbolic destitution of woman as (maternal) placeholder of the void. Her project, as a philosopher, linguist, and psychoanalyst has been to go back through the texts of history, through the "father's story," to examine the ways in which his story is guaranteed or shored up by this (silent) sacrifice of women. She is searching for the double movement of maternal-corporeal repression *and* the appropriation of the maternal procreative role in the male imaginary, on the level of cultural production. Indeed, Irigaray suggests that this denial and appropriation can be read symptomatically as "womb-envy," and that many of our cultural products betray such a desire for the appropriation of "origin":

> ...one might be able to interpret the fact of being deprived of a womb as the most intolerable deprivation of man, since his contribution to gestation – his function with regard to the origin of reproduction – is hence asserted as less than evident, as open to doubt... It does not seem exaggerated, incidentally, to understand quite a few products, and notable cultural products, as a counterpart or a search for equivalents to woman's function in maternity. And the desire that men [*sic*] here displays to determine for himself what is constituted by "origin," and thereby eternally and ever to reproduce him (as) self, is a far from negligible indication of the same thing (Irigaray, 1985a: 23).

However, it is not just Irigaray's negative or critical enterprise, revealing the repressed maternal or the means by which man appropriates the feminine for his own ends, that is crucial for my own engagement with Chronicles. It is also Irigaray's development of a *means* by which one "goes back" or returns to the past, a means that is psychoanalytic in its "setting" or "scenography," that interests me.

In particular, Freud's and Irigaray's conflicting mythics of origins need to be understood as discursive rather than referential or "archaelogical" accounts of history (Grosz, 1989: 206). But they also need to be understood in terms of the function of psychoanalysis as that form of analysis which enables the trauma of the past event first to come to light and then take on its significance in the subject's construction of her history. Psychoanalysis allows for the construction of a history or past for the subject – a return to origins – that *produces* a specific relationship between the present and past, a relationship that enables a shift that alters the subject's future. In Lacanian terms, this is the past that *will have been* for the subject (Lacan's future perfect):

> On the one hand, the unconscious is...something negative, something ideally inaccessible. On the other hand, it is something quasi real. Finally, it is something which will be realised in the symbolic, or, more precisely, something which, thanks to the symbolic progress which takes place in analysis, *will have been* (Lacan, 1991: 158).

> ...what we see in the return of the repressed is the effaced signal of something which only takes on its value in the future, through its symbolic realisation, its integration into the history of the subject. Literally, it will only ever be a thing which, at the given moment of its occurrence, *will have been* (Lacan, 1991: 159).

> I identify myself in language, but only by losing myself in it like an object. What is realized in my history is not the past definite of what was, since it is no more, or even the present perfect of what has been in what I am, but the future anterior of what I shall have been for what I am in the process of becoming (Lacan, 1977: 86).

Psychoanalysis constructs a scene in which the past can be returned to and reworked with the specific intent of envisioning a different future than the one presently imaginable. For Irigaray, this change is possible not simply on the level of the individual, but also on the level of the social. And it is the crucial exercise that feminist daughters must undertake to enable something of a desire for origins to be articulated for their own benefits, particularly in relation to the mother. So, the approach I develop for an encounter with the book of Chronicles, an ancient "sacred" Hebrew text situated as a part of the "origin" of western culture, is one that not only enables an uncovering of the hidden or repressed bodies of women in this literary text concerned with origins or beginnings, but one that also *practices* (as both application and rehearsal) the return to origin as a return to the *maternal* as well as the paternal.

Chapter 2

REMEMBERING THE FORGOTTEN MOTHER:
ENGAGING WITH CHRONICLES IN AN IRIGARAYAN MODE

How, then, can one return into the cave, the den, the earth? Rediscover
the darkness of all that has been left behind? Remember the forgotten
mother? (Irigaray, 1985a: 345).

When women want to escape from exploitation, they do not simply
destroy a few "prejudices"; they upset the whole set of dominant values
– economic, social, moral, sexual. They challenge every theory, every
thought, every existing language in that these are monopolised by men
only. They question the *very foundation of our social and cultural order*,
the organisation of which has been prescribed by the patriarchal system
(Irigaray, 1977: 68).

1. *Introduction: The Task of Analysis*

In the previous chapter, I emphasized that while Irigaray is highly critical of psychoanalytic theory, her own process of interpretive readings
of philosophical, psychoanalytic, and mythological discourses must be
understood as, at least in part, "a *psychoanalytic undertaking* as well"
(Irigaray, 1985b: 75).[1] Although Irigaray is adamant that psychoanalytic
theories of social and individual origins provide us with a *masculine*
relation to origins, she also insists that psychoanalysis, as a specific
form and practice of critical analysis, does offer strong possibilities for
feminist analyses. In light of this complex relationship between Irigaray
and psychoanalytic *theory*, I now turn to Irigaray's own psychoanalytic
reading and interpretive *practice*, which can be characterized as twofold.
On the one hand, she insists upon the negative, critical (psycho-) analysis of the masculine Imaginary and, on the other hand, she is adamant
about the strategic restructuring of Imaginary and Symbolic relations
through the intervention of "woman's" writing and speech.

Listening psychoanalytically for the unconscious of masculine discourses through an analysis of various metaphors, images, contradictions, gaps, repetitions, etcetera, along with an analysis of the function of

the feminine within these discourses, constitutes the negative or critical aspect of Irigaray's interpretive approach. For Irigaray, the purpose of the analysis of masculine discourses is to show how the coherence of those discourses is nurtured and sustained by the construction of the feminine as that which is silent, in order to reveal what should remain unnoticed and unanalysed. However, it is clear from Irigaray's reading strategy that it is just as important to reclaim or take back the feminine, as constructed there, making them "give back what they owe the feminine" (Irigaray, 1985b: 74). Furthermore, analysis of the "father's story" must also involve a return to and reworking of the past to enable an articulation of a feminine relation to and desire for (maternal) origin, which for Irigaray, constitutes the positive possibility of "speaking as woman." Irigaray insists that it is necessary to return to those points of origin (in her case Greek mythology) to analyse the means by which the feminine voice has been silenced, an act that she interprets as matricide. In this chapter, I show how Irigaray's interpretive mode provides us with an important means of returning to those other points of origin, namely the biblical texts of the West, beginning in this volume with the book of Chronicles.

A key category in this discussion is Irigaray's development of the psychoanalytic setting, or *praticable*, as a particular mode (*not* method) of interpretive analysis amenable to feminist inquiry. While Irigaray's analytic technology is heavily indebted to psychoanalytic "discoveries," her own emphasis is on *the efficacy of the psychoanalytic setting*, over and against an orthodox adherence to psychoanalytic theory. Specifically, Irigaray insists that the principal elements of the psychoanalytic setting provide possibilities for a feminist daughter's engagement with the past, one that seeks out the forgotten maternal in order to begin articulating a relation to origin, and to original loss; one that does not perpetuate the "murder of the mother." These crucial elements, to be discussed later, are as follows:

a. the unsettling of the binary arrangement of subject and object of knowledge through the psychoanalytic setting or *praticable*;
b. the dialogically open (and incomplete) structure of analysis, including both the dialogue between analyst and analysand, between theory and practice, and between theory and history;
c. the mode of attentive listening that enables the silences of discourse to be not only accounted for, or critically interpreted, but also to be *heard differently*; and
d. the breaking down of past, present, and future as distinct frameworks.

In particular, psychoanalysis offers the possibilities of enabling feminist critique of masculine representations *and* of setting the scene for a productive and therapeutic dialogue with the past that can begin to articulate a feminine relation to both individual and cultural origins.

I argue that Irigaray provides us with a particular mode, rather than method, of engagement that we can take to our readings of the Hebrew Bible. Such a mode of engagement with the text enables a critical psychoanalysis of the figures and props of the male imaginary that give coherence to symbolic and social structures, at the expense of the feminine and of women. This mode also enables a "return" to the forgotten mother of history and culture: the daughter's mother. As I will explain, this forgotten mother cannot be "found" or located in the past, that is, "she" cannot be recuperated or even reconstructed in the past. Rather she is created *in the present* through an engagement with the past enabled by the psychoanalytic setting or *praticable*. And crucial to this "return" are analytic and poetic modes of language production.

Given what I see to be the importance of Irigaray's reworking of the psychoanalytic setting as an interpretive "mode," I shall open my discussion with her refusal of psychoanalysis as "method" in favour of psychoanalysis as interpretive "mode." I follow this initial discussion with a detailed explication of the *praticable*, as theorized by Irigaray herself. Finally, I discuss the negative, critical and positive, reconstructive aspects of Irigarayan analysis in light of her insistence upon the psychoanalytic *praticable*. At this point in my presentation I also outline my own approach for engaging with Chronicles in an "Irigarayan mode" which, following Michelle Boulous Walker (1998), I am characterizing as "Reading Silence" and "Speaking Silence."

2. *Method or Mode? An "Era of Knowledge Already Over"* *or "the Era of the Spirit and the Bride?"*

According to Irigaray, the majority of practitioners of psychoanalysis, both professional and non-professional (for example, literary critics and theorists), repeatedly privilege the *theory* of psychoanalysis over its *practice*. When psychoanalytic theory is "applied" to the discourse of the analysand, carrying the weight and privilege of a scientific method, nothing new is heard or produced by analysis. This "belief" in psychoanalytic theory as science surfaces because of the refusal of certain analysts to acknowledge any historical and cultural determination behind psychoanalysis and its theories, especially its attitudes toward women and female sexuality, which serve to naturalize and eternalize its own theories.[2] The conditions that lead to the present and presence of psychoanalysis, particularly the *sexualized* status of the framework of theoretical representation, must be kept in the dark to maintain the appearance of the eternal status of the father and his law, concealing the usurpation of the place of material/maternal origins. Although psychoanalytic theory began when Freud decided to listen to women speaking, it is itself a part of the western philosophical tradition and, Irigaray contends, perpetuates the silencing of women that this tradition has repeatedly enacted.[3]

Irigaray asks whether Freud ever heard anything new in the discourses of his female patients, indeed whether he heard them at all:

> He said of women that which he was able to say in describing what he heard, with the ears he had, which probably couldn't hear anything else. What Freud says about feminine desire is heard on the couch. But there are other things that are heard, and the problem is that he stopped at a certain point, that is to say, that he normalized woman in her role, the condition that she had at a certain moment (Irigaray, cited in Whitford, 1991: 32).

Irigaray is pointing here to the inability of the analyst to hear anything *new* in the discourse of the analysand. Rather than acknowledging its place within discursive history, psychoanalysis universalizes its own discourse, thereby already "knowing" what to expect, or what can be heard in the analytic experience. The scene, as it were, has always already been set. However, Irigaray (with a certain irony) points out that this was not the case in the early days of Freudian analysis. Each analysand brought with her the possibility of contributing to both the practice and theory of psychoanalysis. Analysis itself was the space of opportunity through listening and through genuine dialogue. However, once psychoanalysis came to be understood as the science that had finally hit upon the universal law of the unconscious, and analysis became the place of application of that law rather than the place of dialogical engagement between two subjects,[4] "the only status the now complete 'science' can possibly have is that of an era of knowledge already over" (Whitford, 1991: 83; Whitford and Macey's translation).[5]

In other words, the unconscious (which, according to Irigaray, bears a striking resemblance to the "feminine" in western thought) becomes not the reserve of the unspoken, unspeakable, or even "yet to be spoken," but the (silent) guarantee of an already existing language and social order:

> What if the unconscious were at one and the same time the result of censorship and repression imposed in and by a certain history, *and* a not yet come to pass, a reservoir of the still-to-come? Then, your rejections, reprimands, and lack of comprehension would just be turning the future

into the past. What you would be doing is reducing the still unsubjugated
to the level of the already subjugated, the still unspoken or unsaid of language to what *one* language has already paralysed into mutism, or kept
down in silence. Might you be – without your knowledge – the products
and defenders of an existing order, its officials of reprimand and repression, making sure that this order is the only one possible, that there no
other imaginable word, desire or language, aside from the ones already
in place, that there is no other culture authorized but the monocratism
of patriarchal discourse? Are you culturalists without your knowledge?
Some of your statements seem to testify to that...*symptomatically* (Irigaray, 2002a: 207).

Thus, in refusing to acknowledge its own historical debts, psychoanalysis participates within and perpetuates a particular order of language
and knowledge, one which Irigaray claims has consistently functioned
through the repression and denial of sexual difference, that is, the silencing of the feminine. Within this order, "woman" cannot contribute to
the production of knowledge *with* "man"; she functions only as the limit
of masculine knowledge (cf. Lacan, 1998) or as the site of its silences
(Boulous Walker, 1998).

Furthermore, according to Irigaray, the scientific application of theory
to the discourse of the analysand – the psychoanalytic *model* or *method*
– fails to effect change for women and for society because the *virtue* of
the model or analogue is *the reproduction of the same*. In other words,
rather than building upon what is "already known" and by challenging
the "already known" in the process, methods and models can only give
us logical variations of the "already known." In literary-critical terms, an
interpretive approach that simply applies theory to the text as an exegetical tool, and therefore privileges theory over the literary text under
analysis, ensures that neither the theory nor the text expands beyond the
"already known."

In the late 1970s, the literary theorist Shoshana Felman (1977) put
forth most forcefully this critique of the relationship between theory and
method. Felman foregrounds the psychoanalytic notion of transferential
reading within literary criticism, whereby theory is refused its traditionally privileged status over the literary text. Interpretation involves
a mastery of the text and its meaning. However, there is also another
process at work, as psychoanalysis makes clear, that is, the transference
and countertransference that takes place between the analyst/critic and
analysand/reader. Building on both Freud's and Lacan's theories concerning analytic practice, Felman insists that the literary theorist, as analyst of
the text, is never left outside the discourse of the text. The effect of such

an analytic structure is that the literary theorist/analyst, in producing a discourse at the intersection between theory and text, also assumes the place of the analysand. Literary theory is the productive discourse enabled by both interpretation and transference, the dialogue between the two analytic positions (analyst and analysand), but such a dialogue can occur only through the blurring or indistinguishability of these positions effected by the analytic scene. Analytic dialogue is not a dialogue between two distinct, non-complicit or non-implicated subjects. In fact, the analyst "listens" to the discourse of the analysand, *and is affected by it.* This is what Lacan calls "the inmixture of the subjects" (Felman, 1987: 61). As Felman explains, this "new reflexive mode...divides the subjects differently, in such a way that they are neither entirely distinguished, separate from each other, nor correlatively, entirely totalizable but, rather, interfering from within and in one another" (Felman, 1987: 61). In short, the psychoanalytic scene breaks down the hierarchical distinction between subject and object of knowledge.[6]

Toril Moi has argued that such a breakdown of binary opposites is crucial for feminist inquiries:

> There is, then, in the psychoanalytic situation a model of knowledge which at once radically questions and displaces traditional notions of subject/ object relationships and deconstructs the firm boundaries between knowledge and non-knowledge. As this situation of knowledge offers no firmly established binary opposites, it cannot be gendered as either masculine or feminine, thereby offering us a chance to escape the patriarchal tyranny of thought by sexual analogy. As feminists in search of new ways to think about objectivity, knowledge, and modes of intellectual activity, we can ill-afford to neglect the model offered by psychoanalysis (Moi, 1999: 361).

The breakdown of gender binaries effected by the psychoanalytic scene is of course an essential feature of Irigaray's project. However, Irigaray also insists that, because sexual difference is yet to be thought in the West, this blurring of binaries must serve a particular purpose concerning the *construction* of gender and sexuality, a construction of the feminine beyond phallic relations, which preclude any valued and productive relations between women. And, it is perhaps this aspect of her work, the insistence on a production of language *by women* that does not leave them bereft of images, ideals, or divinity, that problematizes an understanding of Irigaray's approach as strictly deconstructive.[7]

Her statements concerning the "reopening" of the figures of philosophy (and psychoanalysis), attest to the necessity of a disruption from women who refuse simply to assume the discursive, symbolic and social (non)positions assigned to them, positions which nourish and sustain the "auto-affection of the (masculine) subject" (Irigaray, 1985b: 123). However, Irigaray does not believe, naively, in the possibility of women speaking outside of phallogocentric discourse. She says, "There is no simple manageable way to leap to the outside of phallogocentrism, *nor any possible way to situate oneself there, that would result from the simple fact of being a woman*" (Irigaray, 1985b: 162). Her strategy of mimesis, whereby various masculine constructions of the feminine are fully assumed in order to *produce* difference, is, as Rosi Braidotti (1989: 99) argues, a tactical strategy that effects a disruption of any understanding of female "nature" as bound up in biological or psychological determinism.

However, Irigaray's "deconstruction"[8] is not, as Elizabeth Hirsh reminds us, identical with Derrida's. It is Irigaray's characterization of her strategy as destroying "with nuptial tools" (Irigaray, citing Rene Char, 1985b: 150) that distinguishes the deconstructive features of her mode from that of the deconstructive method. And as Hirsh astutely acknowledges, Irigaray develops the psychoanalytic *praticable*,[9] the scene or setting of psychoanalysis, as both an instrument of deconstruction *and (re)mediation*:

> Unlike Derrida, Irigaray is a matchmaker – or perhaps more accurately, a couples therapist – concerned to make possible the now universally "impracticable...sexual relation." The deconstructive confounding of oppositions within the scene of analysis is neither an end in itself nor does it set the stage for the eruption of some new term or concept meant to displace the old opposition. Instead, the *praticable* as interpreted by Irigaray (re)mediates the "divorce" of the oppositions that silently govern the production of theory – silently, because they occupy the place of the a priori that stands outside and above any possibility of interrogation. Like a *praticable* connecting two spaces (one onstage and one off, for example), the psychoanalytic *praticable* does not, ultimately, confound or destroy the identity of the two but depends upon preserving them *as* distinct even as it effects their connection (Hirsh, 1994: 289).

There are a number of figures in Irigaray's work that represent the ethico-nuptial work of the *praticable*, notably her (in)famous speculum, the "two lips," the placenta, mucous, and the angel. And in *An Ethics of Sexual Difference*, Irigaray speaks of an era to come, which she calls the "era of the spirit and the bride." This "third era of the West," is a reworking of Joachim of Fiore's three ages of history, the first being the age of the Father (the Old Testament), the second the age of the son (the New Testament and 42 generations thereafter), and finally the age of the Spirit, which sees the conversion of all humanity. Irigaray gives woman a place in this third era as the bride, as she who shares in the spirit as an embodied, sensual, and valued partner:

- The Father, alone, invites, and disappears with Moses and the written law.
- The son (and the mother) invites; but the son remains bound to the Father, to whom he "goes back," to whom he arises.
- The spirit and the bride invite beyond genealogical destiny to the era of the wedding and the festival of the world. To the time of a theology of the breath in its horizontal and vertical becoming, with no murders (Irigaray, 1993b: 149).

The theological language Irigaray favours in her more utopian moments, such as this, are apt to annoy those of us who find such images, while perhaps romantically pleasant and even inspiring, a little weak when placed in the context of an overwhelmingly misogynist Christian history.[10] However, I think we need to place Irigaray's two "eras" alongside one another – "an era of knowledge already over" and the "era of the spirit and the bride" – to realize that Irigaray is less interested in utopian dreaming through Christian romanticism than she is in rethinking epistemological possibilities. The spirit, "as the third term," functions as a *praticable* capable of connecting man and woman, masculine and feminine, as two distinct participants who share and produce the world together.[11] Most importantly, what is *produced* through this *praticable* is "an ethical God," an ethics, in other words, of sexual difference:

> As long as the son is not in mourning for the Father, neither body nor flesh can be transfigured in the couple; as long as the daughter is in mourning for the spirit, then neither body nor flesh can be transfigured in the couple... For woman to affirm that her desire proceeds or wills thus, woman must be born into desire. She must be longed for, loved, valued as a daughter. An other morning, a new parousia that necessarily accompanies the coming of an ethical God.
>
> He respects the difference between him and her, in cosmic and aesthetic generation and creation. Sharing the heaven and the earth in all their elements, potencies, acts (Irigaray, 1993b: 149-50).

So, ultimately, the disruption of the binary construct effected by the psychoanalytic scene is a valuable feature of psychoanalytic practice for Irigaray because it clears a space for a creative production of language *by and for women*, a production made possible by the psychoanalytic *praticable*. In particular, Irigaray develops the *praticable* as a *means* or *mode* of theorizing, interpreting, speaking, and writing that can listen for what currently constitutes the incoherent or unhearable enunciative positions left to women who refuse their Symbolic place as (sexual, intellectual, and theoretical) commodities to be exchanged among men. As Hirsh argues, Irigaray's *praticable* is "an instrument of theoretical discovery, not merely the practical application or instantiation of a (long) finished theory," and it is "an instrument of personal and social transformation, of resistance, not adaptation, to the symbolic status quo" (Hirsh, 1994: 308). It is an instrument, or "nuptial tool," capable of *bringing together* oppositions, rather than destroying them, as the deconstructionists would have it. As Braidotti explains, "(e)ncouraging women to think, say, and write the feminine is a gesture of self-legitimation that breaks away from centuries of phallo-logocentric thought which has silenced women" (Braidotti, 1989: 99).

At this point, I need to stress that, following Elizabeth Hirsh (1994), I am suggesting Irigaray's *praticable* provides us with a *mode* of critical engagement with the book of Chronicles, and not with a model or method of interpretation. The psychoanalytic *praticable* is determined by the specific arrangements of analyst and analysand as two embodied subjects who both intermittently speak and are silent, and who are situated in a particular geography in relation to each other. As an embodied reader and analyst of a *literary* text, it is impossible to argue that such an encounter is analogous to the psychoanalytic scene. However, my own development of Irigaray's approach needs to be understood outside the terms of the analogue, model, or method, and more in line with a *means* or *mode*, as Hirsh suggests. The importance of Irigaray's rereading of the *praticable* is that she offers us a new relationship between theory and practice, and between theory and history, "by proposing new and different criteria of *theoretical* legitimacy derived from an understanding of the relation between theory and therapy in psychoanalysis" (Hirsh, 1994: 300). Irigaray is not anti-theoretical. She is interested in alternative modes, such as that provided by the psycho-analytic *praticable*, which enable a rethinking of the philosophical relations between the empirical and the theoretical, between the *a priori and a posteriori*, and between theory and history. To bring the book of Chronicles into the psychoanalytic scene is not to "psychoanalyse" it (or its author(s)) in the sense of finding an already established (contemporary) theory at work in the ancient text. Rather, it means to enter into a dialogically produced space for analysis of a past in relation to a present produced through the encounter between the two (of us).

3. The Praticable *as Nuptial Tool*

Irigaray distinguishes the setting of psychoanalysis, what determines the analytic *experience*, from other settings such as the philosophical or scientific: "The setting of the analytic scene may not be just another empiric, or just another psychical application, an experience like any other. Who knows? It may be a setting that disorients, and destabilizes the scene of representation" (Irigaray, 2002a: 193). Despite the subjunctive mood in the final sentence quoted here, it is precisely the ability of the psychoanalytic setting to disorient and destabilize the scene of representation that Irigaray perceives as the virtue of this particular setting. Furthermore, she is interested in developing the *praticable* as an instrumental mode for women to engage with cultural representations of the past and present. Briefly, the technical rules that constitute the analytic scene, which I discuss below, ensure that it is "a scene that calls the very condition of representation into question" (Irigaray, 2002a: 193).

Irigaray argues that the current practice of applying the theory of psychoanalysis to other cultural domains (including literary texts), without consideration of the analytic setting that produced the theory, downplays or even negates the importance and efficacy of that scene. It is as if psychoanalysis (as an institution) "wanted to lock up, in the text, in theoretical and scientific interpretations – even those made while 'in session' – a scene that calls the very condition of representation into question" (Irigaray, 2002a: 193). So, for Irigaray, psychoanalysis is a particular form of analysis that destabilizes and disorients the framework of representation which, in the West, is characterized by strict binary oppositions, unified and coherent subjective positions, a tropism of the "front," totalization, and closure. It is a particular setting that generates a theoretical discourse that can only be open-ended and never complete because of the specificity of each analysand in this setting designed to call into question the classic framework of theoretical specul(ariz)ation.

As Irigaray argues, psychoanalytic theory needs to be understood as the discourse enabled by the psychoanalytic setting in the first place, a setting that "was imposed by a *practice* of sexuality" that then "inspired a *theory* of sexuality" (Irigaray, 2002a: 203). To lie on the couch, Irigaray insists, has different connotations for men and women: "It is relatively common for a man, in an erotic situation, to tell a woman to lie down, or to lay her down... It is much rarer, it is in fact exceptional, for a woman to ask a man to lie down, except in therapy" (Irigaray, 1993a: 93-94). In making of his theory a scientific "truth," Freud failed to grasp how that theory was itself the product of a setting that subscribed to a reigning practice of sexuality:

> Where sexual difference is in question, Freud does not fully analyse the
> presuppositions of the production of discourse. In other words, the ques-
> tions that Freud's theory and practice address to the scene of representa-
> tion do not include the question of the sexualized determination of that
> scene. Because it lacks that articulation, Freud's contribution remains, in
> part – and precisely where the difference between the sexes is concerned
> – caught up in metaphysical presuppositions (Irigaray, 1985b: 73).

Most seriously, by universalizing its own discourse as a scientific "truth,"
psychoanalysis misrecognizes the *a posteriori* for the *a priori* (particularly
concerning female sexuality), thus negating its own efficacy as a form
of analysis capable of intervening and effecting change not just for the
individual, but also (and Irigaray is adamant here) for the social. As Hirsh
points out, such a misrecognition indicates that Freud and his followers failed to grasp the virtue of the setting psychoanalysis creates, one
which potentially renders the philosophical opposition between *a priori*
and *a posteriori* obsolete because the distinctions between past, present,
and future collapse. It is a setting that confuses and even disables such
oppositions, precipitating "a new, material/transcendental passageway
between the 'frame' of representation and its so-called content, permit-
ting the one to (re)act upon the other" (Hirsh, 1994: 294).

Importantly, according to Irigaray, the "true" object of analysis is the
(hidden) "framework of all representation" (Irigaray, 2002a: 196), not its
content. In other words, memories themselves, while a crucial feature
of the drama of analysis, are not the objects of analysis. The purpose of
analysis is not to hit finally upon a truth content through remembering, but rather, to *produce* a representational structure and content that
can enable a different relationship between the present, past, and future
to have a meaningful effect on the subject. In Lacan's words, "(w)hat is
realized in my history is not the past definite of what was, since it is no
more, or even the present perfect of what has been in what I am, but the
future anterior of what I shall have been for what I am in the process of
becoming" (Lacan, 1977: 86). For Irigaray, the framework produced in
the analytic scene is one produced *between* analyst and analysand, and
it is a "surrogate frame that they necessarily continue to inhabit" (Hirsh,
1994: 289) while in analysis:

> The form-content (if we can use these terms) of what is to be represented
> – impossible aim in the classical sense of the term – is produced between
> the analysand who speaks and the analyst who sustains the setting of his
> or her word. And, of course, there will almost never be the discovery of the
> setting, or unveiling of what seduces and maintains the word within this

framing. The frame, or the window, determines the form of the appari-
tion; they themselves do not appear, any more than they exist outside the
session (Irigaray, 2002a: 196).

The *praticable* enables the subject of analysis to enter into the "drama of
enunciation" in a present that is *produced* within that scene. Thus, the
hic et nunc of analysis is crucial to analytic practice because it disengages
representation

> from its pretension to a univocal here and now, even an eternal here and
> now, because, once again – despite the hopes of the analysand – there
> will be no model for memory, nor discovery of a memory that would
> equivocally give weight to representation, overdetermining it with tem-
> poral stratifications whose different impacts could be interpreted, giving
> meaning to every moment of the past, up to the present (Irigaray, 2002a:
> 198).

The present in analysis (the *hic et nunc*) is not the logical outcome of *the*
past. It is the effect of the setting itself in relation to *a* past that is also
produced within the representational scene of analysis. As Hirsh (1994:
286-87) points out, Irigaray's revalidation of presence is not an unanalysed metaphysics of presence. Nor is it a form of therapy akin to American ego psychology, in which the analytic present is conceived as a "safety
zone" for the subject so that the trauma of the past is simply ameliorated
through a positive reconstruction of the past by revising the traumatic
scene in an attempt to remove the trauma altogether.[12] The *hic et nunc* of
analysis is a disorienting and destabilizing frame, not a comforting one,
because it challenges everything the analysand "knows" about him or
herself in relation to (self) representation.

Irigaray develops the *praticable* by insisting on the importance of the
three principal rules of analysis: the physical arrangements or "geography" of the analytic scene, the modes of speech (analysand) and listening
(analyst) that take place in analysis, and the transferential relationship.
These three rules of the psychoanalytic scene together constitute the
psychoanalytic setting, enabling the work of that specific setting (the
praticable) to take place. Again, the "work" of the setting is to disorient,
disconcert, and destabilize the scene of representation. More specifically,
the *praticable* disorients the subject of representation who, dependant
on a certain economy of representation, perceives him or herself to be
the source of all knowledge and meaning. In analysis, however, his or her
discursive representation becomes the product of a source that is at least
double. It is a discourse produced *between* analyst and analysand that
can take place only when the "rules" of representation (that it be logical,

rational, coherent, with a single, unified subject positioned as the source of representation, etc.) have been thwarted.

3.1. *The Embodied Geography of Analysis*

The first rule of analysis – the "geography" of analysis, or the arrangements of two bodies in a particular setting – is probably the most difficult to reconcile as a feature of my own development of Irigaray's mode, for reasons I have already mentioned. However, it is probably the most important aspect of the practice of psychoanalysis for Irigaray. In the conventional psychoanalytic setting, the analysand reclines on a couch while the analyst is seated behind the couch outside the analysand's scopic field. Furthermore, the analyst sits behind the analysand and only partially faces him or her. This arrangement of bodies in the psychoanalytic setting is not an arbitrary arrangement; it serves to disrupt the usual setting of representation and communication in specific ways. What I want to draw out in this section is the particular effect the geography has on the relationship between subjectivity and representation. I am also interested in the questions this particular setting gives us concerning the invisible frame of representation, upon which subjectivity is so dependant.

When the analysand is positioned on the couch in a reclining position, the usual coordinates that orient the subject in relation to the world are challenged:

> The subject of representation has a front and a back, an up and a down, and is supposedly upright, forming a right angle with the plane supporting her or him. What happens when the subject lies down and speaks with someone in back?
>
> Imagine the scene. The cardinal points flip over. Where is the subject with respect to front, back, up, down? What becomes of the horizon, for example? The subject's intersection with it is infinite: analysis is interminable (Irigaray, 2002a: 194-95).

Having surrendered the vertical access, now held in trust by the analyst who remains seated upright, the material, corporeal supports necessary for the production of (a) language and (a) meaning are placed into relief. The subject who speaks in analysis, the main producer of language, is the analysand who no longer is positioned as the site of the perpendicular, the (invisible) confluence of the vertical and horizontal axes that orient the subject in relation to his or her world. "The junction point of the two axes is no longer *within* the one who speaks." Instead, in analysis, this meeting point now occurs "between two" (Irigaray, 2002a: 195). The source of language produced in analysis is hence double, rather than single, "(w)hich is strangely disturbing for the proper..." (Irigaray, 2002a: 194).

The reclining analysand is said to be without horizon, no longer the scopic master of the en-framed representational scene in which he or she participates. Instead, the analysand, "immersed in language and in his own history" (Irigaray, 1993a: 93), *is* the horizon, with the analyst holding it all together through his or her visually concealed presence behind. "These two parameters" (one seated behind, one reclining), Irigaray tells us, disobey both social conventions concerning the face-to-face of communication and the relation of signs to language, which are normally "produced in a position orthogonal to the choice and constitution of their meaning. The position adopted in psychoanalysis prevents them from being produced in this manner" (Irigaray, 1993a: 92). In other words, the geography of analysis prevents the analysand from producing rational speech *in the present* of analysis:

> What makes the patient annoyed and nervous when he or she is lying down is first of all the impossibility of producing an exact word or meaning *that relates to the here and now*. This stage has been set for *remembering* (Irigaray, 1993a: 92).

The rambling recollections that the analysand is instructed to produce ("say anything and everything that comes into your head") are enabled by the geography of analysis. The main effect of this geography is the disabling of rational speech in the present so that the analysand "is unable to easily build bridges or platforms that would allow escape" (Irigaray, 1993a: 93). In short, the geography of analysis ensures that the subject of speech *needs the other*.

Importantly, Irigaray insists that both the reclining position of the analysand on a couch and the positioning of the analyst behind the analysand allows the (hidden) behind of representation to contradict the belief that representation has only a "front," which Irigaray calls "the tropism of the front" (Irigaray, 2002a: 202). The subject of representation is imagined as the source of his or her production of language, "with nothing behind him or her. As if he or she had their back to the wall. If there was anyone back there, it would be God: creator of everything" (Irigaray, 2002a: 194). In analysis, however, the pretension that representation only has a "front" is contradicted through "the preoccupation with the backside of the subject." Lying on a couch makes it difficult for the subject to believe that "he or she has no backside, or to imagine some God back there" (Irigaray, 2002a: 197). And the position of the analyst, who occasionally speaks from behind, challenges the presumption that the analysand is the source of a representation that has no behind or underside, and no debts to the other.

Finally, Irigaray draws out the ethical implications of the geography of analysis, particularly the refusal of the face-to-face encounter that generally structures communication between two subjects. In the face-to-face encounter, just as in the mirror, right corresponds to left, and left to right. In analysis, however, because the analyst sits behind, the mirror-like coordinates of the face-to-face are reversed: "they are one behind the other; left corresponds to left and right to right. As if they were looking at themselves, at each other, in the same mirror" (Irigaray, 2002a: 195). The analysand cannot easily use the analyst-other as a mirror reflecting back an image of him or herself as unified and stable subject in the production of language.

The analysand exists in a state of "blindness" with respect to the other, who is positioned behind. Thus, "the gaze that commands object-representation; the gaze that intuits, exposes, reassembles the represented in front of itself, giving it or recognizing its form; the gaze that maintains the privilege of the face-to-face" (Irigaray, 2002a: 200-201) is rendered impotent with respect to the behind. According to Irigaray, "(t)he backside is the impotence of the gaze" (Irigaray, 2002a: 201). What comes to the fore through the geography of analysis, which rejects the face-to-face arrangement that privileges the gaze for something more akin to the body-to-body, is that both the subject and his or her other take on an intellectual and spiritual volume that cannot disavow the corporeal-material support of representation: "In the front-to-back about faces of representation, subjects find their 'volume,' not only the volume of soul, or of mind (circle never constituted except in the face-to-face?), but also of their body, flesh, and story" (Irigaray, 2002a: 197). In the analytic setting, both the epistemological relation, which privileges the "front" (the subject contemplating the world before him or her) and the ethical relation (the face-to-face encounter) which privileges the gaze, are rearranged. This "simultaneous derangement," as Hirsh (1994: 291) puts it, and their effects on the production of language, indicate the mutual dependence of knowledge, representation, and the (non) relation to the other in the face-to-face encounter:

> The psychoanalytic setting makes it obvious that the hierarchy of values of representation corresponds to a perspective, even to an optical illusion. Mastering all representations in the face-to-face, organizing them into the same time-frame, onto the same plane, while maintaining the pretense of respect for their spatio-temporal differences, requires that they be ordered within a perspective with differing degrees or presence,

propriety, and proximity, in accordance with the rigidity of the proper, a perspective that damages, infinitely, through loss of volume (Irigaray, 2002a: 201).

The geography of the psychoanalytic setting is designed "to allow everything to be said without hierarchical judgement, without *a priori* appropriateness or truth" (Irigaray, 2002a: 202). Because of the setting those incoherent features of discourse, which cannot be interpreted according the traditional logic of representation and its production, become meaningful and are given a certain coherence within an analytic framework that is itself an effect of the specific geography of analysis.

According to Irigaray, Freud's most "ingenious idea" is the development of a setting which confounds the traditional logic of representation. Faced with the hysteric's discourse, "facing a sign undecipherable except in paralysis? A sign whose only representation was paralysis," Freud had to "deconstruct the frame of the proper" (Irigaray, 2002a: 202). What Freud came to realize, through his encounter with the hysteric, was the paralytic setting of representation: "Of course, all representations are paralytic, but they do not know it. Whereas hysteria, deprived of its own sense, of common sense – of all sense? – presents in its miming only this remainder of the meaningful sense: its paralytic setting" (Irigaray, 2002a: 202). What the geography of analysis teaches us is that, to effect change, analysis must involve the formulation of a framework that allows the underside of representation (what appears to be excluded or silenced within the scene) to come into play. It can never simply be a matter of importing psychoanalytic theory into the scene, analysing the text with preconceived theoretical formulae. Such an approach can only ensure that the framework of representation, so utterly dependant on what remains silenced or excluded, remains in tact, thus reducing "the still unspoken or unsaid of language to what *one* language has already paralyzed into mutism, or kept down in silence" (Irigaray, 2002a: 207).

3.2. The Rule of Free Association and the Mode of Listening Required
As I have mentioned, one of the effects of the geography of the analytic setting is that it blocks the production of rational speech in the present of analysis. This inability on the part of the analysand is also the effect of the rule of free association, whereby the analysand is encouraged to say anything and everything that comes to him or her without fear of judgement or correction from the analyst. There is no hierarchy of value of representation, no wrong or right when it comes to retelling the past because there "is no rating scale for the appropriateness of memory, no

right or wrong memories, nor even any 'thing' to remember" (Irigaray, 2002a: 195). To "say everything" contributes to the production of meaningless discourse, a construction that enables the framework of representation to dramatically reappear. It is important to point out again that this framework is said to be the "object" of analysis, not the memories or content. The function of the analyst is to act as a passive receptor of the analysand's discourse. The analyst accomplishes this task by making him or herself "the available medium for the inscription of the traces of the analysand, for the time of the drama of analysis, and thus to become what is unfit for the effective presence, unfit for all the edicts of common sense, and unfit for attestations to truth of any kind, etc." (Irigaray, 2002a: 199). However, this role of receptor requires the analyst to surrender any pretension to theoretical knowledge that precedes the analytic scene, which is a very difficult task indeed.

Irigaray is highly critical of the current analytic practice of deferring to an already established system of knowledge (Freudian or Lacanian), which imports a theoretically cohesive language into the analytic scene, a scene that is supposed to suspend all legislation concerning meaning:

> What kind of gesture is it that subjugates the language of the analysand to a system of signifiers that is not his or her own? In other words, even if there is a dictionary or a bible of Freudian or Lacanian discourse, there cannot be a dictionary or a grammar of psychoanalysis, under threat of forcing the analysand into adaptation to a language different from the one she or he speaks. Interpretation and listening on the part of the analyst then become nothing more than acts of mastery over the analysand. They are instruments in the service of a master and of *his* truth. The psychoanalyst is already enslaved, and reproduces his or her own enslavement (Irigaray, 2002a: 209).

Instead, Irigaray insists that the analyst must be prepared to listen without a pre-scripted text, suspending the economy of truth. The first function of the analyst is to receive the traces of the analysand's past, as it is produced in the *hic et nunc* of analysis and to function as the *corporealized* material upon which those memories are inscribed. This, of course, is the body-to-body relationship that analysis is able to produce and sustain because of its unique *praticable*.

There is a resonance here between the analyst's mode of listening in analysis (and the third rule of analysis, transference) and Irigaray's own mimetic strategy of reading and interpretation. To "assume the feminine role deliberately" is Irigaray's way of characterizing the initial path open to women analysing the workings of phallocratic discourses:

> One must assume the feminine role deliberately. Which means already to convert a form of subordination into an affirmation, and thus to begin to thwart it. Whereas a direct feminine challenge to this condition means demanding to speak as a (masculine) "subject," that is, it means to postulate a relation to the intelligible that would maintain sexual difference.
>
> To play with mimesis is thus, for woman, to try to recover the place of her exploitation by discourse, without allowing herself to be simply reduced to it. It means to resubmit herself – inasmuch as she is on the side of the "perceptible," of "matter" – to "ideas," in particular to ideas about herself, that are elaborated in/by a masculine logic, but so as to make "visible," by an effect of playful repetition, what was supposed to remain invisible: the cover-up of a possible operation of the feminine in language. It also means "to unveil" the fact that, if women are such good mimics, it is because they are not simply resorbed in this function. *They also remain elsewhere*: another case of the persistence of "matter," but also of "sexual pleasure" (Irigaray, 1985b: 76).

To assume the feminine, in other words, is to "unveil" the veiling of woman as a necessary function of metaphysical thought. For Irigaray, this entails putting the feminine body into theoretical play, miming the functions assigned to it, while always remaining in excess of that discursive function.

Irigaray's mimetic strategy has been negatively received as essentialist and logocentric by some of her earlier readers. However, Rosi Braidotti (1989) characterizes Irigaray's mimeticism as tactical, with the aim of producing difference. Moreover, Margaret Whitford (1991: 71-72) and Elizabeth Grosz (1989: 132-39) have both highlighted the crucial linkage between mimesis and hysteria in Irigaray's work.[13] Like the hysteric, whose symptoms are an active defiance of the feminine place within which patriarchal society imprisons her, or as Grosz puts it, are "a strategy to ward off the violations with which she is expected to comply" (Grosz, 1989: 137), Irigaray's mimetic strategy can be read as modelled on the hysteric's desperate struggle for autonomous speech:

> The hysteric's symptom is a response to her annihilation as active subject, a resistance or refusal to confirm what is expected of her. Not able to take up an active position by will alone (this would mean, at most, acting like a man), she lives out and uses her passivity in an active defiance of her social position. She (psychically) mutilates herself in order to prevent her brutalisation at the hands of others – hence the tragic self-defeat entailed by hysterical resistance. Irigaray shares the hysteric's *excessive* mimicry, the conversion of her passivity into activity by taking on, in the most extreme forms, what is expected, but to such an extreme degree that the end result is the opposite of compliance: it unsettles the system by throwing back to it what it cannot accept about its own operations (Grosz, 1989: 138).

Both Grosz and Whitford also point to the similarities between Irigaray's mimeticism and psychoanalysis. According to Grosz, Irigaray's mimetic strategy is able to avoid the self-destructive pitfalls of the hysteric because it is a self-conscious undertaking. Irigaray's approach resembles the role of the analyst, whose function is to enable the articulation of the hysteric's discourse:

> Her procedure is not the *acting out*, the *charade* of hysterical expression, where a "script" is performed by the body; it is more like the analyst's facilitation of the hysterical discourse, giving speech to what has remained unspoken and unabreacted in her psychical life. The "cure" is possible only with the social upheavals which grant women autonomy as subjects (Grosz, 1989: 138).

Irigaray's work can be said to include both the hysterical analysand's and the mutely receptive analyst's place within the analytic scene, a scene that confounds the autonomous identity of its participants. Here again, Irigaray is attempting to jam "the theoretical machinery itself" (Irigaray, 1985b: 78) by drawing upon the specific virtues of the psychoanalytic *praticable*.

For Whitford, Irigaray's mimetic reception of masculine discourses functions like the analyst's actively passive reception, which is designed to bring to light the unconscious phantasies operating as supports of those discourses. Whitford suggests, convincingly, that we need to read Irigaray's mimetic strategy "as initiating a process of change at the level of the social unconscious (or imaginary), by offering interpretations of the 'material' offered by society in its philosophical or metaphysical discourse" (Whitford, 1991: 72). So, as analysts or readers of patriarchal discourses, we must first receive the traces of the "father's story" and assume the metaphoric feminine roles assigned to us – masked seducers, treacherous lures, semblances, masquerades, and so on – in order to allow the unconscious phantasmatic structures of patriarchal discourses to come to light.

The importance of this reception of the analysand's discursive past is not the nostalgic preservation of that past or of the "feminine" constructed there. The aim is not to "know" what happened in that past. Or, in the case of ancient texts, the goal is not to "know" what concrete meaning, judged according to an *a priori* economy of truth, resides in a representational language kept dutifully in that past. Rather, as Hirsh points out, the preservation of the past *produced in the present of analysis* is important "only for what it can contribute to a future of difference" (Hirsh, 1994: 295). What can be heard of the past is only what the present conditions of analysis produce, with the analyst willing to admit him or herself into the scene of this production as an active, affected, and effective participant, not as a distant and objective observer:

> We have known for a long time that the language spoken in analysis leaves considerable room for the past, and that the present is immersed in the past: a past that never was present – in the sense of a representable thing – and that never will be (Irigaray, 2002a: 198).

According to Irigaray, the production of this language can only take place when each analysand and each "past" produced in analysis is unrestricted by an *a priori* discourse or theory by which the analysand must be judged.

3.3. *The Rule of Transference*

The importation of an established theory given the status of "universal truth" maintains the discrete status of past, present, and future. However, according to Irigaray, change is only possible (especially for women) when such temporal categories are allowed to merge within and as a result of the analytic setting. For Irigaray it is the third rule of transference which effects such a blurring of temporal categories. The three rules of analysis Irigaray develops in her reworking of the *praticable* – the geography of analysis, the rule of free association, along with the correlate mode of listening, and the rule of transference – are constitutive of and constituted by the psychoanalytic *praticable* and its language and speech effects. Transference has been the one feature of the psychoanalytic setting found to be crucial for feminist politics. According to Irigaray "the projection onto the analyst of what causes the word, or the desire, to reclaim its framework" (Irigaray, 2002a: 196) entails the blurring of the philosophical distinction between subject and object of knowledge and the blurring of temporal categories. Or, as Moi (1999: 361) puts it, the breakdown of binaries effected by the transference provides us with "new ways to think about objectivity, knowledge, and modes of intellectual activity." Significantly, Irigaray explores a particular aspect of the transference that is crucial for my own endeavour here. This is the *enfintinage*, or return to infancy, that takes place as an effect of the psychoanalytic *praticable*, particularly through transference. This blurring of the subject-object and temporal distinctions enables a return to the moment when the subject enters into the Symbolic (becomes a subject of speech). Or rather, it enables the (re)production of that original scene in the *hic et nunc* of analysis.

The particular geography of analysis is important, as I pointed out above, because it turns the habitual scene of representation upside down.

There is no face-to-face in analysis, nor is the analysand given the security of the illusion of him or herself as the sole source of language and meaning production. Instead, the subject's "behind" (on the couch, and in the place of the analyst) comes into play, disconcerting the hierarchy of values of representation, particularly the "tropism of the front." There is no "truth" standard in analysis, no memory model by which to compare the discourse produced in and through that scene, a scene which is itself produced in the *hic et nunc* of analysis and its dialogical modes of speech and listening. What is produced in that scene, through the material geography of the two participants, the modes of speech and listening, and through the analyst's corporeal presence in the transferential exchange is an *excess of meaning* that literally throws the speaking subject into the precarious position of re-entering the realm of language and meaning:

> The subject is *overwhelmed* by language, and, consequently, all signs or signifiers appear, at least for a time, as equally contingent, inappropriate, lacking in specificity, etc. The scene of representation dissolves into confusion. It empties out, even as it loses mastery, both at the same time, within an ever more profuse enunciation. The subject no longer knows where to begin, what goal to aim at, what type of utterence or enunciation to articulate here and now. It is the transference, the projection onto the analyst of what causes the word, or the desire, to reclaim its framework, that maintains what is spoken, the id that is spoken... But in what time? In what confusion of times? (Irigaray, 2002a: 196).

The analysand's illusion of him or herself as a stable, coherent, and masterful subject of representation is stripped away in the setting of psychoanalysis. This precarious subject must reinvent his or her inscription into the Symbolic frame, a frame constituted for him or her by the dialogically transferential scene of analysis, through the use of language:

> How to distinguish "me" from "him" or "her?" Me as the same as him or her? Especially since about the analyst himself or herself (as same) few clues are given. The subject would have to introject the whole analyst? The same questions subsist. Who is *I*? Who is *you*? (Irigaray, 2002a: 197).

Importantly, in analysis the relationship between the past, present, and future is something produced *between two*. This situation contrasts with the usual temporal construct hinged to a single subject of (rational) speech as the nexus of time. *Enfintinage* can only be produced when the distinctions between past, present, and future are no longer stable:

> Try to imagine the beginning ahead of you, and the end behind you, and the habitual scene of representation starts to vacillate. Try to imagine it with no way out, and no hidden agenda, in the following scenario: in an

eternal present, in the future perfect, in a futurable conditional – not some
eternal return of the same – and with absolutely no reappropriation of
the beginning in the origin. What vertigo without our reassuring representation of space! What direction do you move in? How do you begin
speaking?

What do you say anyway? What meaning can language still have? (Irigaray, 2002a: 194).

The analysand is utterly dependant upon the analyst's willingness
also to surrender his or her own subjective certitude, his or her place
as the master of knowledge, to function temporarily as the "feminized"
receptive material (like the tain of a mirror) upon which the unconscious
phantasies of the analysand's representational discourse may appear. The
"Who is *I*? Who is *you*" effected by the transference must be part of the
analyst's experience in analysis as well as the analysand's:[14]

> The analyst theoretically functions as master, guarantor of the discourse
> – analytic discourse, for example. The analyst is supposedly the one who
> knows, guarantees and legislates, and as such, is desirable; what the
> analyst supposedly possesses – knowledge, theory, law – becomes the
> object targeted by the patient. As gratifying as this postulate is, the analyst
> must expose it as a deception, or at least subvert the terms. No one knows
> better than the analyst that "knowledge" and "theory" are phantasmatic
> correlates where one is included, from whence one is excluded, and that
> they cannot function as attributes of any subject (Irigaray, 2002a: 105).

In analysis, the analysand must believe that the analyst holds the hermeneutic key to his or her psychic dilemmas. The role of the analyst is both
initially to reinforce this belief (largely through silence) and then repudi-
ate it by allowing his or her own subjective place of mastery to come into
question.

In analysis, the sexuate body matters precisely because of the *enfintinage* that takes place therein, and as an effect of, its setting, especially
the confounding of the "I" and "You" distinctions through transference.
The analysand is literally forced to (re)encounter his or her own entry
into language, to rebuild, with the assistance of the analyst, the "I" *in
relation to* the "You." For Irigaray, the very power of psychoanalysis lies
in bringing together, in dialogue, the "I" and the "You." Her claim is that
this breech between the "I" and the "You" hinders *all* subjects of speech
within the phallic order, a breech that indicates the problematic relation
to material-maternal origins.

There are two primary forms of this pathological breech, paradigmatically represented by the (female) hysteric (Dora) and the (male) psychotic
(Schreber): the hysteric lacks an "I" while the psychotic lacks a "You."

Both of these deficiencies, for Irigaray, point to the prohibition against an original, feminine interlocutor for the speaking subject. As we saw in the previous chapter, the material-maternal is that which must be rejected if the higher orders of language, law, and culture are to be reached by the subject. Thus, according to Irigaray, (psychotic) man is yet to "know" an exchange with a "you" that is feminine:

> To the extent that men are themselves deprived of their first interlocutrice, the maternal one, and they are without a "you" who is woman and sexualized, they are by the same token deprived of a certain type of exchange (Irigaray, cited in Hirsh, 1994: 297).

Without any sense of a fully sexualized, feminine "you," man can speak to the place of "woman" only as his (masculine) mirror-image and not as his sexual other. Unable to recognize her place in dialogue, "man" speaks in place of the mother.[15]

For women, however, the ban on representing a specific relation to maternal origins outside of phallic logic, that is, a prohibition on representing a separation from a body like her own, means that "women lose the possibility of relating to *themselves* as feminine, of communicating among themselves" (Irigaray, cited in Hirsh, 1994: 297). Without the ability to construct a linguistic relationship "between two" who are recognized as feminine (rather than as the masculine version of the "feminine" as an inverted or atrophied "masculine"), means that any sense of a feminine singular (a feminine "I") or a feminine plural, of "women amongst themselves," remains impossible. The question, then, that seems most crucial for Irigaray is how to build a feminine "I" and "you" for both women and men to engage with in analysis. Irigaray offers an alternative scenario of the entry into language for girls, as a possible *initial* solution to this current discursive and theoretical failure.

Because psychoanalysis is said to effect this *enfintinage*, this (re)appearance of the original scene of the subject's entry into language, the question of the sexed status of the child becomes crucial for Irigaray. In a direct rejection of Freudian and Lacanian theory, Irigaray insists that the subject who enters into language is always an embodied, and therefore sexed, subject (though that nascent subject cannot articulate for him or her self the sexuate status of their body). Furthermore, she challenges the universal status of Freud's famous *fort-da* by arguing that boys and girls enter into language differently. *Fort-da* is the game Freud's grandson, Ernst, plays with a reel on a string, in the absence of his mother. Throwing the reel away from himself and out of sight, Ernst says "o-o-o-o" (interpreted as "fort" or "gone" by Freud), and pulling the reel back to himself, he says "da" ("there"). It is a game that enables Ernst to master the mother's absence (as Freud interprets it) and to rehearse the entry into the Symbolic as "subject," along with the mastery of language (as Lacan interprets it).

For Irigaray, however, the *fort-da* gives us a *masculine* relation to original loss (of maternal plenitude, or the "Real" of his being) upon entry into language:

> Ernst is a boy. When I raised this question of Ernst's maleness one day at a Cerisy conference...someone objected that Ernst could have been a girl. My answer was: he was a boy. *It is important to be faithful to the text.* Not every substitution is possible, especially when sexual difference is involved. In Freud's text, then, the child is a boy. And Freud never wrote that it might have been a girl. Why? A girl does not do the same things when her mother goes away. She does not play with a string and a reel that symbolize her mother, because her mother is of the same sex as she is and cannot have the object status of a reel. The mother is of the same subjective identity as she is (Irigaray, 1993a: 97; my italics).

Focusing on the physical gestures of the different games played by little boys and girls, Irigaray claims that the *fort-da*, with its to-and-fro movement away from and towards the body, is "too linear, too analogous with the to-and-fro of the penile thrust or its manual equivalent, with the mastery of the other by means of an object, it is too angular also" (Irigaray, 1993a: 99). Instead, Irigaray insists that girls enter into language differently because of the daughter's recognition of the similarities between her body and her mother's. Irigaray reads this difference through the reactions that she claims are frequently expressed or performed by the girl child in the absence of her mother. These responses include:

a. throwing herself down on the ground when she misses her mother;
b. losing the will to eat or live, "totally anorexic";
c. playing with a doll and assuming the maternal position in relation to the doll-self ("For mother and daughter, the mother is a subject that cannot easily be reduced to an object, and a doll is not an object in the way that a reel, a toy car, a gun, etc., are objects and tools used for symbolization"); and
d. dancing, which constitutes "a way for the girl to create a territory of her own in relation to the mother... The girl tries to reproduce around and within her an energetic circular movement that protects her from abandonment, attack, depression, loss of self" (Irigaray, 1993a: 97-98).

Irigaray argues further that this circular spatial demarcation articulates the body in relation to the objective world around her. Unlike Freud's Ernst, who attempts to control his subject-object relation by throwing and retrieving, from his presumably stationary body, the object that symbolizes maternal presence and absence, Irigaray's little girl reacts differently. She seeks to attract the other to her by creating her own subjective space protected by the surrounding circle she produces for herself in the absence of her mother:

> Girls do not enter into language in the same way as boys. If they are too worn down with grief they never speak at all. Otherwise they enter language by producing a space, a path, a river, a dance, a rhythm, a song... Girls describe a space around themselves rather than displacing a substitute object from one place to another or into various places; clearly visible in the hand, invisible in the bed, in the mouth in front of or behind the tongue, in the throat, etc. Girls keep everything and nothing. That is their mystery, their attraction. Of course they do play with distance, but in another way. They whirl not only toward or around an external sun but also around themselves and within themselves. The *fort-da* is not their move into language... Girls enter into language without taking anything inside themselves (except perhaps the void?). They do not speak about an introjected her, but talk *with* (sometimes in) a silence and with the other-mother in any case. Girls can find no substitutes for the mother except the whole of nature, the call to the divine or to do likewise. Woman always speaks *with* the mother, man speaks in her absence (Irigaray, 1993a: 99).

While it is all too easy to dismiss this aspect of Irigaray's work on the basis of a reductive essentialism, that is, that boys and girls enter language differently because of the given status and meaning of their "sex," it is crucial to remember Irigaray's own development of the *praticable* as a productive mode of engaging with the discourse of the other, including her own. In the quote above ("Ernst is a boy..."), Irigaray reminds her detractors that "(i)t is important to be faithful to the text." To accept the Freudian and Lacanian interpretation of the *fort-da* as universal ignores the fact that Freud develops his thesis with a male subject (Ernst). In a similar move, Irigaray's thesis concerning the entry into language for little girls is a poetic, even utopian rendering of a different relationship between the body and language, one produced by a woman analyst interpreting the gestures of little girls. She rejects Lacan's insistence that the pre-Symbolic subject in the Imaginary is non-sexed. As she puts it, "Even the child or already the child is considered to be neuter or neutered before he or she begins to speak! What a loss of freedom in the imaginary, the symbolic, in non-verbal expression" (Irigaray, 1993a:

94). Irigaray is attempting creatively to draw out a distinctly feminine or female imaginary within the Symbolic. To do this is not to suggest that this female imaginary is the only one possible. Rather, I think Irigaray is sketching the boundaries of what "woman's" relationship to language may entail, in the sense of a possibly rewarding relationship to language that is yet to be realized. She sketches these boundaries as a woman analyst of the gestures and speech of women *for the purpose of change.* And crucially, her own sexuate female body *makes a difference* in analysis. In other words, I don't think Irigaray is asking us to reject Freud's interpretation of the *fort-da* and replace it with her own theory of language production. She is asking that we reject the universalization of such theories in favour of the "at least two."

To insist on a sexually different relationship to language is to make a space for an alternative relationship to origins. Such a space seeks to include the maternal figure as interlocutor in the drama of enunciation, rather than displace her altogether by taking her place, as is the current theoretical position:

> Woman always speaks *with* the mother, man speaks in her absence. This *with her* obviously takes different shapes and it must seek to place speech *between*, not to remain in an indissociable fusion, with the women woven together. This *with* has to try to become a *with self* (Irigaray, 1993a: 99).

Through her reinterpretation of the psychoanalytic *praticable*, Irigaray develops a mode for women to begin articulating a relationship to maternal origins. This development involves a re-articulation of the necessary separation from her *within and through the virtue of the analytic setting.* For women, the virtue of this setting is the possible production of a symbolic frame that allows language, as that which is produced "between two," to extricate the daughter from the place of the mother, bringing forth through creative production the woman "behind" the mother. For Irigaray, this linguistic production, which functions to allow the mother and daughter to remain distinct (as "speech *between*"), is the primary condition for the production of a Symbolic space for women that does not negate their sexual specificities, which are yet to be produced.

This entire discussion of *enfintinage* as an effect of the transference is crucial for my own approach to engaging with the book of Chronicles. The significance for my interpretive engagement is Irigaray's insistence that it is not simply the analysand who participates in the (re)construction of the initial drama of enunciation. The role of the analyst, first and foremost, is to enable change to take place *between two*:

> No analysand can successfully constitute an irreducible horizon for himself or herself. Such, however, is the goal of analysis – access for the one and the other to their respective horizons, no longer constituted by rejection, hatred or mastery, but fluid and remaining partially open to the other. Permanent construction without closure, of amorous and musical rhythm and scansion.
>
> The goal of analysis could be expressed thus: "Let us invent together that which will allow us to live in and to continue to build the world, and first of all, the world that is each of us" (Irigaray, 2002a: 246).

Furthermore, according to Irigaray, when it comes to the analysis of masculine discourses, women analysts must assert their embodied status as *different* to that of the male analysand. They are obliged willingly to insist upon the site of the feminine as a viable interlocutory site for both men and women.

In other words, it is important to insist on the sexed status of the analyst and her discourse produced *in relation to* the discourse of the analysand. This approach allows for the possibility of the maternal-feminine to take on new symbolic significance for the masculine; "woman" emerges as something other than the pre-symbolic, silent, and problematically both comforting and threatening spaces that currently constitute the feminine in the male Imaginary and Symbolic. But it is also important for the female analyst to allow her own originary drama of enunciation to emerge through the transference. Analytic language can then function as a medium of exchange between herself and her maternal interlocutrice, a figure who emerges in the analytic setting.

Having discussed in considerable detail Irigaray's interpretation of the psychoanalytic *praticable*, I now want to return to Irigaray's specific form of psychoanalytic interpretation of written texts. Again, this approach is twofold: the feminist-critical mode that makes use of psychoanalytic concepts without universalizing those concepts as "truth" and the production of alternative readings that bring a feminine relation to maternal origins into play. The preceding discussion on the importance of modes of interpretation rather than methods, as well as the *praticable* as the setting of analysis, is important background for clarifying Irigaray's own distinct form of psychoanalytic reading. I now want to develop more specifically Irigaray's approach and its importance for reading the book of Chronicles "as woman."

4. *Reading Silence*

The analysis of the means by which the feminine has come to represent the silences of male discourse is crucial to Irigaray's interpretive approach. I have shown how this analysis involves an unrelenting critique of the various discursive mechanisms by which the feminine represents the "unsayable" in Western philosophy. In psychoanalytic terms, women need to analyse the male Imaginary and listen for the unconscious of masculine representation, that is, the "latent content" that resists or is denied formal symbolization. In "The Power of Discourse," Irigaray characterizes her psychoanalytic approach to philosophical texts as a means of uncovering the unconscious processes at work in the philosophical texts with which she engages. Importantly, for Irigaray, psychoanalytic reading is also a form of psychoanalytic listening:

> This process of interpretive rereading has always been a *psychoanalytic undertaking* as well. That is why we need to pay attention to the way the unconscious works in each philosophy, and perhaps in philosophy in general. We need to listen (psycho)analytically to its procedures of repression, to the structuration of language that shores up its representations, separating the true from the false, the meaningful from the meaningless, and so forth (Irigaray, 1985b: 75).

While Irigaray, here, is speaking specifically about philosophical texts, it is clear from her early work that an analysis of *all* written texts of patriarchal cultures, especially "truth" discourses such as the scientific and religious texts of the West, should involve a mode of listening that she characterizes as psychoanalytic. In the description of her approach cited above, Irigaray refers to the rather orthodox, though often ignored, focus of psychoanalysis: on the means by which given texts are *produced*. It is important to re-emphasize that Irigaray does *not* psychoanalyse the authors of philosophical texts. Nor does she impose psychoanalytic theory into the textual worlds that she explores. Irigaray is not searching for the reinforcement of psychoanalytic theoretical "truths." Instead, for Irigaray the focus is on the drama of enunciation itself. Her concern is with how each subject of language production organizes his or her representations within a particular framework or setting within which she herself participates as analyst.

Irigaray explores the means by which major philosophical discourses create and sustain the systematicity and *"position of mastery"* (an internal logic of self-sufficiency) of "philosophy" as a discourse of "truth," at the expense of the feminine. She argues that, in general, the coherence of each philosophy requires the repression of sexual difference, a repression that is symptomatically readable through a masculine desire for the same:

> Now, this domination of the philosophic logos stems in large part from its power to *reduce all others to the economy of the Same.* The teleologically constructive project it takes on is always also a project of diversion, deflection, reduction of the other in the Same. And, in its greatest generality perhaps, from its power to *eradicate the difference between the sexes* in systems that are self-representative of a "masculine subject" (Irigaray, 1985b: 74).

Importantly for Irigaray, patriarchal discourses such as philosophy are structured according to a specular logic, which enables man to see himself reflected everywhere. As I have discussed in the previous chapter, "woman" functions as "the hole in representation." She is what is *unrepresentable*, and therefore threatening, to discursive systems that aim at the representation, and therefore knowledge of, everything in the world. To compensate for this failure or limit of knowledge, "woman" comes to function as man's self-reflecting other. Without her own representations, "woman" thus amounts to the reflective surface of representation, like the tain of the mirror. And so, an analysis of masculine discourses entails a close scrutiny of the means by which this specular logic takes place in representation:

> What allows us to proceed in this way is that we interpret, at each "moment," the *specular make-up* of discourse, that is, the self-reflecting (stratifiable) organization of the subject in that discourse. An organization that maintains, among other things, the break between what is perceptible and what is intelligible, and thus maintains the submission, subordination, and exploitation of the "feminine" (Irigaray, 1985b: 80).

Irigaray's attention is given to the "scene of representation" or "scenography," that is, the structures that organize the masculine subject of speech in his world and that enable his representations to be feasible to himself and others *alike.* She is concerned with how the coherence of that scene is ensured by certain arrangements already in existence. Irigaray writes of

> representation as it is defined in philosophy, that is, the architectonics of its theatre, its framing in space-time, its geometric organization, its props, its actors, their respective positions, their dialogues, indeed their tragic relations, without overlooking the *mirror*, most often hidden, that allows the logos, the subject, to reduplicate itself, to reflect itself by itself (Irigaray, 1985b: 75).

In other words, Irigaray is analysing the prop-like features of the *male* Imaginary that organize and give coherence to "man" in relation to his symbolic world, a world created by and for him. As I have discussed in the last chapter, the mirror is the principal prop in Lacan's elaboration of the dialectical relations between the Imaginary, Symbolic, and Real, a prop that Irigaray insists functions to ensure the non-representation of "woman" outside specular, phallic terms. Analyzing the male imaginary involves a close attention to the details of the representational scene, searching for the means by which the masculine subject ensures that representation contains only a *monosexual* subjective structuration.

And so, Irigaray's own psychoanalytic readings of certain philosophical texts disrupt philosophical discourse precisely because they make visible the "invisible" or silent machinery that supports it:

> What is called for instead is an examination of the *operation of the "grammar"* of each figure of discourse, its syntactic laws or requirements, its imaginary configurations, its metaphoric networks, and also, of course, what it does not articulate at the level of utterance: *its silences* (Irigaray, 1985b: 75).

Thus, while Irigaray is highly critical of psychoanalytic theory, especially because of its apparent refusal to allow women the chance to represent their relationship to and desire for (maternal) origins, her mode of reading can, I have argued, be characterized as *psychoanalytic*. Indeed, working in the mode of the psychoanalytic *praticable* enables the production of an encounter between woman-reader and text that is both therapeutic and ethical. As analytic readers, Irigaray insists that we strive not only to analyse the masculine Imaginary and its appropriation of the "feminine," but to listen *carefully* for the necessary silences of all masculine discourses, to ask how the feminine has come to represent these silences (the unspeakable, the unsayable, the unknowable, the *limit*) of "his" representational frameworks. These silences must be "heard" if we, as women, are to write ourselves into the Symbolic. In other words, we must first understand how we have come to *represent* silence within the masculine Imaginary and Symbolic. As such, Irigaray asks us to rethink the very nature of silence itself. Is silence simply the absence of the spoken word, the absence of voice? In masculine discourses, if women are present and/or are represented as speaking, does this mean they have a voice that can be heard? Do we hear anything of the "feminine," outside its masculine conceptualization, when women speak in Chronicles, as rare as that speech may be?

This question concerning the nature of silence is of the utmost importance for my own study of Chronicles for two reasons. Firstly, while there is a relative dearth of female characters (whether speaking or not) in Chronicles when compared with the Deuteronomistic history (despite the fact that this dearth has really gone by unanalysed in biblical studies; a double silencing?), there are still females who appear in Chronicles, and indeed, speak. Is it fair to claim, then (as I wish to do), that the "feminine" voice is necessarily silenced in Chronicles? Secondly, while Chronicles scholarship is largely dominated by male scholarship, there are women who have written about Chronicles. Is it fair to suggest, then (as I did in the Introduction), that the silence of the feminine voice has successfully been transferred from the biblical text to contemporary biblical scholarship? If we understand silence only in terms of the absence of speech and language, then it is not only unfair, but erroneous, obviously.

However, Michelle Boulous Walker (1998) argues that when it comes to reading the silences of Western discourses, the complexity of the very nature of silence, beyond the understanding of silence as the absence of speech, must be addressed. Boulous Walker explores the silence of the feminine voice in Western philosophy through an engagement with a number of Western philosophers (including Irigaray, Le Doeuff, Kristeva, Althusser, Lyotard, and others). In her study she challenges the conceptualization of silence as simply the absence of speech. Boulous Walker analyses a number of philosophical writings by men (including Plato, Althusser, Freud, Marx, Baudrillard, and Lyotard). She argues that "we can discern a masculine imaginary that works to silence women in quite specific ways" (Boulous Walker, 1998: 1). Employing Althusser's symptomatic reading, guided by the complexities of silence elaborated in the work of Irigaray on the repressed maternal body and Le Doeuff's reading of the mute interiority of philosophy through its images and metaphors, Boulous Walker shows how the silence-speech dichotomy is inadequate for an understanding of women's relation to Western philosophy, specifically, and masculine thinking and writing, in general. Silence cannot be understood only according to a spatial logic that maintains the distinction between inside and outside.

Boulous Walker's principal claim is that the texts of Western philosophy, psychoanalytic theory, and literature all "reveal a masculine imaginary that speaks for the maternal" (1998: 1). She shows how certain strategies of silencing are discernible in these texts, strategies that enable "man" to take the place of the maternal, to speak from that place as "man." The maternal thus constitutes a necessary symbolic site *for man*, and to maintain the monopoly of this symbolic site, a genuinely feminine voice must remain silenced. The strategies of silencing that Boulous Walker uncovers include the simplest form (exclusion) to the more complex forms (denial, disavowal, repression, and foreclosure). Exclusion entails either the proscription against women contributing to the definition and production of discourse or the refusal to hear her when she does speak as "woman," that is, when she does not speak "universally" (masculine discourse). While it is easy to comprehend exclusion in terms of the logic of inside-outside (the excluded remain outside, the included inside), the other, more complex forms of silencing reveal the failure of this logic. Within the logical structures of denial or disavowal, repression and foreclosure, exclusion is internal; the denied, repressed or foreclosed maternal-feminine becomes the (symbolically silent) place from which one speaks *masculine discourse*. In structuralist terms, silence is not simply what remains outside the audible as "unhearable"; it is internal to the very frameworks that *constitute* the audible. Silence *inhabits the symbolic as the necessary guarantee of the audible*. Thus, silence is an internal absence that Boulous Walker insists (along with Irigaray, Le Doeuff, and Althusser) is a *readable* absence. Indeed, silence "entails a spoken yet unheard voice" that is "structured by a logic of repression" (Boulous Walker, 1998: 27). Thus, because the maternal body constitutes the mute interiority of masculine thinking, writing, theorizing, etcetera, according to Boulous Walker, woman is most radically silenced through her association with maternity. For Irigaray, this appropriation of the feminine, particularly the appropriation of the maternal body, constitutes one of the principal means by which women are silenced in philosophical discourse. "Taking back" the feminine, then, is the crucial first step towards speaking from, rather than simply speaking about, the place of "woman."

With respect to Chronicles, then, in light of Boulous Walker's retheorization of silence, that women speak *in* Chronicles (albeit rarely) and that women speak *about* Chronicles (albeit rarely) does not mean that the "feminine" is audible. In other words, silence is not simply reducible to the total absence of speech. Ultimately, what I wish to argue in this book is that the feminine voice is silenced in Chronicles through the association of women with maternity. To hear this voice, I have suggested that we need Irigaray's mode of reading, writing, thinking, and speaking as "woman."

According to Irigaray's interpretation of the psychoanalytic *praticable*, the analysand's construction of the past is a production enabled by the setting itself, particularly by the modes of listening and speaking that take place there. There is no model of memory in analysis. Given this, I think that Chronicles' construction of the past must be allowed to stand on its own without any judgement concerning its historical "truth" in relation to the alternative histories present in the Hebrew Bible (namely, Samuel–Kings). We are listening for the unconscious processes at work in Chronicles, "its procedures of repression, to the structuration of language that shores up its representations, separating the true from the false, the meaningful from the meaningless, and so forth" (Irigaray, 1985b: 75).

In psychoanalytic terms, the unconscious, formed through the primary repressions that take place upon entry into language, is the domain of the unsayable and the unknowable. What constitutes the unsayable and unknowable, however, is determined within a given Symbolic framework. In Seminar XX, Lacan declares that "if the libido is only masculine, it is only from where the dear woman is whole, in other words, from the place which man sees her, that the dear woman can have an unconscious" (Lacan, 1998: 98-99). Lacan's observation suggests that there is nothing unique to the female unconscious, for there can in fact be no such thing as the female unconscious. For Irigaray, however, the unconscious and its mechanics, as theorized by Freud and Lacan, betray many of the characteristics of the "feminine," as constructed within the (masculine) Symbolic frameworks of the West. What Irigaray suggests is that the theoretical formulations of the unconscious themselves betray the phantasmatic symptomologies of the masculine Imaginary. In short, the unconscious theorized by Freud and Lacan is not a *universal* unconscious, but a specifically *masculine* one. This is not to say that the unconscious itself is masculine, or hom(m)o-sexual, but rather that "the commonly reductive interpretation of the unconscious, along with the censure and repression maintained by it, is the hom(m)o-sexual factor" (Irigaray, 1985b: 129).

Instead of formulating a specifically feminine unconscious, therefore, Irigaray stresses that we must first ask to what extent the repressed feminine is included within the masculine unconscious:

> ...before asking about elaborating an unconscious that would be *other* with respect to the unconscious as it is now defined, it is appropriate, perhaps, to ask whether the feminine may not be to a large extent included in that unconscious... Thus many of the characteristics attributed to the unconscious may evoke an economy of desire that would be, perhaps, "feminine." So we would need to work through the question of what the unconscious has borrowed from the feminine before we could arrive at the question of a feminine unconscious (Irigaray, 1985b: 123).

As Margaret Whitford points out, for Irigaray, the distinguishing features of the unconscious closely resemble the masculine constructions of the "feminine": fluidity and mobility; the indifference to the laws of logic (identity and non-contradiction); and the inability to speak about itself (Whitford, 1991: 35). Crucially, because the feminine and the unconscious seem intimately related in metaphysical discourse, with the unconscious consisting "at present and in part, of the repressed/censured feminine element of history, and the repressed/censured component of the logic of consciousness" (Irigaray, 1985b: 124), analysing the unconscious of patriarchal discourses involves an examination of the "feminine" as a different, and *potentially* rewarding economy of representation for women:

> I search for myself, as if I had been assimilated into maleness. I ought
> to reconstitute myself on the basis of a disassimilation... Rise again from
> the traces of a culture, of works already produced by the other. Searching
> through what is in them – for what is not there. What allowed them to be,
> for what is not there. Their conditions of possibility, for what is not there.
>
> Woman ought to be able to find herself, among other things, through
> the images of herself already deposited in history and the conditions of
> production of the work of man, and not on the basis of his work, his genealogy (Irigaray, 1993b: 9-10).

Irigaray's psychoanalysis of certain philosophical texts involves this investigation of the repressed feminine, especially the repressed passionate, sexuate, "woman." As shown in the last chapter, Irigaray is searching for the specular arrangements that sustain male subjectivity, specifically through the buried or unrepresented "woman"; the "woman" beyond the asexual mother (of the son). The task of analysis "as woman" is thus to return this buried, silenced "woman," whom Irigaray casts as the daughter's mother, to the light of day. Irigaray analyses Western patriarchal discourses, particularly "truth" discourses, with the intention of searching for the various phantasies that persist as symptoms of the unconscious of Western patriarchal social order (see Whitford, 1991: 34). Furthermore, these symptomatic phantasies must be studied and analysed for what they can tell us about the means by which "woman" is silenced in cultural ho(m)mo-sexuality.

In light of Irigaray's reading strategy and Boulous Walker's re-theorization of silence, then, my own particular question relates to how a woman is to listen anew, *to read* anew, and ultimately "take back" the feminine as it is rendered in the book of Chronicles. Again, Irigaray is adamant that psychoanalysis provides us with the necessary tools for drawing out what cannot be said or heard within masculine discourses, what *needs to remain silent*. The first step, then, when engaging with the book of Chronicles in the mode of the psychoanalytic *praticable* is to discern the place and function of the feminine in this discursive production of the past by listening *without* historical-critical analysis. As discussed above, the role of the analyst is to draw out the "unspeakable" of the analysand's discourse through a specific mode of listening. To do this requires determining how the analysand's discourse positions the feminine, and therefore, positions me as a woman analyst, in relation to the masculine so that his-story may be allowed its place in the analytic setting. As the geography of analysis teaches us, the virtue of this setting is the mutually ethical dependence of analyst and analysand in the production of discourse. Both analyst and analysand need each other if what is blocking the progress of the subject (individual or social) is to be reworked to enable a different future.

What we are listening for, then, is the "spoken yet unheard voice" (Boulous Walker, 1998: 27) of the text, seeking out "what remains to be discovered, especially the future in the past" (Irigaray, 1993a: 86). Psychoanalysis provides us with critical tools that enable such a voice to be heard in masculine discourses. The two psychoanalytic concepts that are crucial for my engagement with Chronicles are disavowal and repression. Disavowal and repression are quite different processes of defence against psychic trauma. Briefly, disavowal encompasses, simultaneously, both the denial and acceptance of some feature of external reality (namely, according to Freud, the absence of the woman's penis). Repression, on the other hand, relates to internal representations. It is said to be "a defensive process by which an idea is excluded from consciousness" (Moore and Fine, 1990: 166). Following Boulous Walker, through these two concepts of disavowal and repression, in Part II we shall come to understand not only *how* the feminine is silenced in Chronicles, but also *why*.

5. *Speaking Silence Poetically*

It is important to realize that for Irigaray the critical or negative moment of analysis, that is, a feminist critique of the structures of patriarchal thought and its silences, is never enough. The analysis of the male Imaginary of cultural products such as literary texts, as well as the repressions and foreclosures that constitute the unconscious of those texts and the societies that both produce and are produced by them, is utterly necessary if any place is to be cleared within the Symbolic for women to speak "as women" (whatever that might mean). However, as Whitford points out, Irigaray also insists on providing "alternative versions, alternative readings, alternative mythologies, and alternative imaginary configurations, however provisional...which act as holding devices to prevent the immediate reinstallation of the male imaginary configuration" (Whitford, 1991: 103). For Irigaray, then, any reading of ancient stories that seeks to criticise and understand that literature from a feminist perspective falls short unless some attempt is made at offering alternative readings, readings that seek "what remains to be discovered, especially the future in the past" (Irigaray, 1993a: 86).

On the surface, this conjunction of critical analysis and alternative re-readings may sound to biblical scholars a little like a feminist hermeneutics of suspicion. The critique of the structures of historical investigation and the reconstructive agendas of feminists such as Elisabeth Schüssler

Fiorenza, Bernadette Brooten, and Carol Meyers, for example, in many respects resonate with Irigaray's interpretive strategies, particularly the ethical and liberationist criteria guiding their interpretations of biblical material. However, unlike the practitioners of a hermeneutics of suspicion, for whom the reconstruction of "history" is a crucial exercise (though certainly not the only function),[16] Irigaray insists on constructing a different relationship between the past, present, and future, as discussed at length above. She is less interested in "knowing" the past better or more fully (as if it were some concrete "thing"), or in simply revealing, in deconstructive fashion, the gaps and aporias of androcentric histories. Her rereadings are not instances of woman-centered, reconstructive historiography which entail the "discovery" of something in the past previously neglected by patriarchal readings that work according to specific rules and agendas defined by masculine thought.

For Irigaray, rereading the texts of patriarchy "as woman" must entail a reconfiguration of the various figures, motifs, and metaphors of the feminine so that philosophical, cultural, and political interventions by and for women can be made in the present. To speak "as woman" means, for Irigaray, to *speak* or *practice* sexual difference, to speak with "man" from a discursive place that is not appropriable by him. It is not to develop a new theory of woman, to attend to the "What is Woman" question, nor even to elaborate another concept of the feminine, which for Irigaray merely reiterates the masculine obsession with finite concepts and definitions:

> To claim that the feminine can be expressed in the form of a concept is to allow oneself to be caught up again in a system of "masculine" representations, in which women are trapped in a system of meaning which serves the auto-affection of the (masculine) subject. If it is really a matter of calling "femininity" into question, there is still no need to elaborate another "concept" – unless a woman is renouncing her sex and wants to speak like men. For the elaboration of a theory of woman, men, I think, suffice. In a woman('s) language, the concept as such would have no place (Irigaray, 1985b: 123).

Instead, Irigaray argues that "woman" must be able to speak from her own symbolic place(s) and not from the masculine subjective, symbolic positions that are currently available. This means that the given Imaginary and Symbolic structures that are isomorphic with the male body need to be short-circuited to enable a different imaginary construction to be articulated in accordance with a female body linguistically (and therefore, on the level of the Symbolic) conceived in terms other than "lack, deficiency, or as imitation and negative image of the subject" (Irigaray, 1985b: 78):

> Can the word *woman* be subject? predicate? If it can be neither one nor the other, what status does the word have in discourse? The status of "women" as indeterminate plural, as obscure part of the human race... This "women" would amount to a kind of chaotic, amorphous, archaic multiple which, if it is ever to achieve a form, needs some representation of unity to be imposed upon it. "Women" would be like the soup, the clay, the earth and blood, the water, the ocean out of which man emerges as man, and God as God. Woman, the one, single, *unique*, would at best be viewed as a place of procreation or the partition into objects of seduction (Irigaray, 1993a: 69).

> (W)hat other mode of reading or writing, of interpretation and affirmation, may be mine inasmuch as I am a woman, with respect to you, a man? Is it possible that the difference might not be reduced once again to a process of *hierarchization? Of subordinating the other to the same?* (Irigaray, 1985b: 159).

If the very foundation of symbolic and social orders is the silencing of the voices of women, equivalent to matricide according to Irigaray, then the principal question is how to speak "as woman?" Are women only heard when they can adeptly mimic the masculine subjective voice? While critical analysis of patriarchal thought and critical, historical revisionism are necessary elements of feminist interventions, Irigaray maintains that these ultimately fail to effect substantial change for women because there is no real challenge to epistemological structures. Instead, they simply maintain the silence of women. While the content of the Symbolic may shift, the structural relations or frameworks remain the same. Within such phallic frameworks, woman can only ever speak "as man," or remain unheard. And as I have suggested in the previous chapter, Irigaray argues that the silence of women in Western discourses is directly related to the prohibition against women articulating a relation to maternal origins.

So, Irigaray insists that women "challenge every theory, every thought, every existing language in that these are monopolized by men only. They question the *very foundation of our social and cultural order*, the organization of which has been prescribed by the patriarchal system (Irigaray, 1977: 68). Elizabeth Grosz explains:

> At stake for Irigaray are not simply words needed to name female specificity but, more seriously (for a thing does not need a name to be representable), new structures of knowledges, truths and scientificity which authorise and validate different discourses. Femininity cannot simply be added to existing discursive frameworks for there is no space for such an addition. Different ways of knowing, different kinds of discourse, new methods and aspirations for language and knowledges need to be explored if women are

> to overcome their restrictive containment in patriarchal representations...
> Patriarchy does not prevent women from speaking; it refuses to listen
> when women do not speak "universal," that is, as men (Grosz, 1989: 126).

Most importantly, new languages, modes and structures of knowledge
are required which enable women to begin articulating a desire for origin
that does not simply repeat and reinforce the oedipal-phallic desire for
the same, that is, the desire for paternal origination and the obliteration
or silencing of the maternal. Borrowing from Heidegger, Irigaray insists
that women need to invent their own "house of language."[17]

It is clear from Irigaray's poetic style, and her comments concerning
the role of the poet's words (Irigaray, 1999) that she considers poetry to
be a productive, even cathartic linguistic practice because it foregrounds,
rather than disavows, the pleasure of language production, especially
when it comes to the indeterminacy of meaning. Unlike languages and
discourses of truth, poetry enjoys the free play of words and their meanings, refusing to tie down one to the other. For Irigaray, poetic discourse,
like analytic discourse (as discussed in this chapter), has the potential
to explore alternative meanings and pleasures that may begin to speak
the unspeakable desires of "woman" and her body. This potential arises
because in analytic and poetic discourses the emphasis is not upon the
production of a unitary, uncontestable, reflection of some pre-existing
"truth." And, as Grosz points out, such a linguistic practice is of course
threatening to certain masculine discourses:

> Discourses, especially truthful ones, are unable to admit their reliance on
> an active, inscribing language, one which produces rather than reflects
> "reality" or "ideas" – that is, a language which introduces an uncontrol-
> lable, arational principle into every discourse.
>
> Textual practices like poetry, which aim to explore and play with the
> undecidability of language, are socially tolerable when they remain sharply
> divided from other modes of (true, scientific, serious) discourse. When
> poetry is separated from either prose on the one hand, and non-fiction or
> theory on the other, the self-image of phallocentric knowledges is preserved.
> It is only when the poetic text threatens to insert itself into the very heart of
> "serious" theoretical writings, blurring the borders between poetry, fiction
> and knowledge, that discourse more amenable to the positive inscription of
> the female body may be established and explored (Grosz, 1989: 130).

Because poetic and psychoanalytic languages are inventive and both
participate in the production of alternative representational frames that
allow the materiality of language production to come out of the shadows,
both discourses hold the possibility of producing languages that can
speak something of "our body's language" (Irigaray, 1985b: 214).

Of course, Irigaray is not the only feminist to theorize the political possibilities of poetic discourse. Julia Kristeva is no doubt the best known advocate of a radical poetic subject, with poetic language constituting the irruption of what has been necessarily repressed by the Symbolic order, including the maternal.[18] However, unlike Kristeva, for whom the (almost exclusively male) poet's discourse represents a radical and risky speaking *from the place of the mother*, Irigaray insists that poetic language, like analytic language, allows women to produce a language *between* herself and the maternal place. This is a production that constitutes not only radically new Symbolic spaces for women, but also threatens patriarchal social order, which, Irigaray argues, requires both the separation of the mother and the daughter and their lack of subjective distinction as prisoners of the maternal site within the Symbolic.

In the following chapters of this book, then, I am coupling my analytic discourse inspired by Irigaray's work on the *praticable* with a poetic discourse which mimetically evokes the "feminine" as both disruptive and (re)mediative. At certain points in my engagement with Chronicles, poetic language takes over. In other words, when I embrace Irigaray's psychoanalytic mode of reading Chronicles, my own relationship to language and its (logical, rational) production opens out to embrace a more playful and more uncertain form of thinking/writing. To include these poetic responses is, of course, risky. Will too much of myself be given away to the reader? Will the academic reader reject me as a flippant thinker, given the imperial status apportioned to reasoned argumentation in academic thought? Whatever the case, I think this risk is a necessary one. The purpose of the analytic and poetic discourses is both to draw out the "unsaid" of the book of Chronicles and to hear the silences of this discourse in order to recover and to reconstitute the repressed feminine of this particular account of Israelite history. That which constitutes the "unsayable" of this particular masculine relationship to origins, to the present, and to the future provides us with an alternative language, a language "yet to be thought or spoken." Such a language is perhaps intimately related to a "feminine" that patriarchal thought cannot countenance. As such, we must search for the feminine that is buried in Chronicles, a text that functions as one of those points of origin in the West. This buried feminine can then be utilized as a source of (discarded) imagery that enables an analytic and poetic reworking and reinvention of the past *in the present of analysis*, one that can (re)produce the "forgotten" (silenced) mother of history: the daughter's mother.

The poetic discourse begins in Chapter 3, where I initiate my analysis of the first nine chapters of Chronicles, and continues to the end of

Chapter 4, where I conclude my analytic engagement with the Chronicles narrative. The poetic sequence is titled *The Lamentations.* I have chosen to explore the "buried feminine" of Chronicles by employing the broad structure of the first two poems from the Hebrew Lamentations for two main reasons. Firstly, I wish to take an already existing (masculine) structure of poetic lament for the purpose of exploring my own relation to origin and loss, which, as I argued in the previous chapter, is both complex and fundamental to a woman's analysis of her cultural founda- tions. I also think that it is interesting that the employment of a repeti- tious discourse of exclamatory regret, when uttered by the male subject in the West is called "lament" (having been given a valid representational structure in our culture), but when uttered by a female subject is often labelled "whinging" or "nagging."[19] Secondly, given that the principal image employed by the Hebrew (male) poet is that of Israel as an aban- doned woman, I have found that this poem has enabled me to express the anger and sadness I experience when reading Chronicles and Chronicles scholarship, due to the total lack of concern for the relative absence of women in this particular version of Israel's past. On the one hand, then, the image of woman-mother as discarded is useful to the male subject in the production of poetic language, while her absence and silence in the historical discourses of the West largely goes by unnoticed. No doubt, the two are inextricably related. To approach the silencing of "woman" in Chronicles through this poetic lament is, then, actively (and even at times aggressively) to speak from that position of silence, for the purpose of hearing that silence differently. I hasten to add that the two poems I have included here ("Vignettes of a Woman Dead," and "A Daughter, Tied in Her Tongues") are contemporary poems born out of my analytic encounter with Chronicles. They are not revisionist poems.[20] That is, I am not interested in rewriting Chronicles, or the Lamentations for that matter. My poems are very much written in the mode of the analytic present, the *hic et nunc*, as I have carefully theorized it in this chapter, fol- lowing Irigaray's rethinking of the analytic *praticable*. The poems are the means by which I allow the mother as *interlocutrice*, if you like, to emerge in my engagement with the discourse of Chronicles.

6. *Conclusion: Going into Analysis "as Woman" with the Book of Chronicles*

In this chapter I have given a detailed explication of Irigaray's reinter- pretation of the psychoanalytic *praticable*, arguing that she provides us with a particular mode of feminist engagement that we can take to our reading of the book of Chronicles that refuses to maintain the burial of

the forgotten mother of patriarchal history. Her approach is characterized by both the negative, critical analysis of the father's story and the
positive reworking of that story through a reconfiguration of its silences
or readable absences.

I began by stressing that, for Irigaray, to privilege psychoanalytic theory
over the specific analytic practice determined by its unique *praticable*
means that the unconscious offers us nothing new in analysis. Rather,
it functions as the (silent) guarantee of an *a priori* language and social
order. Instead, Irigaray argues that the three rules that constitute and are
constituted by the psychoanalytic *praticable* (the geography of analysis,
the modes of speaking and listening, and transference) effect the collapse
of philosophical distinctions between *a priori* and *a posteriori*, between
the subject and object of knowledge, and importantly between theory
and history. Irigaray's refusal to privilege theory over practice stems from
what she perceives to be the potential of the psychoanalytic setting for
women, as I have mentioned briefly in the last chapter and have developed
further here. Such a setting allows the production of a representational
scene that enables women to return to and rework the past, specifically
by returning "through the masculine imaginary, to interpret the way it
has reduced us to silence, to muteness or mimicry...to (re)discover a possible space for the feminine imaginary" (Irigaray, 1985b: 164).

Moreover, the *praticable* enables the production of a representational
framework that especially enables something of a feminine imaginary
relation to origins to *begin* to be articulated within the Symbolic. I say
"begin" because it is not a case of "digging up" or discovering an already
existing linguistic "thing" in *the* past that has so far remained unheard
within the Symbolic. One of the most important effects of the psychoanalytic setting is the breakdown of rigid temporal categories. What is
produced in analysis is *a* past, and it is produced between the analyst
and analysand in the *hic et nunc* of analysis. And, it is clear from Irigaray's
work that what is *symptomatically* readable or audible in the "truth" discourses of the West, and in the voices and bodily gestures of women, is the
absence of a feminine representation of origin and original loss. As such,
this absence constitutes a *yet to be* thought or spoken. And, according
to Irigaray, the setting of psychoanalysis effects an *enfintinage*, meaning
that women are afforded the opportunity of rewriting themselves into
the Symbolic by speaking *with* the mother rather than speaking in place
of her. As such, the psychoanalytic *praticable* is an enabling and ongoing
process of representational production, and it is a *means* or *mode* of analysis (rather than a method) amenable to feminist theory and practice. And
the importance of such a creation within the Symbolic is "to secure a

place for the feminine within sexual difference" (Irigaray, 1985b: 159). Here, "sexual difference" is understood as that which is yet to be.

Finally, I have argued that Irigaray's particular mode of analysing and engaging with the past texts of various intellectual "traditions" (Western philosophy, science, religion, etc.) can be characterized in terms of her own re-interpretation of the psychoanalytic setting or *praticable*. Irigaray's mode of engagement with past texts is a viable and important mode for feminist engagements with the Hebrew Bible. The relationship between the negative function of critical analysis and the positive, reconstructive function of alternative readings needs to be understood according to the psychoanalytic *praticable* conceived as nuptial tool or instrument capable of bringing together seemingly disparate or "divorced" categories without destroying the identity of either. The critical reading of masculine discourses such as Chronicles first involves receiving the traces of the analysand's discourse, determining the symbolic place that the analysand's discourse designates for the analyst. As a woman analyst, according to Irigaray, this involves functioning as the receptive material upon which the (silent) unconscious mechanisms of the analysand's discourse may appear, with its phantasmatic supports ultimately becoming readable. When functioning in the mode of the *praticable*, the silences of masculine discourses become not only analysable, but are also able to be heard differently. Irigaray insists that the residues of the feminine in the male unconscious (the "scraps" or "debris" of the male Imaginary) provide us with a source of alternative imagery for a productive and therapeutic engagement with the past, one which seeks to bring the "other woman" (the woman buried under her Symbolic mandate as the son's mother) into the light. Building upon Irigaray's emphasis on both the language produced in analysis and poetic language, I employ both of these languages to explore the alternative possibilities offered by this ancient Hebrew text in the analytic setting.

Crucially, the psychoanalytic setting ensures that both of these analytic functions, negative and positive, work together without destroying each other. In other words, the negative and positive tasks of our engagement with the book of Chronicles do not weaken or cancel each other out. Rather, they work together, as viable modes of analysis, seeking "what remains to be discovered, especially the future in the past."

Part II

OUR PRODUCTION OF A PAST, IN THE PRESENT OF ANALYSIS:
ENGAGING WITH THE BOOK OF CHRONICLES

In the last section, I outlined the feminist mode of reading that I wish to bring to the book of Chronicles, a mode heavily in debt to the early work of Luce Irigaray. Based on Irigaray's reinterpretation of the psychoanalytic setting (*praticable*), my own engagement with Chronicles practises a form of psychoanalytic reading that, with Irigaray, I have argued is both ethical and therapeutic. In light of this reinterpretation of the *praticable*, I have argued that Irigaray's own reading practice enables a twofold approach to analysis. On the one hand, the negative, critical analysis of the Imaginary and the unconscious of masculine discourses, by women analysts, must take place so that the silences of those discourses (the *limits* of masculine language and thinking) can not only be heard, but heard *differently*. With respect to this negative, critical aspect of Irigarayan reading practice, and aided by Michelle Boulous Walker's recent work on silence and the maternal body, I shall utilize certain analytic concepts to enable a critical analysis of the means by which the feminine has been silenced in Chronicles. Briefly, in Chapters 3 and 4 I pay close attention to the language of "birthing" and its effects on meaning production, and to the effects that the mother's speech has on the genealogy and the narrative. I am also listening out for what fascinates the analysand, what he chooses to focus on, the things about which he gives us intricate, and sometimes seemingly unnecessary, details. In short, I am listening for the ways in which the "son" (I shall soon explain what I mean by this) borrows from the feminine to construct (t)his "reality" through (t)his specific production of the past.

Thus, in the next two chapters I engage with the genealogies (1 Chronicles 1–9) and the narrative (1 Chronicles 10–2 Chronicles 36) of Chronicles (Chapters 3 and 4, respectively). It is an engagement with Chronicles that utilizes the psychoanalytic mode that Irigaray insists provides us with a means of reading, writing, interpreting, and theorizing the unheard silences of masculine discourses, and of determining the underlying phantasies that support and sustain those discourses. As I have argued in the last chapter, the first step in this process is determining what constitutes the "feminine" for this particular masculine discourse. To address this question entails an examination of both the explicit and implicit constructions of the feminine, and its place and function in this particular patriarchal discourse, a discourse that consists of two distinct, though related genres: genealogy and narrative. No critique or judgement of historical "truth" will be offered here, especially when it comes to the contradictions, anomalies, and linguistic "failures." Again, I am functioning in the mode of analyst willing to listen to *this* story as it stands, "without hierarchical judgement, without *a priori* appropriateness or truth" (Irigaray, 2002a: 202). By this, I mean there will be no judgmental comparisons made with the so-called Deuteronomistic History, which has traditionally been considered by many biblical scholars to be either a more accurate account of Israel's monarchic past, or a more sophisticated literary text, in terms of historical "truth" or literary merit. Any (footnoted) references to biblical texts outside of Chronicles serve simply to undergird the uniqueness of my analysand's discourse. In particular, I wish to receive the place afforded me by this analysand's (the Book of Chronicles) production of his past, here with me. We need to know where we stand with one another. After all, his story begins with an identity line-up, the schematic constitution of a people from the past connected to his present in some way. Where can I, as a woman (indeed a woman who is both the mother of a daughter and the daughter of a mother), find myself here? Is there a place for "woman" in this masculine construction of the past? Obviously this entails a concerted "listening for" the presence of female figures and characters in Chronicles, along with the "use" to which the "feminine-maternal" is put in the production of this story.

Most of the female figures appear in the first nine chapters of Chronicles, which are made up predominantly of genealogies. Within these chapters, it is the Judahite genealogies especially that contain a concentration of female figures and birth reports (small narrative items that usually include a verb "to bear"), so much so that one commentator suggests this to be an indication of "a matriarchal rather than patriarchal bias" (De Vries, 1989: 39). While this may be the case – that certain genealogical records contain remnants of a patriarchal social ordering according to the mother's family, not the father's – my interest with this material, in Chapter 3, is to look at what happens to language and its production when female figures appear. Furthermore, because various forms of the verb ילד ("to bear") appear repeatedly throughout the genealogies, in both masculine and feminine forms, I focus mainly on the effects these verbs have on the genealogical form, given that the verb tends to evoke narrative rather than genealogy, strictly speaking. What I am listening for, in my encounter with the genealogies, are those moments when the analysand (the "you" of my own discursive production here with Chronicles) struggles to make sense or to remain consistent. Given that the primary purpose of this genealogical section in Chronicles is, as many have noted, the production of a sense of continuity with the peoples of the past,[1] these moments where sense and continuity of meaning break down around the figures of women and around the verb ילד alert us to their problematic status in some way.

In Chapter 4, I turn to the narrative production of Israel/Judah's monarchic past. The genealogies give us a picture of Israel's past constructed largely according to the logic of patriliny, and this logic continues with the narrative presentation of the story of Judah's monarchy. In other words, the story flows according to the logic of patrilineal succession: from father to son. But this particular story needs to be understood as the "son's story." Here, in the Chronicles narrative, we have the construction of a past that belongs to *Judah* and its monarchy. For this particular story, the relationship between Israel in the North and Judah in the South can be classified genealogically as "father" and "son" respectively, because in Chronicles, Jacob, who is the "father" of Judah (the "man"), is known consistently as "Israel." Of course, the beginning of the monarchy with David and then Solomon is a period where Israel and Judah are united. But this symbiotic father-son relationship breaks down to give us the story of Judah's monarchy only, with occasional mention of the northern people and their kings. Thus, I can say that here I am in analysis with the son. I am listening to, am engaging with, and am affected by (and am affecting) the *son's* discourse.

My purpose here in Chapters 3 and 4 is to listen analytically for the predominant phantasy in the book of Chronicles, that is, what constitutes and guarantees the "reality" constructed here for the "son," and to determine what this phantasy tells us about the "feminine" in this particular masculine, textual product. I shall argue that the "feminine" is largely reducible to the *place* of the "son's mother" (the woman who bears the son for the father). Given that Chronicles is the "son's" discourse, it is important for me, as analyst, both to allow and reject my positioning as the son's mother (the silent "woman").

Crucial in all of this is my adoption of an "I-You" discourse and my production of a poetic discourse that generates a sense of the mother-daughter relationship. When functioning in the mode of the psychoanalytic setting, the "I-You" discourse serves to build the relationship "between two," between analysand and analyst. Again, Irigaray suggests that this mode is an ethical practice of reading and writing. Indeed, one of the principal virtues of the psychoanalytic setting is that it brings together, in dialogue, the "I" and the "You." As I suggested in the previous chapter, this relation "between" is necessary if "woman" and "man" are able to begin the process of building distinct and non-appropriable symbolic places from which to speak and listen to each other. The poetic text (*The Lamentations*; poems one and two), serves a related though different function. If, as both Irigaray and Boulous Walker argue, "woman" is most effectively silenced through her Symbolic internment as "the son's mother," it is necessary that I insist upon another Symbolic place from which I can be heard: the daughter's mother. However, in assuming the (currently silenced) voice of the daughter's mother, I become aware of another symbolic position appropriate to my "being": I am also the daughter of a mother. Thus, one of the main purposes of the poetic text is to draw out the unsayable of Chronicles (the silenced maternal body and the silenced maternal line) in order to enable the institution of Symbolic spaces that allow me, perhaps, to work through my own dialectical tension, being both the daughter of a mother and the mother of a daughter. Both the analytic dialogue ("I-You") and the poetic discourse effect what I wish to call a "mother-daughter" reading.

Chapter 3

Who Begets Whom? Disavowing the Maternal Body:
1 Chronicles 1–9

1. *According to You (1)… Shall We Begin at a Beginning?*

1 Chronicles 1:1-32

אָדָ֛ם שֵׁ֥ת אֱנֽוֹשׁ׃² קֵינָ֥ן מַהֲלַלְאֵ֖ל יָֽרֶד׃

³ חֲנ֥וֹךְ מְתוּשֶׁ֖לַח לָֽמֶךְ׃

⁴ נֹ֥חַ שֵׁ֖ם חָ֥ם וָיָֽפֶת׃ ס

⁵ בְּנֵ֣י יֶ֔פֶת גֹּ֣מֶר וּמָג֔וֹג וּמָדַ֥י וְיָוָ֖ן וְתֻבָ֑ל וּמֶ֖שֶׁךְ וְתִירָֽס׃ ס

⁶ וּבְנֵ֖י גֹּ֑מֶר אַשְׁכֲּנַ֥ז וְדִיפַ֖ת וְתוֹגַרְמָֽה׃

⁷ וּבְנֵ֣י יָוָ֔ן אֱלִישָׁ֖ה וְתַרְשִׁ֑ישָׁה כִּתִּ֖ים וְרוֹדָנִֽים׃ ס

⁸ בְּנֵ֖י חָ֑ם כּ֥וּשׁ וּמִצְרַ֖יִם פּ֥וּט וּכְנָֽעַן׃

⁹ וּבְנֵ֣י כ֔וּשׁ סְבָא֙ וַחֲוִילָ֔ה וְסַבְתָּ֥א וְרַעְמָ֖א וְסַבְתְּכָ֑א וּבְנֵ֥י רַעְמָ֖א
שְׁבָ֥א וּדְדָֽן׃ ס

¹⁰ וְכ֖וּשׁ יָלַ֣ד אֶת־נִמְר֑וֹד ה֣וּא הֵחֵ֔ל לִהְי֥וֹת גִּבּ֖וֹר בָּאָֽרֶץ׃ ס

¹¹ וּמִצְרַ֡יִם יָלַ֞ד אֶת־(לוּדִיִּים֙) [לוּדִים֙] וְאֶת־עֲנָמִ֔ים וְאֶת־לְהָבִ֖ים
וְאֶת־נַפְתֻּחִֽים׃

¹² וְאֶת־פַּתְרֻסִ֞ים וְאֶת־כַּסְלֻחִ֗ים אֲשֶׁ֨ר יָצְא֥וּ מִשָּׁ֛ם פְּלִשְׁתִּ֖ים
וְאֶת־כַּפְתֹּרִֽים׃ ס

¹³ וּכְנַ֗עַן יָלַ֛ד אֶת־צִיד֥וֹן בְּכֹר֖וֹ וְאֶת־חֵֽת׃

¹⁴ וְאֶת־הַיְבוּסִי֙ וְאֶת־הָ֣אֱמֹרִ֔י וְאֵ֖ת הַגִּרְגָּשִֽׁי׃

¹⁵ וְאֶת־הַֽחִוִּ֥י וְאֶת־הָֽעַרְקִ֖י וְאֶת־הַסִּינִֽי׃

¹⁶ וְאֶת־הָֽאַרְוָדִ֥י וְאֶת־הַצְּמָרִ֖י וְאֶת־הַֽחֲמָתִֽי׃ ס

¹⁷ בְּנֵ֣י שֵׁ֔ם עֵילָ֣ם וְאַשּׁ֔וּר וְאַרְפַּכְשַׁ֖ד וְל֣וּד וַאֲרָ֑ם וְע֥וּץ וְח֖וּל
וְגֶ֥תֶר וָמֶֽשֶׁךְ׃ ס

¹⁸ וְאַרְפַּכְשַׁ֖ד יָלַ֣ד אֶת־שָׁ֑לַח וְשֶׁ֖לַח יָלַ֥ד אֶת־עֵֽבֶר׃

¹⁹ וּלְעֵ֥בֶר יֻלַּ֖ד שְׁנֵ֣י בָנִ֑ים שֵׁ֤ם הָֽאֶחָד֙ פֶּ֔לֶג כִּ֤י בְיָמָיו֙ נִפְלְגָ֣ה

הָאָ֑רֶץ וְשֵׁ֥ם אָחִ֖יו יָקְטָֽן׃

²⁰ וְיָקְטָ֣ן יָלַ֗ד אֶת־אַלְמוֹדָד֙ וְאֶת־שָׁ֔לֶף וְאֶת־חֲצַרְמָ֖וֶת וְאֶת־יָֽרַח׃

²¹ וְאֶת־הֲדוֹרָ֥ם וְאֶת־אוּזָ֖ל וְאֶת־דִּקְלָֽה׃

²² וְאֶת־עֵיבָ֣ל וְאֶת־אֲבִימָאֵ֑ל וְאֶת־שְׁבָֽא׃

²³ וְאֶת־אוֹפִ֥יר וְאֶת־חֲוִילָ֖ה וְאֶת־יוֹבָ֑ב כָּל־אֵ֖לֶּה בְּנֵ֥י יָקְטָֽן׃ ס

²⁴ שֵׁ֣ם ׀ אַרְפַּכְשַׁ֖ד שָֽׁלַח׃

²⁵ עֵ֥בֶר פֶּ֖לֶג רְעֽוּ׃

²⁶ שְׂר֥וּג נָח֖וֹר תָּֽרַח׃

²⁷ אַבְרָ֖ם ה֥וּא אַבְרָהָֽם׃ ס

²⁸ בְּנֵי֙ אַבְרָהָ֔ם יִצְחָ֖ק וְיִשְׁמָעֵֽאל׃ ס

²⁹ אֵ֖לֶּה תֹּלְדֹתָ֑ם בְּכ֤וֹר יִשְׁמָעֵאל֙ נְבָי֔וֹת וְקֵדָ֖ר וְאַדְבְּאֵ֥ל וּמִבְשָֽׂם׃

³⁰ מִשְׁמָ֣ע וְדוּמָ֔ה מַשָּׂ֖א חֲדַ֥ד וְתֵימָֽא׃

³¹ יְט֥וּר נָפִ֖ישׁ וָקֵ֑דְמָה אֵ֥לֶּה הֵ֖ם בְּנֵ֥י יִשְׁמָעֵֽאל׃ ס

³² וּבְנֵ֨י קְטוּרָ֜ה פִּילֶ֣גֶשׁ אַבְרָהָ֗ם יָֽלְדָה֙ אֶת־זִמְרָ֣ן וְיָקְשָׁ֣ן וּמְדָ֔ן וּמִדְיָ֥ן וְיִשְׁבָּ֖ק וְשׁ֑וּחַ וּבְנֵ֣י יָקְשָׁ֔ן שְׁבָ֖א וּדְדָֽן׃

Your story is moving swiftly (*so let's move swiftly with it*), from Adam at *the* beginning:

Adam, Seth, Enosh; Kenan, Mahalel, Jared; Enoch, Methuselah, Lamech; Noah, Shem, Ham, and Japheth. The sons of Japheth: Gomer, and Magog, and Madai, and Javan, and Tubal, and Meshech, and Tiras. And the sons of Gomer: Ashkenaz, and Diphath, and Togarmah. And the sons of Javan: Elishah and Tarshish, Kittim, and Rodanim. The sons of Ham: Cush and Mizraim, Put and Caanan. And the sons of Cush: Seba, and Havilah, and Sabta, and Raama, and Sabteca. And the sons of Raamah: Sheba, and Dedan. And Cush begot (?) Nimrod; he began to be a mighty man on earth. And Mizraim begot (?) Ludim, and Anamim, and Lehabim, and Naphtuhim, and Pathrusim, and Casluhim – from whence came the Philistines – and Caphtorim. And Canaan begot Zidon his first-born, and Heth; and the Jebusites, and the Amorites, and the Girgashites, and the Hivites, and the Arkites, and the Sinites, and the Arvadites, and the Zemarites, and the Hamathites. The sons of Shem: Elam, and Asshur, and Arpachshad, and Lud, and Aram, and Uz, and Hul, and Gether, and Meshech. And Arpachshad begot Shelah, and Shelah begot Eber. And to Eber were born two sons: the name of the one was Peleg, for in his days the earth was divided; and his brother's name was Joktan. And Joktan begot Almodad, and Sheleph, and Hazarmaveth, and Jerah, and Hadoram, and Uzal, and Diklah, and Ebal, and Abimael, and Sheba, and Ophir, and Havilah, and Jobab. All these were the sons of Joktan. Shem, Arpachshad,

Shelah; Eber, Peleg, Reu; Serug, Nahor, Terah; Abram – he is Abraham. The sons of Abraham: Isaac and Ishmael. These are their generations: the first-born of Ishmael, Nebaioth; and Kedar, and Adbeel, and Mibsam, Mishma, and Dumah, Massa, Hadad, and Tema, Jetur, Naphish, and Kedem. These are the sons of Ishmael (1 Chron. 1:1-31). [2]

So far, not a woman in sight, not even at the beginning of your people. All of this rapid production of sons on their (masculine plural) own? The names pile up, sometimes in a simple list ("Adam, Seth, Enosh, Kenan. Mahalalel, Yered, Chanoch, Methuselah, Lemech. Noah, Shem, Ham, and Japheth"; 1 Chronicles 1:1-4), but at other times with an introduction ("The sons of Japheth..."; 1:5). The males here seem to be producing quite well on their own, moving swiftly through the generations, often lingering across a generation before returning to the movement of time we are beginning to recognize as your favoured motion, here from the beginning: father to son. A motherless-daughterless world? Time passes, as your title suggests ("The Word-Things of the Days") producing history through the mere listing of male names, vertically and horizontally. No acts required, just generations.

But you seem to recognize that the production of generations is precisely that – a production – and a pertinent verb appears for the first time:

וְכוּשׁ יָלַד אֶת־נִמְרוֹד הוּא הֵחֵל לִהְיוֹת גִּבּוֹר בָּאָרֶץ׃

And Cush begot (bore? יָלַד) Nimrod. He was the first to be a mighty man (גִּבּוֹר) on earth (1 Chron. 1:10).

Cush's name takes the privileged place of first word in this sentence, giving weight to him as he who begot (יָלַד; bore?) Nimrod. But who is the mightyman (גִּבּוֹר)? Is it Cush or Nimrod? Syntactically, Nimrod's name immediately precedes the masculine pronoun, thus making him the first to be a mighty man on earth. But Cush, too, seems fairly mighty, being the first one here in the genealogies to be ascribed a verbal act (and what an astonishing one it is!). And, we note, momentarily, that the genealogical form brakes here, with the introduction of a verb, and significantly narrative erupts for the first time.

*

(Will the verb "to bear," in your simple trail of men and their names, speak your desire for a complexity of time whose movement bends backward to seek the forward, needing an original act to keep the machinery well-oiled? Unspoiled? An act which you will only ever see as your own? Where is she, that original genetrix? And where will that place me with her?)

*

Indeed, you continue to use this masculine verb (ילד, "begot") of reproduction flawlessly, that is, without any syntactical difficulty:

וּמִצְרַ֗יִם יָלַ֞ד אֶת־(לוּדִיים) [לוּדִים֙] וְאֶת־עֲנָמִ֔ים וְאֶת־לְהָבִ֖ים וְאֶת־נַפְתֻּחִֽים׃

And Mitzraim begot (bore?) Ludim, Anamim, Lehavim, and Nephtuchim (1:11).

וּכְנַ֗עַן יָלַ֛ד אֶת־צִידֹ֥ון בְּכֹרֹ֖ו וְאֶת־חֵֽת׃

And Canaan begot (bore?) Sidon, his first-born, and Cheth (1:13).

וְאַרְפַּכְשַׁד֙ יָלַ֣ד אֶת־שָׁ֔לַח וְשֶׁ֖לַח יָלַ֥ד אֶת־עֵֽבֶר׃

And Arpachshad begot (bore?) Shelach and Shelach begot (bore?) Ever (1:18).

וְיָקְטָ֣ן יָלַ֗ד אֶת־אַלְמֹ֤ודָד֙ וְאֶת־שָׁ֔לֶף וְאֶת־חֲצַרְמָ֖וֶת וְאֶת־יָֽרַח׃

And Yoktan begot (bore?) Almodad, Sheleph, Chatzarmaveth, and Yerach (1:20).

Everything seems to flow smoothly when the masculine verb appears, despite the fact that no verb is really required by this form that you have chosen to begin your story. Furthermore, in each of these cases the masculine subject is given emphasis, appearing before the verb. *The verb to bear.* So far, the act itself takes secondary place in relation to the father and his name. Does man, in your story, birth his children, his sons? And his sons (birthing) his sons? Or are you simply speaking metaphorically?

In 1:19, the pu'al form– יֻלַּד , "X was brought forth" – appears once (1:19). Like the יָלַד verbs you have preferred up until this point, the pu'al verb does not include the name of a maternal figure, and reads as follows:

And to/for Ever were born two sons (וּלְעֵ֥בֶר יֻלַּ֖ד שְׁנֵ֣י בָנִ֑ים): the name of the first was Peleg, for in his days the land was divided; and the name of his brother was Yoktan (1:19).

Given the passive form of the verb here, we might expect a named source. However, the names of the two sons (and the etymology of the first) seem to be more important to you.

So what of 1 Chronicles 1:32, when a woman steps into view? Well, not quite a woman (אִשָּׁה), but Abraham's *pilegesh* (פִּילֶגֶשׁ), his not-quite-wife (*Is it concubine? I am not sure what you mean.*). You tell me that "she bore" (יָלְדָה), the feminine form of the verb. Since I am now familiar with your use of the masculine form of the verb (יָלַד), the expression has become a little awkward:

וּבְנֵי קְטוּרָה פִּילֶגֶשׁ אַבְרָהָם יָלְדָה

And the sons of Keturah, Abraham's *pilegesh* (she) bore (יָלְדָה)…(I Chron. 1: 32).

The syntax seems to be struggling when this woman enters your history (or your pre-history).[3] Syntactically, the subject of this sentence appears to be וּבְנֵי קְטוּרָה פִּילֶגֶשׁ אַבְרָהָם, "the sons of Keturah, Abraham's פִּילֶגֶשׁ," given that so far, in each case where the ילד verb appears, the subject is placed at the beginning of the sentence. I would expect, then, a masculine verb. However, the summary formula in verse 33 – כָּל־אֵלֶּה בְּנֵי קְטוּרָה, "all these were the sons of Keturah" – implies that Keturah is the subject of verse 32, in agreement with the gender of the verb. Is this syntactical clumsiness due to the presence of a verb in a story-telling form that does not really require one? The introductory formula, followed by a simple list (the form favoured up until this point), and appearing here again (וּבְנֵי "And the sons of…"), would have sufficed without the verb that seems to confuse. Or, even the 3ms Qal, יָלַד, which so far hasn't caused us any trouble when it comes to the production of meaning and comprehension, would have met your requirements. Actually, I expected that the verb "to bear," appearing in a discourse concerned with the generation of generations, would have sat comfortably here with Keturah, given that birthing is an activity usually associated with women. But, this is not the case. And indeed, this is not the first appearance of the verb "to bear," despite the fact that this *is* the first appearance of a female character.

So far in this story, this verb has appeared a number of times (1:10, 11, 13, 18[2], 19, 20) mainly in the Qal, third person, *masculine* singular.[4] There has been no struggle so far with יָלַד. Actually, your sentences flow smoothly, from an emphatic moment with the father's name, followed by his verbal act (יָלַד) and then the names of his sons. All appear with the marker of the definite object (אֵת). No deviations from this formula. No struggle when it comes to meaning and understanding between us. Until Keturah, your first woman (or rather, פִּילֶגֶשׁ, or something distinct from, אִשָּׁה, woman?) intrudes unexpectedly into the scene, bringing a *feminine* form of the verb "to bear" with her?

There is one more occurrence of יָלַד, however, and it is somewhat problematic, to say the least, and as unexpected as the appearance of Keturah. In 2:48, יָלַד appears with a *feminine* subject:

פִּלֶגֶשׁ כָּלֵב מַעֲכָה יָלַד שֶׁבֶר וְאֶת־תִּרְחֲנָה׃

The *pilegesh* of Caleb, Maachah, (he) begot/bore Sheber and Tirhanah (2:48).

The syntax struggles here again with the appearance of the פִּלֶגֶשׁ, Maachah, just as it did when the פִּילֶגֶשׁ, Keturah, unexpectedly appeared in 1:32. Syntactically, the subject of this verb has to be Maachah, the *pilegesh* of Caleb. The verb, however, is masculine, suggesting that Caleb begets/bears Sheber and Tirhanah. While the 3ms verb, יָלַד, follows conventional grammatical expectations in the early stages of the genealogies, and adheres to a strict syntactical ordering (subject-verb-direct object), in this verse (just as with Keturah in 1:32) the gender of the subject does not match the gender of the verb. Furthermore, Sheber is the only offspring in the verses that use יָלַד whose name (and status as a direct object of the verb) is not marked by אֵת. It is clear, then, that with the appearance of women, or in these cases, פִּלַגְשִׁים, syntactical difficulties and anomalies also appear. These complications are associated with "birthing verbs" using the root יָלַד, problematizing meaning production. But importantly, the appearance of פִּלַגְשִׁים associated with grammatical problems when used with the verb root יָלַד, points to a problem with the use of this verb root from the very beginning that is mostly overlooked in traditional scholarship. The use of a verb concerned with birthing, a verbal act only women's bodies are capable of, is appropriable by a masculine subject in your discourse. Indeed, this "birthing act" with masculine subjects functions in the production of this past as its underlying machinery; it provides the logic of temporal movement through time, what pushes the story forward. Does the slippage we have just discussed point to nervousness on your part concerning this act of birthing as an appropriative masculine act?

2. *Birth Pangs?*

But we have gotten ahead of ourselves. Let us return to Keturah. Following the list of her sons ("Zimran, Yokshan, Medan, Midian, Yishbak, and Shuach") and the lists of Yokshan's and Midian's sons (32b-33a) is a summary formula: כָּל־אֵלֶּה בְּנֵי קְטוּרָה, "all these were the sons of Keturah" (1:33b). This expression is somewhat strange, given the overwhelming emphasis so far on masculine production and paternal lineage. But even stranger is that you follow this with a marker of narrative intrusion or connection, despite the fact that we seem to be well and truly functioning in the mode of genealogy, not narrative. The next verse opens with וַיּוֹלֶד. This form is a Hiph'il of יָלַד meaning "he caused to bear" and is commonly translated "he begot." It is also a waw consecutive imperfect typical of narrative. But why the narrative form of the root יל"ד in the Hiph'il, a verbal form you have not yet used? Previously you used the Qal perfect, יָלַד. Actually, why is this Hiph'il form typical of narrative used in a genealogy? Its seeming intrusion makes one wonder about a missing narrative, about what has not been said. The intrusiveness of the form is clear from the text. Beginning with the summary formula of 1:33b, and followed by verse 34, our text is as follows:

כָּל־אֵלֶּה בְּנֵי קְטוּרָה:

וַיּוֹלֶד אַבְרָהָם אֶת־יִצְחָק ס בְּנֵי יִצְחָק עֵשָׂו וְיִשְׂרָאֵל:

All these were the sons of Keturah. And Abraham bore (וַיּוֹלֶד) Isaac. The sons of Isaac: Esau and Israel (1 Chron. 1:33b-34).

Immediately following a summary formula for the sons of Keturah, the verb to bear, יל"ד, in the Hiph'il 3ms, appears in a narrative form (waw consecutive), although what precedes and what follows this verb is a fairly standard genealogical arrangement. Unless, of course, a line of sons belonging to a woman evokes a narrative detour from the strictly father-son movement of this discourse? A stagnation in the movement of this history? It is intriguing, also, that narrative seems to erupt around these females, given that women and their stories are given very little space in your narrative that follows.

*

(There are stories here, untold. Silently, they dwell together, swishing their skirts for movement underneath your own obsessions, constituting an existence. I am beginning to hear something of them, in a voice that can only come from you and me, here together. If I think about it long and hard, I'm actually quite sad. Shall I begin my Lamentations?)

*

Following Esau's genealogy, rather than moving straight to "Israel," your main character, if you like, you decide to take us on a detour through the descendants of Esau through Seir, this time according to the *non-verbal* arrangements of...בְּנֵי ("The sons of...") and...וּבְנֵי ("And the sons of..."). I presume that "sons" is gender specific here, given that in 1:39 we encounter a name we know is feminine because you insist on making this clear:[5]

וּבְנֵי לוֹטָן חֹרִי וְהוֹמָם וַאֲחוֹת לוֹטָן תִּמְנָע:

And the sons of Lotan – Chori, and Homam; and the sister of Lotan (was) Timna (1 Chron. 1:39).

Timna is not included in 1:38, which lists the "sons" of Seir (who himself has not appeared prior to this verse, but still gets the honour of a significant line of production!), including Timna's "brother," Lotan. The connection between a female figure and her brother, not her father, suggests a particular form of familial and social arrangement. There has, so far, been no real picture given, concerning the setup of your families (patrilocal or virilocal, for example). The only female figure mentioned prior to Timna, Keturah, is afforded her own line (of "sons," of course). Does this appearance of a woman afforded both subjective status in relation to the verb "to bear," and a summary formula that credits her as ancestor, indicate that in your distant past, the recognition of a production (of "sons") by a maternal figure depends upon a familial setup where daughters belong to the brother and not to the father? In other words, are Keturah's "sons" associated with her name because her children belong to her kin and not to Abraham's?

*

1. *Vignettes of a Woman Dead*

> 1. *When was this city full of people?*
>   *She simply can't say, but only that the*
>   *ghosts of those she may have known*
>   *have moved there,*
>   *but move no more.*
>   *There's not even*
>   *a floating to be had in this city of sump.*
>   *And the house? What of it and*
>   *the swellness of it all? Well,*
>   *she has long been a widow in her own abode,*
>   *the stone always left unturned.*
>   *When he breathed his blooded breath*
>   *over her and her children,*
>   *she was the bride of life*
>   *taken to matrimony by death himself,*
>   *and thus a bride no more.*
>   *Perhaps she was great among her people,*
>   *a princess among her kind,*
>   *but vassalage seems to be her only*
>   *workable movement, the only way her eyes*
>   *can bend themselves away from the ground.*
>   *Or so she's told.*

*

3. *An Intriguing Inclusion on your Part*

In fact, you follow Seir's genealogy with a king list (1 Chron. 1:43-54), "the kings who reigned in the land of Edom before a king reigned over the children of Israel" (1 Chron. 1:43a). One feature of this list is non-patrilineal succession. "Prior"[6] to the Israelite monarchy (about which you will tell us later), which progresses according to patrilineal succession, is a monarchic system that does not work according to the favoured son. All we are told is that these kings come from places that were different to the place of origin of the former king. And extraordinarily, in verse 50, nestled within the Edomite king list (1:43-51) is a short matrilineal construct: Mehetavel, the daughter of Matred, the daughter of Me Zahab. Whether there are three female figures named here or two is unclear as Me Zahab appears nowhere else in the Hebrew Bible. If we entertain the idea that Me Zahab is the mother of Matred, then we have a three generational maternal line. If not, then the maternal line of Mehetavel is thwarted, returning to the paternal origin of her mother. Nevertheless, we note that a non-patrilineal model of monarchic succession also includes a mother-daughter genealogical relationship. Let's read them literally for a moment by giving the possible English meaning of the names:

מְהֵיטַבְאֵל֙ בַּת־מַטְרֵ֔ד בַּ֖ת מֵ֥י זָהָֽב׃

Mehetavel ("God benefits"), the daughter of Matred ("the continuing one?"), the daughter of Me Zahab ("waters of gold") (1 Chron. 1:50).

This line of succession is worth noting, given that up until this point only one mother (of "sons") and one sister (of a "son") has been mentioned amongst an overwhelmingly masculine genealogical picture of your distant past. When Israel's patrilineal monarchic order "takes over," what will happen to mothers and their daughters? What happens to the benefits of God (El) if their continuity and valuable fluidity ceases? This inclusion on your part is intriguing, given that continuity is important for you, as we shall see.

*

2. *You think she's wept bitterly in the night?*
She'll tell you truly she's shed nothing more
than the clothes of habitual undress
so her skin might sense something of the night
that tried to get past him, get through him,
to soothe her as he blocked the door.
Lovers, she's had none among them all, and

expects she'll see his drooping skull
in heaven with his Lord,
patted and pasty in his Sunday bests,
his shoes a piety that seemed
good enough to get him there in the first place.
　　Little bastard schemer,
　　　he's even tricked his god.
And friends, well who's to say?
Do work mates count?
If not, her heart went only on the trail of milky children,
now wondering why this lunatic fringe of hers hangs low.

*

4. From Edom to Israel, a Sharp Turn?

Again, a list of sons – "Reuven, Shimeon, Levi, Judah, Yissachar, and Zevulun. Dan, Joseph, Benjamin, Naphtali, Gad, and Asher." The first of these sons to be given a line is Judah. This time the line of descent is made by using a passive birthing verb (ילד in the Niph'al) and a maternal figure is mentioned:

בְּנֵי יְהוּדָה עֵר וְאוֹנָן וְשֵׁלָה שְׁלוֹשָׁה נוֹלַד־ לוֹ מִבַּת־שׁוּעַ הַכְּנַעֲנִית

The sons of Judah – Er and Onan and Shelah, the three born to/for him (נוֹלַד־לוֹ) from Bath-Shua (מִבַּת־שׁוּעַ) the Canaanitess (2:3a).

Unlike the previous passive verb (1:19, יֻלַּד), the possessive prepositional construction here is with the pronominal suffix (לֹו, "to/for him") rather than with the preposition attached to the proper name (וּלְעֵבֶר, "to/for Ever"). Furthermore, the maternal "source" of this production is included, with the sons of Judah coming *from* Bath-shua. Her name is Bath-Shua the Canaanitess (or is it the daughter (בַּת) of Shua the Canaanitess. Is this another brief maternal line; is this passive form followed by mention of the maternal figure remarkable?) In your first chapter most of the verbs "to bear" are 3ms Qal, יָלַד, "he bore." It is also interesting that, just as with Keturah's appearance in 1:32, a narrative form follows, though this time there is a narrative sequence, not the simple use of the waw consecutive followed by genealogy. The account concerns Er: "Now (וַיְהִי) Er, the first-born of Judah was evil in the eyes of YHWH, and he killed him" (2:3b). Why does the appearance of a maternal figure, in conjunction with a birthing verb (albeit a passive one), generate a shift of form, a desire for narrative? This repetition of narrative intrusion is beginning to look like a symptom, one which will speak despite your desire for silence.

*

3. *You built this little bowl for her*
   to cook up her exile, her affliction,
   her servitude and gratitude. You, her Lord,
   her keeper,
   "yeah thanks very much for all that,"
   she'd say, "but I've never known
   another dish." She did, however,
   hear of other tastes
   out there for the tasting,
   but her tongues always turned on her and
   licked willingly from your bowl.
   Incidentally, no-one has ever overtaken her.
   She simply lay down,
   exhausted by day and exhumed by night.
   Was she distressed, she hears you ask? Not sure.
   Her memory heaves every now and then,
   but the television, she recalls, did take her out
   and untangle the knots of her nerves
   with forgotten promises well within
   the realms of the possible.

*

Following this narrative intrusion, I see that you name another maternal producer for Judah, but this time you use a feminine verb "to bear":

וְתָמָר֙ כַּלָּתוֹ֙ יָלְדָה לּוֹ אֶת־פֶּרֶץ וְאֶת־זָרַח כָּל־בְּנֵי יְהוּדָה חֲמִשָּׁה׃

And Tamar, his daughter-in-law, bore for him (יָלְדָה לּוֹ) Peretz and Zerach. All the sons of Judah, five (1 Chron. 2:4).

This is the second appearance of יָלְדָה, after Keturah in 1:32. Here, however, I notice that you do not struggle syntactically. Indeed, you assert confidently that these are the sons of Judah, not Tamar. Perhaps the social laws here are less threatening to you. Is your grammar clearer here because there is no פִּילֶגֶשׁ (concubine?) to throw your meaning awry? Just a woman's name producing sons for her man, contributing to his line of production – five in all.

*

4. *Here's a secret she's prepared to float:*
   She is the aperture that binds the lonely.
   Her flesh looks to her for advice, but
   even she cannot entertain it. She cast herself out
   of it long ago, too tired even for
   a somnambulist's regular throwing of the dice.

The bones of her feet are multitudes of fish,
smashed onto the floor in a rhapsody only for you,
but you would never feast there. You
just laughed at their jerky insignificance
and cringed small when she
dragged herself to the front gate
at the end of a tiny path,
a Labrador,
and nothing more.
She's always been desperate for company,
only to retire when the horizons shot something off.
Her fingers thought they could count the days,
but they too bear her affliction.

*

5. A Smooth Production Line

You continue smoothly, listing the sons of Peretz first (2:5), followed by the sons of Zerach (2:6). Then the sons of Carmi are given (2:7). Next you mention the sons of Ethan (one of Zerach's sons; 2:8), followed by the sons of Hezron. Here, you return again to a passive verb, the Niph'al of יָלַד:

וּבְנֵי חֶצְרוֹן אֲשֶׁר נוֹלַד־לוֹ אֶת־יְרַחְמְאֵל וְאֶת־רָם וְאֶת־כְּלוּבָי:

And the sons of Hezron who were born to/for him (נוֹלַד־לוֹ) – Yerach-meel, Ram, and Cheluvai (1 Chron. 2:9).

Hezron's sons may be born to or for him, like Judah's first three, only here no maternal figure is mentioned. Actually, the use of אֵת to mark the direct objects of the verb is problematic, given that the verb is passive! Did you forget to include a maternal figure with a feminine verb – such as x bore (יָלְדָה) Yerachmeel... – after the passive verbal clause? Or, perhaps you forgot to use the preposition מִן with the maternal name, as you did with Bath-Shua the Canaanitess in 2:3a? And as if to compensate for this peculiar sentence, which lists the sons as if they were the direct objects of an active verb "to bear," the next three verses introduce a masculine form of the verb "to bear" in the Hiph'il, connoting causality as they lead us toward a crucial figure:

וְרָם הוֹלִיד אֶת־עַמִּינָדָב וְעַמִּינָדָב הוֹלִיד אֶת־נַחְשׁוֹן נְשִׂיא בְּנֵי יְהוּדָה:

And Ram begot (הוֹלִיד, caused to bear?) Amminadav, and Amminadav begot (הוֹלִיד, caused to bear?) Nachshon, prince of the sons of Judah (2:10).

וְנַחְשׁוֹן֙ הוֹלִ֣יד אֶת־שַׂלְמָ֔א וְשַׂלְמָ֖א הוֹלִ֥יד אֶת־בֹּֽעַז׃

And Nachshon begot (הוֹלִיד, caused to bear?) Salma, and Salma begot (הוֹלִיד, caused to bear?) Boaz (2:11).

וּבֹ֙עַז֙ הוֹלִ֣יד אֶת־עוֹבֵ֔ד וְעוֹבֵ֖ד הוֹלִ֥יד אֶת־יִשָֽׁי׃

And Boaz begot (הוֹלִיד, caused to bear?) Oved, and Oved begot (הוֹלִיד, caused to bear?) Jesse (2:12).

וְאִישַׁ֣י הוֹלִ֣יד אֶת־בְּכֹר֞וֹ אֶת־אֱלִיאָ֗ב וַאֲבִֽינָדָב֙ הַשֵּׁנִ֔י וְשִׁמְעָ֖א הַשְּׁלִישִֽׁי׃

And Jesse begot (הוֹלִיד, caused to bear?) his first-born Eliav, and Avinadav the second, and Shimea the third (2:13).

נְתַנְאֵל֙ הָֽרְבִיעִ֔י רַדַּ֖י הַחֲמִישִֽׁי׃

Nethanel the fourth, Raddai the fifth (2:14).

אֹ֚צֶם הַשִּׁשִּׁ֔י דָּוִ֖יד הַשְּׁבִעִֽי׃

Otzem the sixth, David the seventh (2:15).

What can this Hiph'il form of the verb ילד "he caused to bear" possibly mean, particularly when there is usually only a masculine direct object of the Hiph'il verb? As a causative form of the verb ילד it seems to carry a greater sense of agency for the masculine subject. However, in terms of sense, one would expect the sentence to read "he caused a mother to bear a son." It can not mean "he caused his son to be born," for the verb is active, not passive. And yet, in the genealogies the object of the verb הוֹלִיד is always masculine (except for one remarkable instance which we will encounter soon). The father causes his son to bear? A very strange verb indeed, and one that you use time and time again. For now, however, let us focus on the rapid temporal movement that this verb generates. Actually, it is as if you are in a hurry to move through the generations towards your most important figure, David, only lingering across his generation once the verb ceases its movement forward. Each use of the verb הוֹלִיד generates a single son who in turn produces a son until we come at last to Jesse in verse 13. His name אִישַׁי gives him the honour of being associated with the word for man אִישׁ. This genealogy leading up to David is an economical linear progression through time. It is only slightly less economical than the simple list of names that opens your historical discourse, beginning with Adam, the first man, whose name means "earth," and moving swiftly for ten generations to Noah (1 Chron. 1:1-4). While the simple list generates a rapid movement forward, away

from the first man whose name evokes some sense of material origins
(אָדָם; Adam), the Hiph'il form of the verb "to bear" moves us rapidly
forward *toward* another man (Jesse), who will produce the royal house.
Indeed, as we shall see later, the royal house and its "beginning" constitutes the "beginning" of history proper and the "beginning" of the narrative form "proper." In other words, the use of ילד in the Hiph'il, 3ms
(הוֹלִיד) indicates origins distinct from the material (maternal). "Man," in
this particular reconstruction of the past, is responsible for all production, all origin.

*

5. *Apparently we are born into the arena, with*
   clapping and lemonade keeping our keepers
   on the ball.
   On her tiny feet were placed
   the softest and bounciest of shoes
   to spring her forward, always forward,
   and visors everywhere, every time,
   to keep shame lunging at her tiny frame.

   (she's never really felt the crowded surface of an apex,
   and doesn't think she'll be starting for there
   any time soon).

   Dig her a hole in the dirt,
   for that is where her fish-feathers warm.
   Oh, and please take these shoes from her feet
   - she requests you throw them back to the sea
   for she needs them not in a pit of shallow defile,
   of this she knows you'll see.
   You could also, if you choose, catapult that visor
   through the air,
   and with a rotation of your elegant hips,
   blast that beast to kingdom come.
   But, she knows, you won't.
   Your addictions are the same as hers,
   from birth, your shared decree.

*

At this point the "sisters" of Jesse's sons, Tzeruiah and Avigail are
given. We note that they are known as the sisters of Jesse's "sons," not
the daughters of Jesse. Again, as with Timna in 1:39, the distance from
the father is greater for the females of the line than it is for the sons,
with the sister tied genealogically to their brother not their father. Unlike

Timna, however, Tzeruiah and Avigail are given a list of "sons." Tzeruiah's sons are given according to the וּבְנֵי formula ("And the sons of…"), while Avigail appears as the subject of a birthing verb:

$$\text{וַאֲבִיַּיִל יָלְדָה אֶת־עֲמָשָׂא וַאֲבִי עֲמָשָׂא יֶתֶר הַיִּשְׁמְעֵאלִי׃}$$

And Avigail bore Amasa, and the father of Amasa was Yether the Ishmaelite (1 Chron. 2:17).

An Ishmaelite reproducing with a Judahite? Is this why Avigail is made the subject of a verb to bear? So far, only two women have been afforded the honour of being subjects of a verb "to bear." The first, Keturah, is a פִּילֶגֶשׁ whose presence disrupts your syntax (though, like Tzeruiah, she is given a list of sons) while the second, Tamar, is bearing to or for Judah. That is, her reproductive capacity is related to the man for whom she produces. Here with Avigail, however, the syntax is in order (subject-verb-direct object), with emphasis given to the birthing subject, and there is no possessive construct for the father. Instead, we simply have a note concerning the father of Amasa, giving us his name and his people of origin (Ishmaelites).

*

6. *You speak of things that depart from her*
   as if she, in her majesty,
   has any hold whatsoever in
   your mental schemes. All these things
   that apparently
   set her heart racing, you speak.
   And yet, when she lifts her hand out
   to even the smallest leaf from the sky,
   you blow your black breath on the ends of
   a laughter cultivated
   especially for her and her leaf-loving kind.
   Take it all, for she is old and
   her majesty awaits her
   exactly in the space cleared by
   the logic of your throat.

*

6. *The Cracks Are Starting to Show*

Immediately, with the next verse, we encounter what would have to be your strangest construction so far:

וְכָלֵב בֶּן־חֶצְרוֹן הוֹלִיד אֶת־עֲזוּבָה אִשָּׁה וְאֶת־יְרִיעוֹת

And Calev, the son of Hezron, begot (הוֹלִיד , caused to bear?) Azuvah, a wife, and Yerioth (1 Chron. 2: 18a).

Calev, whose name is not listed in 2:9 as one of the sons of Hezron (instead he is called כְּלוּבָי, Cheluvai?), begets his own wives (well, one wife, the other a...)? We might think that אֵת in this sentence means "with," which is possible. Yet, so far in your discourse, this syntax of masculine subject – birthing verb – direct object marked by אֵת has been fairly consistent. And, in the case of the verses with הוֹלִיד there has been no deviation from this ordering. Were you nervous about the in-mixture of peoples, (royal) Judahites and Ishmaelites? So nervous that you let slip a particular fantasmatic desire for a masculine birthing of women? If men could bear on their own, would not in-mixture be guaranteed against?

*

7. *There is nothing can be told your ear*
   of a time when she was more than just
   one of the feathered little holes buried in this pit.

   She might say that
   it was the space of promises forever
   kept in the darkness of her flesh. That she cooed
   for what she might become, knowing only that
   its metallic failure
   would be the first of many deaths to come.
   She might say that the sun never burnt her flesh there,
   nor did the wind tear the hole between her legs,
   or suck her up into it,
   making for her an exit route
   of the introductory passage to the world.
   She might say how she knows
   our hands
   met in a poetry
   whose lyric beats
   you have interred.
   She might say how she knows
   her limit,
   and that yours is her.
   There is nothing she can tell your ear

about her time of precious things
from days of old. Only those with
ears to hear...........................?
Don't make her laugh. Her words
are your only guarantee down here
in the Jerusalem pit.

*

As it turns out, Yerioth is given a line of sons (2:18b; "And these are her sons…"), while Azuvah, a wife, dies in v. 19, causing Calev to take Ephrath for himself:

וַתָּמָת עֲזוּבָה וַיִּקַּח־לוֹ כָלֵב אֶת־אֶפְרָת וַתֵּלֶד לוֹ אֶת־חוּר׃

And Azuvah died and Calev took for himself Ephrath, and she bore for him (וַתֵּלֶד לוֹ) Chur (1 Chron. 2:19).

Again, the narrative verbal forms appear, this time following the death notice of Calev's woman/wife (אִשָּׁה), one he himself has begotten. Calev's taking of Ephrath for himself (וַיִּקַּח־לוֹ כָלֵב אֶת־אֶפְרָת), and Ephrath's bearing of Chur for Calev (וַתֵּלֶד לוֹ אֶת־חוּר), are both, strictly speaking, in excess of the form you have chosen to begin your story. Once again, narrative erupts within genealogy around the figure of a woman, this time a dead one. And Ephrath, the one he took for himself, bears a son *for* him. This is the only "son" of Calev who has been born for him (Yerioth's sons, we are told in 2:18b, are hers), and it is this son who is given a line of descendents.

Not only that, Chur's production of descendents (only two, for now) comes about with a return of the causative verb הוֹלִיד:

וְחוּר הוֹלִיד אֶת־אוּרִי וְאוּרִי הוֹלִיד אֶת־בְּצַלְאֵל׃

And Chur begot (הוֹלִיד, caused to bear?) Uri, and Uri begot (הוֹלִיד, caused to bear?) Betzalel (2:20).

The last time this verb was used with Calev, it was to beget, or "cause to bear" (?) two female figures, one of whom dies while the other is given a line of her own. This time, however, Calev takes a female figure for himself, a figure who then bears for him. And the product of this legitimate (?) arrangement is a return to the intensified masculine production of a masculine figure who successfully reproduces his father's act (just as in 2:10-13). It seems we are back on track.

*

8. *Her house is spotless*
    and her dreams are
    empty of everything
    but an operatic note.

    She always sits on the
    sofa with a full-face
    of Sabbath mornings
    for those chilly girls
    who read the news.

    Her looks, impeccable.
    Her hair, the colour of
    May. But her words
    have hung themselves
    from the rafters, and
    wait for someone to
    bag them like mangoes.
    Take them to market.
    No-one ever comes,
    and they rot on the floor.

    Her shame is electric dust,
    her reflection a simple, discrete
    failure in your cluttered room.
    You say that she was honored
    but now crouches at the tip?
    She'll tell you, truly, her charms
    have long despised her,
    and your voice has always
    gleaned for her the virtue
    of sticks and stones.

*

But not for long. Suddenly, you interrupt this progress with a return to Hezron, Calev's father:

וְאַחַ֗ר בָּ֤א חֶצְרוֹן֙ אֶל־בַּת־מָכִיר֙ אֲבִ֣י גִלְעָ֔ד וְה֥וּא לְקָחָ֖הּ וְה֣וּא
בֶּן־שִׁשִּׁ֣ים שָׁנָ֑ה וַתֵּ֣לֶד ל֔וֹ אֶת־שְׂגֽוּב׃

And afterwards, Hezron came to the daughter of Machir, the father of Gilead, and he took her when he was sixty years old, and she bore for him (וַתֵּ֣לֶד ל֔וֹ) Seguv (2:21).

וּשְׂג֖וּב הוֹלִ֣יד אֶת־יָאִ֑יר וַֽיְהִי־ל֗וֹ עֶשְׂרִ֤ים וְשָׁלוֹשׁ֙ עָרִ֔ים בְּאֶ֖רֶץ הַגִּלְעָֽד׃

And Seguv begot (הוֹלִיד , caused to bear?) Yair; and there were for him twenty-three cities in the land of Gilead (2:22).

I note the mirror-like construction here: the son and father each "take" a woman who then bears a son for him. The verbal form "and she bore" (וַתֵּלֶד) indicates the narrative status of this birthing. Furthermore, in each instance, the product of these unions then goes on to "beget" (הוֹלִיד) on his own. However, there is a notable difference in the father's story. Unlike Calev's taking of Ephrath for himself, Hezron is empha-sized as the subject of his action through the double use of the masculine pronoun הוּא (he): "and he took her" (וְהוּא לְקָחָהּ), as well as "and he (וְהוּא) was the son of sixty years" (וְהוּא בֶן־שִׁשִּׁים שָׁנָה). Why, I might ask, is the father's act and age privileged through the emphatic use of the masculine pronoun?

*

9. *How many years have you all*
   searched among her skirts for a filth
   that could steady the little bones in your hands?

   How many years has her sartorial lounging
   spat up against the wall for you?

   How many years have her skirts been a dirty joke
   for you and yours up there,
   where woman is death in drag
   doing Bassey or Garland?

   How many years has she bent over the tub,
   with icy water spearing the politics of her hands
   as they scrub and scrub and scrub your reflection
   from an invitation to the dance?

   "O Lord, behold my affliction,
   for the enemy has triumphed!"

   How many years has she lay down
   in embrace with sorrow,
   for sweet miss alone has known
   how to soften her skin
   into the textures of another garment?

*

But before we can contemplate this, a question mark suddenly appears over the issue of Hezron and genealogical "ownership":

וַיִּקַּח גְּשׁוּר־וַאֲרָם אֶת־חַוֹּת יָאִיר מֵאִתָּם אֶת־קְנָת וְאֶת־בְּנֹתֶיהָ
שִׁשִּׁים עִיר כָּל־אֵלֶּה בְּנֵי מָכִיר אֲבִי־גִלְעָד׃

Now, Geshur and Aram took Chavvoth Yair from them, Kenath and her dependencies (lit. "daughters"), sixty cities. All these were the sons of Machir, father of Gilead (2:23).

וְאַחַר מוֹת־חֶצְרוֹן בְּכָלֵב אֶפְרָתָה וְאֵשֶׁת חֶצְרוֹן אֲבִיָּה וַתֵּלֶד לוֹ
אֶת־אַשְׁחוּר אֲבִי תְקוֹעַ׃

And afterwards, Hezron died in (against?) Calev Ephrathah, but the wife of Hezron was Aviyah, and she bore for him Ashchur, father of Tekoa (2:24).

So, what is happening here? First of all, Calev's line is interrupted with a return of the father. But the father has taken a woman from Machir, who, through the inclusion of a fairly standard genealogical summary (בְּנֵי מָכִיר אֲבִי־גִלְעָד כָּל־אֵלֶּה)– "all these were the sons of Machir, father of Gilead"), seems to be the "owner" of the line his daughter produces for Hezron. And then, we are told, Hezron dies "in Calev Ephrathah" but his wife produces another son for him, perhaps posthumously. So, does Hezron's line end in Calev and Ephrath (now called Ephrathah), only to be begun again with the production of another son by Aviyah? Actually, this verse is difficult to translate because of its unusual syntax. However, again I note the language of narrative here, especially with the feminine verb "and she bore" (וַתֵּלֶד) which this time follows a death notice of the father. And again I note my struggle to understand you. Is Calev Ephrathah a place which coincidentally bears the names of Hezron's son and his woman?

But didn't you provide Hezron's line earlier (2:9), along with his descendents through Ram, including David (2:10-15)? Indeed, following all this untidiness with Calev/Hezron, you return to Hezron's line through Yerachmeel (2:25-33). But this also confuses me because all of these descendants are the sons of Yerachmeel, the son, not Hezron, the father. And unlike his father, Yerachmeel's line through his first-born, Ram, is attributed to Yerachmeel (not Ram), through the summary formula in verse 33, "These were the sons of Yerachmeel." What 2:24 implies, then, is that the father potentially both lives and dies through the production of sons. The tension that this verse symptomatically displays, through its strained syntax and its subordinate clauses, which struggle to keep the father's name alive, is the tension between father and son concerning genealogical ownership. In other words, genealogical "ownership" (a line belonging to a name) is not set in this discourse. Not only are certain women given their own line, but also only certain males are given the status of line-owners. The tensions here are both male-female and male-male. However, women play a crucial role in this masculine, father-son struggle. As you have just shown, with Hezron's line, women sustain the father's name and potentially guarantee the continuation of his story through their production of sons. However, at the same time these sons may also be what potentially terminates his story, becoming both greater and more well known than the father.

*

10. *Will the beginning always be the end*
    of our story?
    Are the beginning and end always
    to be
    the wedded content of her abject place
    down here in the Jerusalem pit?
    The nuptial contract of her dusty disappearance?
    Are our precious things
    destined
    to be
    man-handled
    and pan-handled
    and turned outside-in
    to form a sanctuary
    for a foreigner's commerce?

*

Immediately following the summary formula for Yerachmeel in 2:33, you give us another narrativized moment concerning yet another female and her production for men. This time, however, the problem of a man having no sons rears its head:

וְלֹא־הָיָה לְשֵׁשָׁן בָּנִים כִּי אִם־בָּנוֹת וּלְשֵׁשָׁן עֶבֶד מִצְרִי וּשְׁמוֹ יַרְחָע:

Now, Sheshan had no sons (lit. "there was not for Sheshan sons"), only daughters, but Sheshan had an Egyptian slave and his name was Yarcha (2:34).

וַיִּתֵּן שֵׁשָׁן אֶת־בִּתּוֹ לְיַרְחָע עַבְדּוֹ לְאִשָּׁה וַתֵּלֶד לוֹ אֶת־עַתָּי:

So, Sheshan gave his daughter to Yarcha his slave, and she bore for him Attai (2:35).

Whose "son" is Attai? The question is important because, for the next six verses (2:36-41) you offer a masculine production of sons according to the formula using הוֹלִיד ("he caused to bear"); twelve generations swiftly told. Surely the honour of this lengthy genealogical inclusion cannot be accorded to an Egyptian slave, given that we are still amongst the Judahites (your favoured line)? And, does the 3ms Hiph'il form of the verb "to bear" seek to compensate (twelve times!) for the genealogical failure that a father faces if he does not have any sons? Will this be the end of his name? Symbolic death? Ironically, this situation is not unlike the usurpation of the place of the father by the son, is it? Tricky business, given that man needs his sons to hold genealogical weight, but the son may himself hold more fame when the line is attributed to him.

*

11. *Her daughters put their hats on*
    and headed for the city.
    She now hears their pitted groans,
    their grinding bones,
    their university credit card,
    their careless disregard
    of pasts forever unknown.
    Forgotten, she casts her eyes to the sea.
    "Look, O Lord, and behold,
    for I am despised."

*

Actually, these two verses (2:34-35) combine three issues: gender, ethnicity and class (to use a problematically modern term) that coagulate here. When there are no sons to keep a man's name going, it is possible to give his daughter to a slave, a man stripped of his status as exchanger (and therefore not a man at all?), and together they keep a man's name alive. And his status as an Egyptian does not seem to be an issue for you, beyond its mention.

But the concentration of the causative verb הוֹלִיד, which, with Sheshan's line, occurs twelve times, also interests me. The verb is used seventy-six times in 1 Chronicles 1–9[7] (and the Hiph'il waw consecutive form וַיּוֹלִיד appears three times [1:34; 5:37; and 8:9]), making the Hiph'il of ילד by far the most common *verb* used to express, explicitly, the masculine production of generations of predominantly male children. But it is the concentration of this verb in certain lines that is interesting. As we have already seen, the verb is used seven times in succession for the line that leads to Jesse and David. Furthermore, 1 Chronicles 5:30-40, a gene-alogy of the descendents of Aaron through Eleazer (supposedly a list of the High Priests from the time of Aaron until the destruction of the first temple) employs the הוֹלִיד formula in the production of sons; the verb is used twenty times! Given, then, that the verb is used to produce the line up to David, and the important priestly Aaronite line (the two major themes of a centralized monarchy and cult in the narrative to come), why, I ponder, is Sheshan's line, through his daughter and his Egyptian slave afforded such an honour? Are not the issues of genealogical continuity and purity, which understandably seem to concern you when it comes to the monarchic and priestly lines, made extremely problematic by 2:34-35?

*

12. *"Many is the number of toxins*
    that constitute a body.
    But tell me, truly,
    all you who pass me by,
    have you ever smelt such a thing as me?
    Worm your way up close to me,
    test your capacities,
    your audacities,
    might you keep this corpse some company?"

*

And where are we, at the end of your line of masculine causative production, recalling that the last time this formula was used it was to move me swiftly towards Jesse and David? Calev himself returns with yet more genealogical production, only (once again!) you seem a bit con-fused. First of all, we are told that Calev's first-born was Mesha (2:42), despite the earlier indication that Calev's first-born was Chur (2:19). Or, was it Azuvah and Yerioth (2:18)? Furthermore, another פִּילֶגֶשׁ, Ephah, is introduced into Calev's service, producing Charan, Motza, and Gazez (2:46a). But, then, you suggest that Charan begets (הוֹלִיד) Gazez (2:46b). In verse 48 Calev's concubine, Maacah, produces sons for him. Or does she? As I have discussed above, the meaning is ambiguous here, with the gender of the subject and the gender of the verb contradicting one another:

פִּלֶגֶשׁ כָּלֵב מַעֲכָה יָלַד שֶׁבֶר וְאֶת־תִּרְחֲנָה׃

The *pilegesh* of Caleb, Maacah, (he) begot/bore Sheber and Tirhanah (2:48).

In the next sentence, the same problem occurs, though with a reversal of genders:

וַתֵּ֣לֶד ֒שַׁעַף֒ אֲבִ֣י מַדְמַנָּ֔ה אֶת־שְׁוָ֛א אֲבִ֥י מַכְבֵּנָ֖ה וַאֲבִ֥י גִבְעָ֑א
וּבַת־כָּלֵ֖ב עַכְסָֽה׃

And Shaaph, father of Madmannah, bore (וַתֵּ֣לֶד, "and she bore") Sheva, father of Machbenah, and the father of Givea. And the daughter of Calev was Achsah. (2:49).

A masculine subject, שַׁעַף appears with a feminine verb וַתֵּ֣לֶד, "and she bore!" And as if this wasn't enough confusion, the first part of the following verse confuses the father with the son:

אֵ֣לֶּה הָי֞וּ בְּנֵ֤י כָלֵ֙ב בֶּן־ח֔וּר בְּכ֖וֹר אֶפְרָ֑תָה

These were the sons of Calev, the son of Chur, the first born of Ephrathah... (2:50a).

At this point there follows a list of the various descendents of Calev through Shoval, the father of Kiriath Yearim, and Salma, the father of Bethlehem, all Judahites.

So, Calev's return, after his father's "death" in Calev Ephrathah(?) and the extensive line of Yerachmeel (not Hezron, the father), brings about a question mark over the productive source of Gazez (Ephah, the פִּילֶגֶשׁ, or Charan?), a remarkable breakdown of syntax and sense around gender and the verb "to bear," and the reversal of Calev's and Chur's familial relationship. Calev is now son to Chur and grandson of Ephrathah, who earlier was the one he took for himself, and who produced Chur *for Calev* (2:19). Given Calev's reappearance after a succession of verses using the verb form הוֹלִיד (like Jesse, the father of David), and given the attention to detail concerning his production through his women (including פְּלַגְשִׁים), and indeed, given his very production *of* women in 2:18, one wonders why he is so important. His line is not the one that will produce the future king, David. Yet, so much of this chapter is devoted to him. And, why all these women and why the non-sense that erupts when they appear?

*

13. *"It is not from on high
    that you sent fire into
    my bones;
    you did not descend
    but merely crossed the room with style.
    Stepping around the furniture
    like a gambler in an Italian suit,*

you petrified my shuffling feet –
their bones arranged as a
52 pick-up joke upon the uninitiated,
wondering what to do.
You spread a net for my feet,
the catch of the day,
to be gutted and scaled,
consumed without a second thought
for their previous wanderings.
But you turned them back into the wool-fibred sea,
left them stunned and faint, all day long.
Not even curious if they'd
ever known the gambler's arrangements
of paths to and away."
You always loved the sadist's economy,
and she could only love that you loved.

*

There are only three other places in the genealogies where there is a similar concentration of female figures: David's women (3:1-9), the second genealogy of Judah (ch. 4), and the genealogy of Menasheh (7:14-19). I want to move to these places in your discourse to see if something similar is happening there. I'll begin with Menasheh because, while this is the only place where there is a concentration of female figures *outside* of the Judahite lines, within this genealogy we have a connection to the Judahites through Hezron. For it is here, amongst the descendents of Menasheh, that we find Machir, whose daughter Hezron "took" in 2:21.

7. Father → Son?

Your text begins as follows:

בְּנֵי מְנַשֶּׁה אַשְׂרִיאֵל אֲשֶׁר יָלָדָה פִּילַנְשׁוֹ הָאֲרַמִּיָּה יָלְדָה
אֶת־מָכִיר אֲבִי גִלְעָד:

> The sons of Menasheh, Asriel, whom she bore. His Aramean concubine bore Machir, the father of Gilead (7:14).

Already, I struggle to understand you here. In this verse, there are two 3fs verbs "she bore" (יָלְדָה), but syntactically, only one named subject (Menasheh's Aramean concubine). The feminine subject of the first verb (the mother of Asriel) is not named here, nor has she been mentioned immediately prior to this verse. The feminine pronoun (here included in the 3fs form of the verb) makes it difficult to place the subject with certainty. Furthermore, in the second part of the verse, you mention that Machir's mother is a פִּילֶגֶשׁ (an Aramean, this time) who is the subject of a verb "to bear" (3fs, Qal). There is no prepositional clause with 3ms pronoun לוֹ ("for him"). In other words, Menasheh's paternity is not emphasized. Is this why Hezron's line is uncharacteristically named as Machir's in 2:23? Is there the hint here of a social system wherein the daughters are important because the products of their unions belong to the daughter's father and not to their husband's family? But the overarching line in your discourse is the patrilineal one, from father to son. Is this father-daughter line of descent an older social system? But, when you begin at *the* beginning with Adam, for ten generations you give us a strict father-son construct. This is your favoured motion in the genealogies, which is mainly concerned with the past (although your present is ushered forth in places). Do you speak of times past or present?

*

14. *"You took me to the streets,*
    before all who knew my name,
    and you tied my sins as treats
    around my throat, a scarf of shame.
    I remember your hands there at my neck
    tenderly working my knotted ahead,
    and the magic you bore by the hands of your clock
    saw me painted and tarred without red.

    Gone is my blood to the dirt, you see,
    and my stamina faints to the ground,
    but while this casual beatly rhyme
    is all that's left of me,
    my blood took with her the warmth of her sound,
    and to the rest she tossed a decree."

*

For now, let's continue with Machir:

וּמָכִיר לָקַח אִשָּׁה לְחֻפִּים וּלְשֻׁפִּים וְשֵׁם אֲחֹתוֹ מַעֲכָה וְשֵׁם הַשֵּׁנִי צְלָפְחָד וַתִּהְיֶנָה לִצְלָפְחָד בָּנוֹת:

And Machir took a woman/wife to/for Huppim and to/for Shuppim, and his sister's name was Maacah, and the name of the second was Tzelophchad, and Tzelophchad had daughters (7:15).

וַתֵּ֫לֶד מַעֲכָה אֵֽשֶׁת־מָכִיר֙ בֵּ֔ן וַתִּקְרָ֤א שְׁמוֹ֙ פֶּ֔רֶשׁ וְשֵׁ֥ם אָחִ֖יו שָׁ֑רֶשׁ
וּבָנָ֖יו אוּלָ֥ם וָרָֽקֶם׃

And Maachah, the woman/wife of Machir, bore a son and she called his
name Peresh and the name of his brother Sheresh; and his sons – Ulam
and Rekem (7:16).

וּבְנֵ֥י אוּלָ֖ם בְּדָ֑ן אֵ֚לֶּה בְּנֵ֣י גִלְעָ֔ד בֶּן־מָכִ֖יר בֶּן־מְנַשֶּֽׁה׃

And the sons of Ulam – Bedan. These are the sons of Gilead, the son of
Machir, the son of Menasheh (7:17).

וַאֲחֹת֤וֹ הַמֹּלֶ֙כֶת֙ יָֽלְדָ֔ה אֶת־אִישְׁה֖וֹד וְאֶת־אֲבִיעֶ֑זֶר וְאֶת־מַחְלָֽה׃

And his sister, the ruling one, bore Ish Hod, Aviezer, and Machlah (7:18).

Firstly, verse 15 virtually makes no sense to me. I would have expected
Machir to take a woman/wife *from* (מִן) Huppim and Shuppim, but here
he takes one "to" or "for" (לְ) them. After this we are given the name of
"his" sister, Maachah. But whose sister is she? I presume she is Machir's
sister because you are currently dealing with his family (though, syntactically, she could be the sister of Shuppim). And there was the earlier
"taking" of Machir's daughter by Hezron, a Judahite, so the inter-tribal
"taking" of a woman/wife to Huppim and Shuppim (who are either of
Yissachar or Benjamin) would not be uncharacteristic. And yet, in verse
16 you say that Maachah is the woman/wife of Machir! Perhaps they are
related, which of course is not unheard of. But what, then, am I supposed
to make of the first part of verse 15? Did you mean to say "from" Huppim
and Shuppim after all? And what of the strange clause "and the name
of the second was Tzelophchad?" The second what? The second sister?
Is not Tzelophchad a male? A male who, like Sheshan in 2:34, has only
daughters?

In verse 16, Maachah (by the way, is there a dearth of women's names
available to you?), the woman/wife and perhaps sister of Machir, bears a
son (well, two, actually) and explicitly names the first, and implicitly the
second. No bearing *for* Machir. Again, this absence of paternal possession
suggests that Maachah has some kind of status as producer of a line. This
possibility is strengthened because she names her son (or sons) and by
the ambiguous ending of the verse – "and his sons – Ulam and Rekem."
Are Ulam and Rekem the sons of Sheresh, giving us a matrilineal construct? Or, are they the sons of Machir, in which case there is a distinction
between the mother's sons and the father's sons? And given that verse
18 introduces a female figure known as "the ruling one" (or, "Queen"), a

sister of Gilead, we could be forgiven for thinking that women have some
kind of power (political and social) in this family. Contrarily, however,
you say that all of these are the "sons" of Gilead the son of Machir the son
of Menasheh (7:17b)! While this summary formula adheres to a strictly
patrilineal form, it is somewhat problematic for a number of reasons.
First of all, Gilead has only been mentioned in the birth report[8] of his
father in verse 14. All early indications pointed to the ensuing genealogy
being Machir's (not Gilead's), with all the problems concerning women
coming into play around Machir. Furthermore, Machir's woman/wife/
sister is granted genealogical status for the reasons discussed above.
The summary formula thus contradicts the genealogical narrative that
precedes it. Gilead appears from out of the blue to receive the honour
afforded those who genealogically "possess" descendents. Machir and
Menasheh are granted some status as Gilead's father and grandfather,
but Maachah is denied status by the patrilineal construct.

*

15. *"It was my first awakening,*
    my first sensual embrace outside.
    The smell of it in the afternoon sun, drying.
    I can't tell you where I am,
    back there at the door
    to my world and to my place in it.
    I'm floating 'round chamomile and
    the Summer of the Rose,
    intoxicated, in love.
    She always let me comb it for her,
    as she lay silently with her eyes
    blinking to the light.
    So I must be behind her,
    there in the afternoon sun with
    its chamomile and rose-dressed Summer
    breathing its breath upon us.
    Mother's virgin in love.

    Dad's at the pub again
    and I'm just back from the afternoon plains –
    back to my real first love.
    I'm caught up in Mother's hair
    drying in the sun.
    She's sad and quiet with eyes shutting us out,
    thinking of him
    who will soon run his fingers
    through that hair of ours.

Hers, I mean.
It's Her hair, not mine,
but it was the first thing
that knotted me into the world.
Its touch and its smell.
Of all the days in the sun,
the drying days in the sun with Her,
this is the only one I cannot forget.
It is the day I never got to wave goodbye
to that hair of Mother smell."

*

All the same, the genealogies of both Hezron and Menasheh have notable similarities. Both have reduced ancestral status because of their sons who are given the honour of the formula of ownership ("these are the sons of..."), both have a number of female figures named who "bear," and both are incredibly difficult to interpret with any clear sense. And further, was not Hezron's genealogical and patrilineal status actually directly challenged in 2:23 by Machir, the son of Menasheh, himself? But the patrilineal formula, here, reminds me of how efficient the father-son line of descent is when it comes to meaning and sense. No difficulties here when the "son of" (בֶּן) formula is used. Gilead is clearly the son of Machir, who is clearly the son of Menasheh. But, as will become apparent, this is not always the case.

8. The Passive of David

The Judahite line, as has already been pointed out, begins officially in chapter 2, focusing mainly on Hezron (son of Peretz, son of Judah, son of Israel) and his son Calev. Chapter 3 continues the Judahite geneal-ogy, this time through David (a descendent of Ram, son of Hezron, son of Peretz, son of Judah, son of Israel). David and his son Solomon are arguably your most important characters in the narrative that follows the genealogies, and so it is no surprise to find an entire chapter devoted to this line. And, indeed, there are a collection of women at the begin-ning with David, all women who produce children for him. Curiously, the Davidic line is devoid of any active verbs "to bear."

David's "sons" are divided between those "born for him" (נוֹלַד) in Hebron (3:1-4), and those "born for him" (נוֹלַד) in Jerusalem (3:5-8). Distinguished from these are the sons of the פִּלַגְשִׁים, and Tamar, "their sister" (3:9). What follows in verse 10 is a list of monarchic succes-sion through Solomon (3:10-16). The rest of the chapter contains the genealogies of David's line for several generations (up to a period of time understood by scholars to be post-exilic Israel). The only form of the verb ילד, "to bear," that appears in this important phase of your genealogical production is the Niph'al (passive) form נוֹלַד, "X was born" – and it appears three times, each time with reference to the sons of David (3:1, 4, 5). No Qal perfect 3ms (יָלַד) production here, and no Qal perfect 3fs (יָלְדָה) birthing either. Only a passive verb is used for the sons of David, with David himself the indirect object of this passive verb "to bear?" David, the future ideal king of Israel's past? And, with most of the maternal women named, we might have expected for this great man and his line the feminine verb followed by the possessive prepositional phrase (יָלְדָה לוֹ: "she bore for him"), or perhaps the 3ms, mono-productive verbs יָלַד ("he bore") or הוֹלִיד ("he caused to bear").

*

16. *"Dad's at the pub and*
    Mother's putting on makeup.
    Standing at the vanity,
    her cigarette ornamenting its edge,
    She's glossing her lips and
    moistening her lashes for him,
    the him for whom She will leave me.
    I can only imagine he knew
    I simply couldn't share her,
    not when I hadn't come to know
    the very matter that required some sharing.
    I was still only at her hair,
    and there was so much more to go.
    But I wouldn't get past it.
    It was my only addiction away from the grasses.
    It was my first addiction,
    the one that led me to the grasses.
    To the possibilities of self.
    I was in the process of separating –
    but with the sun, She left.

    Dad's back and he's reading the note she left.
    Just enough time to scribble the misery,
    not enough to wave that smell goodbye.
    He's poured himself a scotch,
    though he can barely stand after the session.
    I'm standing beside him, my heart

not knowing whether to break or flee.
Who's going to help me through the bleeding?
Who's hair will keep me knotted to the world
when I need to be knotted right there in it?
I read it over his shoulder and
wish my eyes knew better.
There's talk of loneliness,
of forgotten flesh,
of unheard words,
of days washed with gray.
Then there's "the business" of me.
Make sure she stays Catholic.
Find her a man better than yourself.
Somehow,
with his thirteenth drink for the day,
he took Her to mean immediately.

'I know a man here in town.
Wouldya be a woman yet?'

The first death is always the hardest
there in the land of the living."

*

But, then again, when you use verbs "to bear" in the presence of female figures, they generate contradictions and syntactical difficulties. But, with David, his sons, and his women, meaning is never in danger of falling apart. We know that Amnon is his first born to (לְ) Achinoam the Yez-reelitess (3:1b). The second is Daniel to (לְ) Avigail the Carmelitess (3:1c). The third is Avshalom, who is the son of (בֶּן) Maachah, the daughter of Talmai, king of Geshur (3:2a). The fourth is Adoniyah, son of (בֶּן) Chaggith (3:2b). The fifth is Shephatiah to (לְ) Avital (3:3a), and the sixth is Yithream to (לְ) Eglah, his woman/wife (3:3b). Why Eglah is the only female to be afforded the titular honour of woman/wife (אִשָּׁה) is unclear to me, especially since Bath-Shua, the mother of Solomon, is not afforded the same honour (if indeed it is intended as one).[9]

In this chapter, only one female figure is mentioned outside of 3:1-9. Her name is Shelomith (3:19), and she is named as the sister of the "sons" of Zerubavel. One named woman amongst all the later people of the Davidic line, possibly the time of your "present." Women do not appear to be all that important in the present for you, particularly in this line of great importance. Furthermore, in 3:21, which gives us the sons of Chananiah (one of Zerubbabel's sons), the once dependable "son of" formula goes awry:

בְּנֵי שְׁכַנְיָה: וּבֶן־חֲנַנְיָה פְּלַטְיָה וִישַׁעְיָה בְּנֵי רְפָיָה בְּנֵי אַרְנָן בְּנֵי עֹבַדְיָה

And the sons of (lit. "the son of") Chananiah, Pelatiah and Yisaiah. The sons of Rephaiah, the sons of Arnan, the sons of Obediah, the sons of Shechaniah (3:21).

At this point, we have approached the "present" of your past,[10] and it seems your language of patrilineal progression is struggling! While you are incredibly focused on giving the most important male names of this present, with only one female named (as a sister), this is not enough to guarantee the successful generation of sense. If women cause you problems in your reconstruction of your past, then, the father-son construct (the underlying logic of your genealogical and narrative production!) disconcerts you when you encounter your present! In other words, the logical machinery of your movement through time, from father to son, breaks down when you approach your present. Leaving us where?

*

17. *See her now, she's*
   young and sold –
   from the grasses long
   to the red-gone pit,
   and an allegory
   has its hold
   on her fleshy tongue
   and its sounds unwrit.

   No wonder she's filthy-down,
   alone, uncomforted,
   her scrubbed hands reaching up -
   two birds without their cage.

*

9. Discontinuity

After devoting chapter 3 to the Davidic genealogy, we end in your "present." Chapter 4 then quickly returns us back through time to Judah and his descendents. For a brief period at the beginning, following a list of the "sons" of Judah (Peretz, Hezron, Carmi, Chur, and Shoval) you set off down the line of Reaiah, son of Shoval (4:2). However, rather abruptly, you return to the line of Chur (son of Calev, son of Cheztron), beginning with the "fathers of Etom,"[11] including a sister's name (Hatzlelponi). And, just as swiftly, you move to the line of Ashchur, who was named as one of the sons of Hezron in 2:24. He is the son whom Hezron's wife, Aviyah, bore for him after he died "in Calev Ephrathah" (?). With the return of Hezron's lineage, female names also return along with the active forms of the verb ילד. But at this point I also find myself in a very problematically disjointed production line.

In 4:5, you point out that Ashchur had two women/wives (נָשִׁים), Chelah and Naarah. That this information constitutes a narrative deviation from the genealogical form is apparent by the waw consecutive form of the verb וַתֵּלֶד "she bore" in the following verse:

וַתֵּלֶד לוֹ נַעֲרָה אֶת־אֲחֻזָּם וְאֶת־חֵפֶר וְאֶת־תֵּימְנִי
וְאֶת־הָאֲחַשְׁתָּרִי אֵלֶּה בְּנֵי נַעֲרָה:

And Naarah bore for him Achuzzam, Chepher, Temeni, and the Achashtarites – these were the sons of Naarah (4:6).

Another genealogical moment that tells us how many women a man has is understood to be narrative, while the number of his sons is strictly genealogical. Here again, the appearance of women in your discourse evokes narrative, without any story being told.

*

18. *"I could not help the urge to run*
    without the ribbons and the silks
    he liked to watch me run in
    only in my skirts of oldest cotton
    that could sister-well the grass
    my mother knows what I mean
    ask her if you know her
    and she'll tell you what I'm like
    christ I'm lonely for her
    she left me cut me dry
    and my spirits they're
    in fleshless chains that smile."

*

Unlike Naarah, who is the subject of a narrative verb "to bear" for Ashchur, and is given a summary "these were the sons of" formula (אֵלֶּה בְּנֵי־), Chelah's line is given according to the standard "sons of" (בְּנֵי) introduction followed by a list of names (4:7). What is odd about this return to the line of Hezron is that this narrative moment with the women of Ashchur generates a series of broken genealogies. Verse 8 begins with Kotz, a hitherto unheard of figure, begetting (הוֹלִיד, "he caused to bear") "Anuv and Hatzovevah, and the families of Acharchel the son of Harum" (4:8). It is followed by a narrative sequence concerning Jabez (4:9-10), another figure who has not appeared previously (I will return to this narrative shortly). Verse 11 introduces Cheluv, the brother of Shuchah, neither of whom has been mentioned before. Cheluv is the subject of the verb הוֹדִיל, "he caused to bear," producing Mechir, the father of Eshton. Eshton himself becomes the subject of הוֹדִיל, producing "sons" (4:12). But again, with verse 13, a figure (Kenaz), who is not a part of any preceding genealogical line, is encountered. So too, in 4:14, with Meonathai, 4:15 with Calev ben Yephunneh, 4:16 with Yehallel, 4:17 with Ezrah, 4:19 with the wife of Hodiah, and 4:20 with Shimon and Yishi. Actually, verse 19 once again presents a problem concerning sense:

וּבְנֵי֙ אֵ֣שֶׁת הֽוֹדִיָּ֔ה אֲח֣וֹת נַ֗חַם אֲבִ֤י קְעִילָה֙ הַגַּרְמִ֔י וְאֶשְׁתְּמֹ֖עַ הַמַּעֲכָתִֽי׃

> The sons of the wife of Hodiah, the sister of Naham, father of Keilah the Garmite and Eshtemoa the Maacathite (4:19).

It is not clear whether the sons of Hodiah's wife are the nameless father of Keilah and Eshtemoa, or, if Naham is the father of Keilah and Eshtemoa, in which case the sons of Hodiah's wife are never named, and the sentence trails off without conclusion. Did you get caught up placing a woman within your patriarchal schema? Were you so nervous about getting her family's male credentials correct that you forgot to give us the names of her sons? It seems, then, that the narrative note in 4:5 concerning the two wives of Ashchur introduces an incredibly disjointed and discontinuous picture of these Judahite families who descend from Hezron (4:5-20). And once again the presence of women disconcerts your ability to produce sense.

*

19. *"He was not a bad man*
    but I feared him awful
    for he did as he chose
    as was his right.
    I ate the dirt
    for it pleased me so

licked from my teeth
digestibly light.
He thought me mad
from the day we met
but ever so pretty
and ever so tight.
I was his burden,
He'd say to all,
And they understood
his loathsome plight.
I was unformed
in a social way,
but I was so pretty
and baptised right.
They understood,
they understood,
those holy ones
never lose their bite."

*

Amidst all of this concentrated fragmentation, there are two very interesting sections that include female figures both of whom confound you
in some way: Jabez's mother (4:9-10) and Mered's wives (4:18). Mered
and his wives are significant because, like the problems I have noted so
far, this verse struggles to make sense. This time the confusion concerns
maternal identity. Jabez's mother, on the other hand, is unusual in the
geneaologies because the account is the only instance of a woman speaking in the genealogies, and it is speech that includes the verb root ילד "to
bear." In this passage, it is paternal identity rather than maternal identity
that is ambiguous.

Let me begin my discussion of these two passages with Mered. Mered
is introduced in 4:17 as one of the sons of Ezrah. The problems begin with
the second part of verse 17:

וּבֶן־עֶזְרָה יֶתֶר וּמֶרֶד וְעֵפֶר וְיָלוֹן וַתַּהַר אֶת־מִרְיָם וְאֶת־שַׁמַּי
וְאֶת־יִשְׁבָּח אֲבִי אֶשְׁתְּמֹעַ׃

And the son of Ezrah – Yether, Mered, Epher, and Yalon. And she conceived Miriam, and Shammai, and Yishbach, father of Eshtemoa (4:17).

To whom does the third feminine singular form of the verb "she conceived" (וַתַּהַר) refer here, Ezrah or Yalon? Or, has the female subject of
this verb been left out altogether (as with 7:14a)? And why is there no
verb using the root ילד ("to bear"). Or, to put it another way, why is the

verb root, הרה ("to conceive") used instead of the verb root ילד ("to bear?") Digressing for a moment, וַתַּהַר appears in only one other place in the genealogies, 1 Chronicles 7:23:

וַיָּבֹא אֶל־אִשְׁתּוֹ וַתַּהַר וַתֵּלֶד בֵּן וַיִּקְרָא אֶת־שְׁמוֹ בְּרִיעָה
כִּי בְרָעָה הָיְתָה בְּבֵיתוֹ:

And he came to his wife and she conceived (וַתַּהַר) and she bore (וַתֵּלֶד)
a son, and he (Ephraim) called his name Beriah for in evil was in his house
(הָיְתָה בְּבֵיתוֹ כִּי בְרָעָה) (7:23).

Again, with 7:23 and its language of feminine production, I struggle to understand you ("for in evil [בְרָעָה] was in his house"). At least here, however, the presence of the two verbs together does seem more in line with your focus on the production of sons, that is, the verb "to conceive" does not, on its own, include the act of birth. Perhaps, you use the verb this way in 4:17 because an ambiguous mother also produces a daughter (Miriam, presuming Miriam is a female), and because the birthing act is understood as a masculine affair, the production of "sons." But let me now proceed to the following verse concerning Mered and his wives:

וְאִשְׁתּוֹ הַיְהֻדִיָּה יָלְדָה אֶת־יֶרֶד אֲבִי גְדוֹר וְאֶת־חֶבֶר אֲבִי
שׂוֹכוֹ וְאֶת־יְקוּתִיאֵל אֲבִי זָנוֹחַ וְאֵלֶּה בְּנֵי בִּתְיָה בַת־פַּרְעֹה
אֲשֶׁר לָקַח מָרֶד:

And his Jewish wife bore Yered, father of Gedor, and Chever, father of
Socho, and Yekuthiel, father of Zanoach, and these are the sons of Bithiah,
the daughter of Pharaoh, whom Mered had taken (4:18).

The rather obvious problem here is that the introductory note concerning the children born by Mered's Jewish wife is contradicted by the summary formula, which states that these are the sons of Bithiah, the daughter of Pharaoh. The problem of maternal identity is here supplemented by ethnic distinction. Now it appears obvious, theoretically at least, that the issue of ethnic difference or purity does not really concern you. As has been the case so far, a number of your genealogical figures, while not "Israel-ites," are included in your lists, which are said to constitute the people of the past: Bath-Shua the Canaanitess (2:3a), Yether the Ishmaelite (2:17), Yarcha, Sheshan's Egyptian slave (2:34), and Machir's unnamed Aramean concubine (7:14). Even David's wives come from elsewhere: Maachah, the mother of Avshalom, David's son, is the daughter of Talmai, king of Geshur (3:2a). So, if ethnic difference is not an issue for you, if you are willing to admit the past mixtures of blood in your picture of "Israel," then are your language difficulties here – your struggle to make sense – due to the presence of *maternal* bodies? Actually, this verse brings together certain features of interest – ethnic difference, the problematic status of genealogical ownership and continuity, combined with the verb root ילד ("to bear") in association with a female figure.

*

20. *"a sock full of meat that's turned in the street*
    hangs down from the last of my bony cage
    these juices in wool, a burning treat
    for flesh that takes the stench of age

    a sock full of meat that's turned around
    swings stench in flight from plotted day
    he sought my mind but found my mouth
    and now does hiss at my clotted decay

    a sock full of meat that's turned across
    swings heavy low as an old woman's breast
    and traces only the memory of loss
    for words of speech and folded detest

    a sock full of meat that's turned in the street
    hangs down from the last of my bony cave
    these juices in wool, a burning treat
    for she who consumes both past and grave"

*

But, let us now turn to our final birthing verb and maternal figure of interest, Jabez's mother. In 4:9, Jabez's unnamed mother is given direct speech, and her speech concerns the acts of birthing and naming. This speech is followed by Jabez's prayer to the god (אֱלֹהִים) of Israel. In nine long chapters of genealogy, only these two figures speak directly. To be sure, direct speech is not a defining feature of genealogies. Indeed, it is an anomaly, like Jabez himself, who seems to dangle without a clear paternal line. While he is included in the Judahite line, there is no explicit mention of his father, nor of any line of males issuing from him. There are no connecting male names for Jabez, no clear line of descent through men, and yet, he "was more honoured than his brothers." Perhaps his name was left off the list of the sons of Ashur (1 Chron. 4:5-8), and his mother was either Helah or Naarah? Nevertheless, he appears only in relation to his nameless mother, his indirect partner in speech in the genealogical material:

וַיְהִי יַעְבֵּץ נִכְבָּד מֵאֶחָיו וְאִמּוֹ קָרְאָה שְׁמוֹ יַעְבֵּץ לֵאמֹר כִּי יָלַדְתִּי בְּעֹצֶב׃
וַיִּקְרָא יַעְבֵּץ לֵאלֹהֵי יִשְׂרָאֵל לֵאמֹר אִם־בָּרֵךְ תְּבָרֲכֵנִי
וְהִרְבִּיתָ אֶת־גְּבוּלִי וְהָיְתָה יָדְךָ עִמִּי וְעָשִׂיתָ מֵּרָעָה לְבִלְתִּי
עָצְבִּי וַיָּבֵא אֱלֹהִים אֵת אֲשֶׁר־שָׁאָל׃

Now Jabez (יַעְבֵּץ) was more honoured than his brothers; but his mother
called his name Jabez, saying, "Because I bore (יָלַדְתִּי) in pain (בְּעֹצֶב)."
Jabez called on the god of Israel, saying, "Oh that you would bless me and
enlarge my border, and that your hand might be with me, and that you
would keep me from evil (מֵּרָעָה) so that it might not hurt me (עָצְבִּי)!"
And god (אֱלֹהִים) granted what he asked (1 Chron. 4: 9-10).

His mother calls his name, Jabez, a play on the word for pain (עֹצֶב).
Jabez's mother plays with letters and words. She turns them over and
around, bringing poetry to the least poetic of forms, genealogy. Indeed,
consonantally, this word עֹצֶב can also mean "to shape or fashion," giving
subjective status to the maternal body in pain as a productive, creative
subject; an agent of creation. Related to this verb root is the noun, עָצָב,
"idol." So, Jabez's mother's creative play with words, which speaks to the
productive body in pain, also evokes a mediating figure between the
human and the divine. One created by her? Her speech act not only refers
directly to her body in pain but also evokes the creativity of fashioning
an object of divinity, one of your most hated things, as I shall point out
in the next chapter.

*

21. *"Bring on the day of the end of all*
  for I am alone with the bitter,
  bring 'em all down and cut their tongues
  see if they speak to the letter."

*

All this, for Jabez, is problematic. He must immediately call on his
surrogate father, his instrument of change who has the potential power
to negate the symbolic authority of the mother's play with words – words
about her body and its experience. An experience no man can truly
"know." The mother's play with words will stick to her son in the form of
a name. This name from a mother who speaks poetically, who is interested in turning letters around, seducing and seduced by word-things to
make meaning of her life at a certain point is rich in meaning. It speaks

of her experience, some how. It identifies a man without a clear paternal history; his name binds him to his mother, to her body and its language (of the divine?) In the act of naming, this woman speaks of her body and its experience without any mention of him at all ("for I bore in pain"). No wonder he is nervous.

*

22. *"I began with you on the day after blood,*
     you held me to the word,
     now all of you can let me go
     to the sing-song of unheard.
     But know that you can never know
     not of judgement but of bliss,
     you've built your shrine of limits denied
     with woman, shit, and piss."

Clearly, I am faint.

*

Of course, the *mater delorosa*, the suffering mother, is an old favourite in the masculine Imaginary. The maternal body in pain, especially, is a particular bodily experience pertaining to "woman" that man can imagine, with more or less accuracy, and he is able to convince himself that he may know something about the one thing his body will never do. It is no real surprise that Jabez's mother is given birth pain as the experience upon which she will draw, for it comes at the moment when a male is born. The birth itself is generally the only experience of the production of life that is given direct, symbolic reference in masculine representations (the womb, as we shall see, will saturate his Imaginary universe). But the female body has bled, had intercourse, stopped bleeding monthly, swollen with fluids, produced hormones that effect the moods through which experience will filter, and so on. Jabez's mother, potentially, had a wealth of corporeal experiences with which to play. But she was given (and she gives us) only one, the most important, because it is the most comprehensible, one. She contributes to the genealogical economy through the production of a son. Her "experience" must speak to that.

Even so, what does Jabez want? What can the father grant him? The father can bless him (בָרְ) and enlarge his boundaries (וְהִרְבִּיתָ אֶת־גְּבוּלִי), provide for him in needy times (וְהָיְתָה יָדְךָ עִמִּי; lit. "your hand might be with me"). The father can also offer him protection from the evil brought upon him by his mother's interpretive and creative speech. Something about his name and its relationship to maternal-corporeal pain spoken poetically by the mother seems to insist that wealth and paternal assistance are not forthcoming for Jabez, only suffering. With a mother whose interruptive narrative of naming connects the son to the incontrovertible fact of biological birth, of feminine-maternal corporeal production, he finds himself in exile from the Symbolic paternal line and its mono-production. Given this banishment from masculine mono-production, why might Jabez be the most honoured among his brothers? In tearing himself away from the mother, in turning to the father (the god of Israel) for intercession, does his honour enlarge along with his borders (i.e. his material claim)? Apparently.

*

2. A Daughter, Tied in her Tongues

1. *Moisture for the pit of Jerusalem?*
   Oh, but your generosity astounds.
   Set under water, your heroine
   is sure, but sure, to drown.
   Your filthy foot has rested
   long enough for those of us
   to know that mildew settles
   itself down
   into the very fabric of a thing thus
   scorned and battered upon.
   She's too tired to speak now,
   and I am yet to allow her fragrances
   a place beyond me and mine,
   so I speak without guarantees
   of ethical anomalies.

   Do I speak-bury her once again,
   or forever hold my peace?

*

The mother's creative words threaten the coherence of patrilineage and require intervention by the father of fathers. On the surface, here in the genealogies of Chronicles, the son's words to the father ultimately seem to have greater power than the mother's words to or for herself. 'Elohim grants Jabez his requests. But is not the god of Israel's intervention somewhat limited? Honour, blessings, enlarged borders, assistance in the times of need, and protection from evil may have been issued to

Jabez, but his story has ended. There is no line of sons (not even any lesser sons, i.e., daughters) issuing from Jabez. Ultimately (as the genealogies teach us) this production of sons is the only guarantee of historical success. Jabez is frozen in history with a mother who dared to play with words, dared to speak her experience, dared to bring her body into language; dared, seemingly, even to equate this body with the divine and her representation. And you forgot to name her. Perhaps you were anxious?[12]

10. Summary Analysis

While a number of issues have arisen in light of this analytic engagement with the genealogies of Chronicles, I want to focus on the figure of the mother in 1 Chronicles 1–9 and on the ילד verbs. First of all, this anxiety around the figure of the mother in 4:9-10 is rather strange, given that for our analysand, as we have already heard, women are mainly understood as mothers of sons. The mothers of sons in 1 Chronicles 1–9 are as follows: Keturah, 1:32; Bathshua the Canaanitess, 2:3; Zeruiah and Abigail, 2:16-17; Jerioth and Ephrathah, 2:18-19; the daughter of Machir, 2:21; Abiah, 2:24; Atarah, 2:26; Abihail, 2:29; Sheshan's daughter, 2:34-35; Ephah, 2:46; Maacah, 2:48; Ahinoam and Abigail, 3:1; Maachah and Haggith, 3:2; Abital and Eglah, 3:3; Bathshua, 3:5; David's concubines, 3:9; Helah and Naarah, 4:5; Ezrah(?), 4:17; Mered's Jewish wife and (?) Bithiah, daughter of Pharaoh, 4:18; the wife of Hodiah, 4:19; the many wives of the bands of the host for war, 7:4; Manasseh's Aramean *pilegesh*, 7:14; Maacah, 7:16; the ruling sister, 7:18; Ephraim's wife, 7:23; Hodesh, 8:9; Hushim, 8:11; and Maacah, 8:29/9:35, whom we can only presume is the mother of the sons listed from 8:30/9:36. There are also two, perhaps three instances of women being the mothers of daughters: Matred and Mezahab, although we have no way of being certain of the gender of the latter, 1:50; and the ambiguous mother (perhaps, Ezrah) who conceives Miriam, 4:17. Women who appear in the genealogies without reference to their status as mothers are Timna, 1:39; Mehetabel, 1:50; Azubah, 2:18-19; Achsah, 2:49; Tamar, 3:9; the six daughters of Shimei, 4:27; Sheerah, 7:24; Serah, 7:30; Shua, 7:32; and Baarah, 8:8. Clearly, women are understood mainly as the mothers of sons.

But women also seem to cause great problems when it comes to the production of meaningful, genealogical sense. These problems generally erupt around the use of the verb ילד ("to bear"), and may be characterized as

1. grammatical and/or syntactical breakdowns (1:32; 2:9, 48, 49; 4:19; 7:14);
2. contradictions (2:19, 21, 23, 46, 50a; 4:18; 7:15, 17); and
3. a breakdown of realism (2:18a).

10.1. *Grammatical and/or Syntactical Breakdowns*

There are, in this genealogical discourse, three instances of gender confusion around a ילד verb. In 1 Chronicles 1:32, the verb is feminine, singular (יָלְדָה) but syntactically the subject of this verb could in fact be the masculine, plural וּבְנֵי קְטוּרָה פִּילֶגֶשׁ אַבְרָהָם ("And the sons of Keturah"). 1 Chronicles 2:48 and 1 Chronicles 2:49 both contain a subject and a verb with contradictory genders:

פִּלֶגֶשׁ כָּלֵב מַעֲכָה יָלַד שֶׁבֶר וְאֶת־תִּרְחֲנָה׃

The *pilegesh* of Caleb, Maachah, (he) begot/bore Sheber and Tirhanah (2:48).

וַתֵּלֶד שַׁעַף אֲבִי מַדְמַנָּה אֶת־שְׁוָא אֲבִי מַכְבֵּנָה וַאֲבִי גִבְעָא וּבַת־כָּלֵב עַכְסָה׃

And Shaaph, father of Madmannah, bore (וַתֵּלֶד, "and she bore") Sheva, father of Machbenah and the father of Givea. And the daughter of Calev was Achsah (2:49).

These syntactico-grammatical struggles draw our attention to an important feature of the genealogies. It seems as though our analysand is, in these verses, reluctant to admit that it is only women who are, in reality, capable of birthing. While the verb in 1:32 is feminine, the somewhat unnecessary inclusion of the standard introductory formula וּבְנֵי ("And the sons of") makes the gender of this possible subject masculine. Even if we read 1:32 as "And the sons of Keturah, Abraham's pilegesh: she bore…," the clumsy syntax still makes the gender of the subject fairly nebulous. In 1 Chronicles 2:48 and 49, it is simply the case that the gender of the subjects contradicts the gender of the verbs. In both verses the direct objects of the verbs are marked with אֶת־. This means that the subjects of the verses are פִּלֶגֶשׁ כָּלֵב מַעֲכָה in 2:48 and שַׁעַף אֲבִי מַדְמַנָּה in 2:49. In other words, 2:48 and 49 present us with the gendered subject of the birthing verb in direct contradiction with the gender of the verb, in contravention of the grammatical laws of this gendered ancient language, unlike 1:32 where the clumsy syntax makes for a more ambiguous relationship between the genders of the subject and verb.

In 1 Chronicles 2:9 we encounter a grammatical problem with the ילד verb in the Niph'al form:

וּבְנֵי חֶצְרוֹן אֲשֶׁר נוֹלַד־לוֹ אֶת־יְרַחְמְאֵל וְאֶת־רָם וְאֶת־כְּלוּבָי׃

And the sons of Hezron who were born to/for him (נוֹלַד־לוֹ) – Yerachmeel, Ram, and Cheluvai (1 Chron. 2:9).

As I indicated earlier, the problem in 2:9 concerns the inclusion of אֶת־ to mark the definite objects of the verb, which in this case is a passive form. I contend that we read this slip as indicative of the problematic status of the maternal body in this discourse, for if a woman's name was included, along with an active form of the verb (e.g. וַיֵּלֶד), there would be no grammatical problems with this sentence. Without the feminine verb and the maternal name, however, the inclusion of אֶת־ effectively functions as the "slip" through which we may recognize both the fantasy sustaining this discourse, and the maternal silence required for this fantasy. That body is absented, *silenced*, to enable the fantasy of masculine (re)production.

With 1 Chronicles 7:14 we encountered a difficulty in determining the subject of the feminine verb:

בְּנֵי מְנַשֶּׁה אַשְׂרִיאֵל אֲשֶׁר יָלָדָה פִּילַגְשׁוֹ הָאֲרַמִּיָּה יָלְדָה אֶת־מָכִיר אֲבִי גִלְעָד׃

The sons of Menasheh, Asriel, whom she bore. His Aramean concubine bore Machir, the father of Gilead (7:14).

With this verse, it seems as if there is one too many verbs "to bear" (ילד "she bore"). The "she" of the first 3fs יָלְדָה has no prior proper name, while the second verb does. We could interpret the subject of both verbs to be Menasheh's פִּילֶגֶשׁ, with the second verb and the production of Machir being something of an afterthought. However, in every other instance where ילד appears, the subject precedes the verb (1:32; 2:4, 17, 46; 4:18; 7:14), meaning that the subject of the second verb is most likely פִּילַגְשׁוֹ הָאֲרַמִּיָּה, leaving the first verb without a named subject. Of course, Hebrew verbs do not need named subjects to make sense. However, in this instance, given the pattern of named subjects in conjunction with the verb ילד this verse at best struggles to make sense. And this verse is followed by a verse that is almost impossible to translate with any sense (1 Chron. 7:15; see above). Compared with the relative ease with which our analysand constructs his past when women are not present (for example 1 Chron. 1:1-31), and compared also with the

infrequent problems when a masculine form of יָלַד is used (see below),
a certain nervousness around women and the feminine act of birth is
betrayed by these verses.

*

2. *You there, the destroyer,*
   beckon me back
   to show me her, your pettly prize
   as if for the first of times.
   Your anger,
   it does shift her feet
   from their little homes,
   through the streets,
   walking 'cross flat smooth stones,
   seducing her at your camel's gate
   with grand ideas and weighty tomes.

   Our kingdom lies behind.
   Freezing cold and full of salt.

*

10.2. *Contradictions*

Apart from the moments where the gender of the subject and the verb
of certain verses are in contradiction, there are several other instances
where our analysand seems to contradict himself. With 2:46 we encounter a possible contradiction:

וְעֵיפָה פִּילֶגֶשׁ כָּלֵב יָלְדָה אֶת־חָרָן וְאֶת־מוֹצָא וְאֶת־גָּזֵז וְחָרָן
הֹלִיד אֶת־גָּזֵז׃

And Ephah, the pilegesh of Calev, bore (יָלְדָה) Haran, Moza, and Gazez;
and Haran begot (הֹלִיד caused to bear) Gazez (2:46).

Now, of course, there may be two characters named Gazez. Haran may
beget a son and name him after his brother. What interests me about
this verse, however, is that it is almost as if the masculine causative verb
contradicts the feminine verb which precedes it.

With 1 Chronicles 4:18, on the other hand, we seem to face an undeniable contradiction, this time concerning maternal identity:

וְאִשְׁתּוֹ הַיְהֻדִיָּה יָלְדָה אֶת־יֶרֶד אֲבִי גְדוֹר וְאֶת־חֶבֶר אֲבִי
שׂוֹכוֹ וְאֶת־יְקוּתִיאֵל אֲבִי זָנוֹחַ וְאֵלֶּה בְּנֵי בִּתְיָה בַת־פַּרְעֹה
אֲשֶׁר לָקַח מָרֶד׃

And his Jewish wife bore Yered, father of Gedor, and Chever, father of Socho, and Yekuthiel, father of Zanoach, and these are the sons of Bithiah, the daughter of Pharaoh, whom Mered had taken (4:18).

Who is the mother of Yered, Chever, and Yekuthiel? Is it Mered's Jewish wife or his Egyptian wife? According to this verse, it is both. Rather than offer possible explanations, as many scholars have before,[13] I suggest instead that this contradiction like all the other problematic features concerning women and the verb ילד in the genealogies may be understood as symptomatic of the difficulties this masculine discourse faces when women enter this representational framework. Immediately following this verse is more evidence of this struggle:

וּבְנֵי אֵשֶׁת הוֹדִיָּה אֲחוֹת נַחַם אֲבִי קְעִילָה הַגַּרְמִי וְאֶשְׁתְּמֹעַ הַמַּעֲכָתִי:

The sons of the wife of Hodiah, the sister of Naham, father of Keilah the Garmite and Eshtemoa the Maacathite (4:19).

With this verse, as I mentioned earlier, it is as if our analysand got so caught up situating a woman within his patriarchal schema that he forgot to finish his sentence and give us the names of her sons.

*

3. *You there, the destroyer,*
   You give her but no choice.
   Your strength is breath
   on her still-young flesh
   wherein you'll store your voice.
   And what of her own, her virgin ruach?
   With a straw to her mouth
   Did you syphon it and make your own?
   Is it this with which you wish to kiss me?
   To blow some of her back to my mouth;
   is this your only commerce?

   Your kisses burn off my breasts,
   "consuming all around."

*

The nervousness around the figures of women is particularly noticeable in the genealogies of Hezron and Meneshah. When Hezron takes the daughter of Machir, this line is given to Machir himself. Thus 2:21

and 2:23 are in contradiction. And yet, what begins as Machir's line in 7:15 is attributed to Machir's son Gilead in 7:17. But even more obviously problematic is the explicit contradiction concerning Calev and Chur. According to 2:19, Chur is Calev's first born, while 2:50a makes Calev the son of Chur. These contradictions alert us to the tension between father and son when it comes to genealogical "ownership." The father must produce a son to hold any genealogical weight. And yet, the son must himself become a father of a son. Once he does so, there is a chance his name will be greater than his father's. "Woman," then, comes to symbolize this tension. She is necessary for the production of sons and the continuation of the father's story. Yet when she appears, she disconcerts our analysand's logic of representation. Perhaps this disruption results because her very production threatens the father with the end of his story? Her success in producing sons for the father also guarantees the end of the father's story.

*

4. *Oh, now, but you are fine.*
   Your skin a glossy Irish beer
   in someone else's hand.
   You bend your bow like an enemy,
   *   pierce the flesh of her stillborn heart*
   to fill it with your own.
   And you succeed, you always do.
   You become her originality
   and it truly, truly does suit you.

*

10.3. *A Breakdown of Realism*
Finally, we have the very interesting case of 1 Chronicles 2:18a:

וְכָלֵב בֶּן־חֶצְרוֹן הוֹלִיד אֶת־עֲזוּבָה אִשָּׁה וְאֶת־יְרִיעוֹת

And Calev, the son of Hezron, begot (הוֹלִיד, caused to bear?) Azuvah, a wife, and Yerioth (1 Chron. 2: 18a).

In this verse a man "causes to bear" (הוֹלִיד), with the direct objects of this causative verb being his own women/wives. Given that in the seventy-five other cases where הוֹלִיד is used the direct object of this verb is always marked with אֶת־, I insist that we read this verse as a slip pointing to the fantasy of male birth; in this case, a man bears those who "in reality" are the only ones who can bear.

In total, of the ninety-one uses of the masculine forms of the verb ילד,
there are only three problematic instances (2:9, 18a, 48). While this suggests that our analysand is very comfortable with the masculine birthing
verbs, the instances where these masculine verbs are struggling for clear
meaning all relate to the problem of gender. The problem of sense in 2:9
occurs because the sons' names appear as the definite objects of a passive
masculine verb (ילד in the Niph'al). Without a maternal source named
(as in 2:3a and 3:1ff.), in conjunction with an active feminine form of ילד,
the "slip" here indicates a certain jarring. "Man" understands himself as
the active subject of birth, but in "reality," he is really the indirect object
of that feminine act. Children are born "to or for" him. Or, of course, "he"
is the direct object of that act; he is the son born by a woman's body. In
1 Chronicles 2:48 there is a feminine subject of a masculine verb יָלַד, "to
bear," and 2:18a has a man begetting women. In other words, we can say
that at certain moments in this genealogical discourse biological "reality"
is proving problematic for our analysand.

11. *Conclusion*

In Chapter 1, I discussed Irigaray's thesis that masculine thinking and
writing in the West function through an unacknowledged silencing of
women. For Irigaray, it is the extrication or "forgetting" of maternal-
corporeal origins that enables "man" to construct an image of himself
as self-made, or at least in debt only to the father who bears an uncanny
resemblance to himself. Irigaray insists that we read and analyse
masculine texts in search of the means by which man accomplishes this
"murder of the mother." She insists we first determine what constitutes
"the feminine" in masculine discourses, and then ask what aspects
of the feminine must remain silenced? In other words, why is one
particular construction of the feminine necessary, and why must other
aspects remain unacknowledged? In Chapter 2, I argued that Irigaray's
re-theorization of the psychoanalytic setting (*praticable*) offers women
a viable mode of reading, writing, thinking, and speaking *as women*, a
mode that refuses to participate in and perpetuate the silence of the
feminine through the simple acceptance and practice of masculine
theoretical and methodological approaches. Such a mode, Irigaray
argues, enables the silences of masculine discourse – what cannot be
said – to be heard. Furthermore, Michelle Boulous Walker's argument
that silence needs to be understood as more than just the absence of
speech has enabled me to listen psychoanalytically for the strategies of
silencing the feminine at work in the genealogies.

According to 1 Chronicles 1–9, what constitutes the feminine? In this chapter I have shown that in the genealogical discourse of Chronicles the feminine is largely reducible to a social-symbolic function: to (re)produce sons for both the father and for Israel. However, whilst "woman" is overwhelmingly constructed as the son's mother in the genealogies (with only a few possible instances of the mother-daughter line: 1:50; 2:3a; 4:17), it is *masculine (re)production* which is dominant, both through the far greater use of masculine forms of יָלַד (ninety-one times: eighty-five active forms and six passive compared to seventeen active feminine forms) and through the largely (though not always) successful use of these masculine verbs in terms of meaning-making. Furthermore, the verb "to bear" is appropriable by the masculine subject. Thus, we can say that woman is largely restricted to her socio-symbolic function of producing *for* men, but without any real recognition of a debt to her body's role in (re)production. Thus, the dominant phantasy, here in the genealogies, is *the phantasy of mono-sexual, masculine (re)production.*

Why must the feminine be restricted to the symbolic function of the production of sons for the father, while the maternal body itself remains unacknowledged? The psychoanalytic concept of disavowal is instructive here. The orthodox Freudian definition of disavowal is the denial and acceptance of some external feature of reality, usually the absence of the mother's penis. For Freud, disavowal is the defense mechanism that underwrites fetishism and the psychoses. However, in the genealogies, it is the debt to maternal origin that clearly is being disavowed. That is, material-maternal origin is (seemingly paradoxically) both denied and affirmed in the genealogical discourse. In "reality" only women can birth children. Indeed, maternal origin does seem to be acknowledged in several cases, with "woman" overwhelmingly being understood as the son's mother. And yet, the genealogical discourse in Chronicles not only presents patrilineage as the standard, with fathers and sons presented as constitutive of almost all of Israel's past and present familial make-up, but also presents masculine reproduction as the standard through the overwhelming dominance of masculine subjects of the verb "to bear." The silent machinery of this discourse is the father's production of the son; the discursive movement through time in 1 Chronicles 1–9 largely consists of a phantasmatic, non-corporeal mechanical movement from father to son, to his son, and so on. In other words, corporeal origins are remarkably unacknowledged and are replaced instead by the generative succession of male names.

One of the principal symptoms of this phantasy of mono-sexual, masculine production occurs in 1 Chronicles 4:9-10. When a woman speaks of *her body* and one of its corporeal experiences – precisely, the one bodily act that only a woman's body is capable of performing in "reality" – genealogical identity, which hangs desperately on the father-son line, ceases to function well. Indeed, the story of the son ends. The effects of this self-referential maternal speech, along with the effects of the feminine forms of the verb to bear in the genealogies, alert us to the fact that the affirmation of maternal origin in this masculine dis-course is purely symbolic. In other words, it seems that *the necessity of the material-maternal* must remain silent so that patrilineal, patriarchal, symbolic order is sustainable and hegemonic.

While women are present in the genealogies, their silence is main-tained through this disavowal. The silence of maternal-matter functions as a necessary silence for the masculine subject of this production of the past. Indeed, the disavowal of this material-maternal debt is readable pre-cisely through the slips, contradictions, and breakdowns of meaning we have heard from our analysand, here in the present of analysis. However, it is 1 Chronicles 4:9 that most dramatically reveals how problematic the mother's self-referential speech is for the masculine subject of this dis-course. I have argued that it is the type of speech given by Jabez's mother that is important to hear. Jabez's mother not only speaks about her birth-ing body, but she also plays with those words concerning the birthing body when she names her son, even evoking a relationship between the mater-nal body and the representation of divinity itself. Her speech is a poetic play with words and meanings, an act that both acknowledges the (un-representable) maternal body and allows for the suggestion of a feminine relationship to the divine, one created by herself. Jabez's mother's speech causes the masculine subject grave fears for his own socio-symbolic sur-vival. In fact, 1 Chronicles 4:9 asserts, if you like, that there is a direct con-nection between women's speech and this disavowed maternal-corporeal origin which sustains the phantasy of masculine mono-production. In this particular recounting of the past, when a woman speaks *poetically* about her body in birth (without any mention of the son at all in relation to this verbal act), the son is given no paternal heritage, and no sons who will continue *his* story. It would seem that poetic maternal speech shat-ters the continuity and certainty of patrilineal discourse, with its smoothly functioning logic of progress from the father to the son.

I suggest that 1 Chronicles 4:9, while generally considered of minor rel-evance or importance in traditional Chronicles scholarship, in fact reveals the logical kernel at the heart of this literary production of the past, first in the genealogies and later (as we shall see in the next chapter) in the narrative of Chronicles. The logic of this discourse, its silent machinery, is the progression from father to son which relies upon an unacknowledged or silenced debt to original materiality/maternality. This maternal origin is thus effectively silenced through the disavowal of Mother-matter (both the acceptance and denial of the biological fact of maternal birth) and instead, "woman" is interned as the symbolic (re)producer of the son for man.

*

5. *Your anger, poured from a fire-proof vessel*
   makes you her enemy, her father, her lover.
   And in the chemistry of it + me
   is the mystification of mourning.
   It is you now, your turn, you consume.
   Me and you now, my obsession.
   And together we both throw her the scraps
   of our delicate, lovely mornings.

*

Finally, before I move to my reading of the narrative section of Chronicles (1 Chronicles 10—2 Chronicles 36), I want to conclude this chapter by returning to those moments in the genealogies where women are associated with narrative. I am not suggesting that narrative only appears in the genealogies when a woman's name or a feminine birthing verb appears. Indeed, large sections of narrative appear without any reference to women at all (for example, the "giving" of land parcels to various priestly families in 6:39-55). Furthermore, narrative sometimes immediately follows some masculine forms of the verb "to bear" (1:10, 19; 2:3). And yet, so often in this discourse we hear of how narrative erupts around the figures of women and the feminine birthing verbs associated with them (1:32; 2:19, 21, 24, 35, 49; 4:6, 17; 7:16, 23), as if birth itself belonged somehow to narrative, not genealogy (ironically).[14] Strictly speaking, verbs are not a necessary feature of genealogical lists, as I pointed out at the beginning of this chapter.

It is interesting to note that in biblical genealogy studies and Chronicles scholarship, the genealogies are said to be a less interesting form of story-telling than narrative or poetic forms. Of course, it is recognized that genealogy is a literary form, one that, according to Johnson, "could be used as an alternative to narrative or poetic forms of expression, that is, as one of several methods of writing history and of expressing the theological and nationalistic concerns of a people" (Johnson, 1969: 82). But genealogy is a less desirable form than narrative or poetry. In fact,

according to Siedlecki (1999: 234), it is the *dearth* of narrative that contributes to the general consensus that the first nine chapters of Chronicles
are "one of the more tedious parts of the second history...any dynamic
narrative elements that might contribute to anything even remotely
resembling a plot are kept to an absolute minimum." So, too, Ackroyd,
who writes that the "opening chapters do not provide exciting reading:
they consist almost entirely of lists and names with relatively few historical notes or narrative fragments..." (Ackroyd, 1973: 30). And De Vries,
in his form–critical commentary, asks the following question of the first
nine chapters of Chronicles:

> Apart from a few isolated birth and conquest stories, it contains no narra-
> tive whatsoever, so what is its *organic* connection, if any, with the lengthy,
> complex, *organically* constructed narrative that follows upon it? That nar-
> rative is, unmistakably, the core of the work. It could quite readily stand
> by itself, for it has a clearly marked theme beginning with the death of
> Saul and reaching to the exile of Judah under Nebuchadrezzar. But the
> genealogical introduction needs the narrative, for it has no meaning in
> itself (De Vries, 1989: 14; my italics).

If narrative is a "superior" form of story-telling, then, what are we to make
of this association between female figures, birthing verbs and narrative
in the genealogies? Why does the desire for narrative make itself heard at
these points in a form that does not require narrative machinery at all?
As I suggested earlier, with regard to the unnecessary and problematic
use of a narrative form of the verb "to bear" in 1 Chronicles 1:32, it makes
one think that there is another story which remains untold here, silent.[15]

I suggest that this association is symptomatic of the principal form of
women's silence in the narrative section itself. Earlier, I stated that when
compared with the other history of Israel, namely Genesis—2 Kings, the
number of women absent from this version of the past in the Chronicles
account is remarkable. Initially, if we consider the silence of women in
Chronicles, it is, on the surface, due to this absence. However, in this
chapter I have shown how women's association with maternity is directly
related to their silence. Through the psychoanalytic concept of disavowal,
we have heard how women are effectively silenced because the maternal body itself is both affirmed (though barely) and denied to enable
the phantasy of mono-sexual production. Furthermore, when a mother
speaks, patrilineal progress ceases. That we also have a symptomatically
readable relationship between narrative and the maternal body in the
genealogies suggests that women's silence in the rest of Chronicles (the
narrative itself) is directly related to this body of hers which must remain
unrepresented. Thus, I turn now to listen for the means by which the

maternal body has been appropriated by this masculine narrative discourse. I shall show that the maternal body is repressed in the narrative, that this repressed body is directly related to the issue of women's silence, and that this silence is necessary to enable the maintenance and continuation of the phantasy of mono-sexual (re)production.

Chapter 4

THE DEBT-FREE MASCULINE SUBJECT: THE REPRESSED MATERNAL
BODY IN 1 CHRONICLES 10–2 CHRONICLES 36

1. *According to You (II)... Shall We Begin Again?*

We now have an assembled cast, the peoples of the past who define the present from which your past is imagined. Effectively, the stage for the story in narrative form has been set, along with a well-crafted litany of family lines connecting the present with the past. However, the family tree is overwhelmingly masculine. The genealogical form of the past unfolds largely according to masculine mono-sexual production, from father to son in swift successions. Yet, when women do appear, it is predominantly to produce sons. What is most interesting to note is that women, nevertheless, have the ability to shatter the continuity of this discourse; they disrupt your flow. This ability is indeed significant given the discernible phantasy of mono-sexual production underwriting this production of the past through the form of genealogy. When the maternal body is evoked, especially through the feminine forms of the verb root ילד ("to bear") and, in one instance, through a woman's speech, continuity and meaning become distorted. It is as if this language cannot cope when "she" and "it" (the specter of her maternal body) appear.

*

6. *Now we're all burning.*
    Set alight.
    Your sweet success.
    Even your own fear you.
    They loathe her, your daughter-bride.
    She speaks your words in public,
    but in private
    your words pattern her little
    like a dolly-whore, deeply fried.

*

Moving on now from your genealogical prologue, in this chapter I need to listen carefully for the use to which the "feminine," especially the feminine-maternal body, is put in the narrative account of Israel's monarchic and cultic past given in Chronicles. As I argued in the last chapter, in the genealogies material-maternal origins are necessarily silenced through the disavowal of the maternal body as origin of the male subject (readable through the slips, contradictions and breakdowns of meaning in the genealogies). This silent maternal body enables "man" to sustain his identity as sole-producer, as he who is eternal begetter, never begotten. In this chapter, however, I wish to show that in the Chronicles' narrative the maternal body is necessarily *repressed* and silenced. That is, while on the surface it seems as if it is the father who is silenced to enable the story of the son to unfold (as I shall explain later), it is in fact maternal origination, as "conceivable" idea, which has been cast beneath the surface of symbolic representation. The idea of the maternal body as origin belongs to, and constitutes, the masculine unconscious. I shall argue that it is the repression of the maternal body that most effectively silences the feminine in this particular re-narration of the past. In other words, that silence of the feminine-maternal body is fundamentally constitutive for this narrative discourse of the past. I suggest that this repression is readable through the description of the temple in Chronicles and through the description of certain male bodies in the narrative: Saul, Jehoram, Asa, Uzziah. The murder of Saul and his sons (1 Chronicles 10) may be read symptomatically as a narrative of the original repression of the maternal body. The diseased bodies of Jehoram, Asa, and Uzziah are abject bodies that, I shall argue, are readable as the *return* of the repressed maternal body. Their bodies actually make audible what is supposed to remain inaudible: the debts to nature in general, and the maternal body specifically. Furthermore, I shall argue that these three kings suffer their particular afflictions for a specific reason. Both Jehoram and Asa are associated with mothers who actually speak (verbally in the case of Athaliah and visually in the case of Maacah). This maternal speech is in breech of the silenced Symbolic place of the maternal body. And Uzziah, while not associated with a mother who speaks, is a lover of nature, which is also heavily repressed in Chronicles. Thus, by listening to these seemingly curious aspects of the narrative, I suggest that we will hear what is not supposed to be heard: our debts to nature and to the maternal body.

2. *Ideal Israel Born of Man*

This story you offer us, of times and places past, makes little room for women. Once again, the story, this time narrative in form, begins without a woman. From the very beginning of this narrative account men are at war, a father and his sons battling in vain against the uncircumcised Philistines. Are they not your real enemy, those men who do not bear the mark of ritual separation from the mother? But this father, Saul, and his sons must perish so that the "proper" line of men may rule your story of wars and worship. After all, this is a story about Yahweh's men organizing themselves (socially, politically, religiously, economically), yet straying with monotonous repetition from the prescribed path, and rewarded or punished accordingly by a consistent, though largely absent father figure/legal instrument. Finally, your story ends with a glimmer of hope. Your people, punished by exile from the land for their disobedience, are allowed to return home.

*

7. *Why won't you let her go?*
   When sweet meats and feast days
   surely would suffice?
   You've tired, even, of your holy things,
   the spaces and places that embrace in your name
   (fatigued? in chains?)
   You love your enemy because he loathes your own.
   I've seen you cry the ugly cry.
   Not pretty.

   At least your salt is moist, alive.
   A solid column on your body, lithe.

*

However, at the beginning of your story you appear to be worried. For some reason, you indicate that Saul and his sons are not ideal. Instead, David and his son Solomon, whose stories constitute a substantial amount of narrative space (1 Chronicles 11–2 Chronicles 9), are presented as the ideal patrilineal dyad. The father, David, will be the greatest of the kings, consolidating the kingdom and laying the pragmatic foundations for his son's success as temple builder. Neither will really falter in your eyes, apart from David's love of war and blood that prevents him from becoming the temple builder (ironic, perhaps, given the sacrificial logic of both the cults of war and of Yahwism). An ideal movement through time, from father to son, from "beloved" (דָּוִיד) to "peace" (שְׁלֹמֹה), with no obvious tensions between them or between Solomon and David's many sons. These two men are Yahweh's perfect instruments born out of the destruction of Saul and his line:

וַיָּ֣מׇת שָׁא֗וּל בְּמַעֲלוֹ֙ אֲשֶׁ֣ר מָעַ֣ל בַּֽיהוָ֔ה עַל־דְּבַ֥ר יְהוָ֖ה אֲשֶׁ֣ר
לֹא־שָׁמָ֑ר וְגַם־לִשְׁא֥וֹל בָּא֖וֹב לִדְר֑וֹשׁ׃וְלֹֽא־דָרַ֥שׁ בַּֽיהוָ֖ה
וַיְמִיתֵ֑הוּ וַיַּסֵּ֥ב אֶת־הַמְּלוּכָ֖ה לְדָוִ֥יד בֶּן־יִשָֽׁי׃

And Saul (שָׁא֗וּל) died on account of his unfaithfulness with which he acted against YHWH, according to the word of YHWH which he did not keep; and also for inquiring (לִשְׁא֥וֹל) of the necromancer (א֖וֹב) for guidance (לִדְר֑וֹשׁ). He did not inquire (דָרַ֥שׁ) of YHWH, so he killed him and turned the kingdom around (וַיַּסֵּ֥ב אֶת־הַמְּלוּכָ֖ה) to David, son of Jesse (1 Chron. 10:13-14).

Yahweh turns (סבב) the kingdom over to David, the beloved, after the destruction of Saul (שָׁא֗וּל), the one who forgoes the guidance of Yahweh, the "father." Saul, instead, asks or inquires of the underworld. This nether world is a world associated with שְׁא֗וֹל ("Sheol"), a feminine noun meaning the underworld, which has the same consonantal spelling as Saul's name and which is related to the verb root שׁאל meaning "to ask or inquire." This story of origin moves from one who inquires of the feminine (via a masculine source, א֖וֹב, a masculine, singular noun meaning "necromancer")[1] at the beginning, to one whose murder by the "father" leads to the beloved one, and then on to peace. What functions, then, as narrative "origin" of your past, your history, is the removal of the man who inquires of the feminine, who seeks a response from the place you understand as feminine; a silencing, in a way, of the type of analytic relationship we are engaged in here. Nevertheless, I shall dwell a little longer with this "man" who inquires of the feminine and whose murdered body plays an important role in the institution of your precious and blessed Davidic monarchy.

*

8. *You've turned on me,*
turned around to measure
a temple space for us
with one door for your escape.
Come and go as you please,
I'll not make a single sound.
But know you'll always find me
slightly breathless
at your return
not strong enough for love
not weak enough for amnesia.

Still alive
with death to learn.

3. *A Body in Bits and Pieces: The Murder of the (M)other?*

Unlike your genealogical discourse (1 Chronicles 1–9; which prefers names to bodies) you begin your narrative past (1 Chronicles 10) with the somewhat disconcerting, gruesome *corporeal* beginning: the suicide/murder of Saul and his sons.[2] Somewhat suddenly, the narrated story begins with war, with men after each other's bodies. The story of Saul's death opens with information about a battle between the Philistines and Israel. The "men of Israel" flee from the Philistines and, we are told, "they fell slain on Mount Gilboa" (וַיִּפְּלוּ חֲלָלִים בְּהַר גִּלְבֹּעַ; 1 Chron. 10:1). The Philistines pursue Saul and his sons, and after they strike down (נכה) Jonathan, Abinadab, and Malchishua (10:2), the Philistines find and wound Saul (10:3). Saul asks his armour bearer to pierce him with his sword, to protect him from whatever deeds the uncircumcised might have in mind. This is how Saul understands his situation (10:4a). After his armour bearer refuses, Saul does the job himself, falling on the sword (10:4b). His armour bearer sees that Saul is dead and falls on the sword and dies (10:5). In verse 6 we find a statement concerning the deaths of Saul, his three sons and "his whole household."

The men of Israel in the cities in the valley flee when they hear of the deaths, and the Philistines move in (10:7). When the Philistines find the corpses (הַחֲלָלִים; lit. "the pierced" or "the slain"; 10:8) of Saul and his sons on the following day, they strip Saul, take his head and his armour and send it about the land as a victory lap for their idols (עֲצַבֵּיהֶם) and their people (10:9). His armour they hang up in the house of their gods,[3] and his head they fasten to the house of Dagon (10:10). The valiant men of Jabeth-Gilead collect the headless body (גּוּפָה) of Saul and the bodies (גּוּפֹת) of his sons (presumably with their heads still connected?), and bury the bones of these fast decaying bodies (עַצְמוֹת; 10:11-12). In verses 13 and 14, we are given the reasons for Saul's death: he did not keep the word of the Lord (10:13a) and also for "inquiring by necromancy" (שָׁאוֹל בָּאוֹר ל; 10:13b). Because of this second transgression, we are told, the Lord slew Saul and turned the kingdom over to David (10:14).

War will be a familiar story in your history, but the question here, at the beginning, is this: why does the body of Saul present such a problem in 1 Chronicles 10, and what exactly do the Philistines do to Saul in verse 3?

וַתִּכְבַּד הַמִּלְחָמָה עַל־שָׁאוּל וַיִּמְצָאֻהוּ הַמּוֹרִים בַּקָּשֶׁת וַיָּחֶל מִן־הַיּוֹרִים׃

> The battle weighed heavily upon Saul, and the archers found him with the bow and he was wounded/he became frightened of the archers (וַיָּחֶל מִן־הַיּוֹרִים; 1 Chron. 10:3)

I find it difficult to understand you when you say מִן־הַיּוֹרִים וַיָּחֶל. It is possible to translate the final clause as "and he was wounded."[4] Or it is possible to translate the final clause as "he became frightened of the archers" or "he writhed in fear from the archers."[5] Has Saul been wounded yet? Has the enemy penetrated him at this early point? Or is Saul simply fearful of what is to come?

Actually, with verse 4, Saul himself is worried lest those men whose bodies are different, the uncircumcised (הָעֲרֵלִים), do something unspeakable/unimaginable to his own. Now, this word, וְהִתְעַלְלוּ, is the Hithpael waw consecutive perfect 3rd common plural of עלל, meaning "to act arbitrarily." In the Hithpael, the word means "to deal wantonly" or "to humiliate." However, עלל can also mean "to insert or to thrust in." Given the semantic range of עלל does Saul fret that the Philistines will humiliate him by raping him in some way?

*

9.   *You could have fed me*
     run cool-skinned lumps
     over my love-dense lips
     always apart, always awaiting
     the birth of words
     to sway your hips.
     But, you withheld.
     You are the mono-man,
     the monopoly-man
     with an autonomous hold on the cord.
     Only one, (but bereshith),
     always only one?
     My securities are sinking,
     searching for the mud,
     the blood
     that will stir my lips, return
     my vision from the Lord.

*

And again, in verse 4, the problem of penetration concerning Saul's body appears when his armour-bearer refuses to put the sword through him. In verse 5, the armour-bearer falls on the sword, along with Saul, or so it would seem. While it is not entirely clear as to whether there is one sword or two, what seems clear to me is that the problem around the body of Saul is one that involves *penetration*. The Philistines may or may not have penetrated him with an arrow in verse 3. And penetration is perhaps also what Saul fears in verse 4, the humiliation of penetration by

the uncircumcised. His armour-bearer is too scared (יִרָא מְאֹד) to penetrate him with the sword. In the end, Saul has to penetrate himself. Well,
so we think. In verse 14 you give Yahweh credit for the fatal penetration of the body of Saul, an act that generates the turning around of the
kingdom and the beginning of the story of David. All in all, I would say
that the question of Saul's penetration is thoroughly ambiguous. Actually, not only ambiguous, but clearly problematic in that it serves to focus
(masculine) anxiety, and significantly, to alter the narrative drive.

But what is the significance of Saul's body? I think the key to understanding the use of Saul's death in the service of narrative origin is located
in the use of the curious Hebrew word for "body," a word found nowhere
else in this story.[6] In 1 Chronicles 10:12 we have a direct reference to the
"body" of Saul and the "bodies" of his sons. The Hebrew word used is
not the usual (גְּוִיָּה)[7] but גּוּפַת (the feminine singular construct form of
גּוּפָה).[8] גּוּפָה is a strange word that has a semantic range that includes
hollowness[9] and closed-ness (גּוּף).[10] In other words, the word you choose
here to represent the bodies of Saul and his sons is a word that evokes
the *male* body as an enclosed, empty container, an exterior shell encas-
ing an empty space. Rather clean when you consider the mess that bodies
and corpses can make. But more than this, this hollow, contained body,
under threat of penetration from the enemy men, evokes the maternal
body – that container for the father's seed. This maternalized body is
murdered, beheaded, displayed and paraded by one group of men (the
Philistines) as victory over another (the Israelites).

And what of Saul's principal crime? His death, you tell us, is the deserved
consequence of his faithless acts against Yahweh: for not observing the
word/command of Yahweh (עַל־דְּבַר יְהוָה אֲשֶׁר לֹא־שָׁמָר; 10:13), for
consulting a necromancer for guidance (בָּאוֹר לִדְרוֹשׁ וְגַם־לִשְׁאוֹל; 10:13)
and for not seeking out Yahweh (וְלֹא־דָרַשׁ בַּיהוָה; 10:14). Saul, it seems,
is guilty of going to a *different* source for knowledge. Instead of Yahweh,
Saul seeks guidance from someone who has access to the world of Sheol.
Of course, as I have mentioned, Saul's very name (שָׁאוּל) indicates a preference for inquiring of that world of nebulous existence.

What I want to suggest is that it gradually becomes clear that Saul
is heavily associated with the feminine in this version of your past, and
more subtly with the maternal. Although the word for his murdered body
seems to be suggesting something beyond the reality of a body (as all
words must do), in this case it is a body that is pure exterior envelop-
ing nothing but space, an empty, *feminine-maternal* body as you might
imagine it. Furthermore, the problem concerning this body is one of

penetration, and it is a problem that is thoroughly overdetermined in your representation of monarchic origins. Thus, for you, what instigates the story of Israel's monarchic and cultic past, what functions as narrative "origin" for you, is the murder of this feminized and maternalized body of Saul, along with the (feminized, maternalized) bodies of his sons. Importantly, however, your story of origins has already silenced the maternal, for it is not the mother whose murder serves as origin of patrilineal, patriarchal history.[11] These are men whose bodies are maternalized. Already, the mother is absent from the story; she is already silenced.[12] There are no women in this first story about men, and yet I want to suggest that their silence is audible and readable right here at the beginning: the repression of the maternal body constitutes, for you, the generative origin of narrative hi(story). Indeed, this repressed maternal body constitutes the foundation of your discourse. The maternal body (even a genealogy of maternalized bodies) serves as a prop for the retelling of this past concerning the institution of patriarchal, socio-political and religious history. In other words, the story of the murder of Saul and his sons can be read symptomatically as a narrative of this *original repression of the maternal body* that generates the properly patrilineal succession narratives that follow.[13]

*

10. *My sisters and I are on the ground –*
     daughters, tied in our tongues.
     We rub the earth through our lifeless hairs
     grind sackcloth into our skins.
     We bend down low
     lick dirt caked by tears
     passing the lumpen words upon our tongues
     in kisses filled with fears.

*

4. From Father to Son, a Blessed Machine

David's story is one of successful consolidation – consolidation of the people of his god, of his reign, of the land, and of the Jerusalem cult. But David's story also serves as the introduction of the story of his son Solomon, whose narrative destiny is to build a house for Yahweh's name. Here in Chronicles the stories of the father and the son are intertwined in a productive and seemingly harmonious embrace. During this golden era (and *only* during the glorious reigns of David and Solomon), the two kingdoms of Israel and Judah are united under one king. But, as we also know from the genealogical chapters that introduce Chronicles, "Israel" (Jacob) and "Judah" are father and son. In your version of the past Jacob is repeatedly known as Israel, not Jacob.[14] Thus, undergirding your ideal monarchic arrangement is the symbiotic, unconflicted familial dyad of strict patriliny – father and son, Israel and Judah (only possible once he who seeks knowledge from the feminine has been removed?). In this period of great wealth, warrior successes (David), peace (Solomon), and cultic adherence, there are no narrated tensions between father and son, no explicit usurpation, by the son, of the symbolic place of the father. The succession of Solomon is smooth and there is no war between Israel in the North and Judah in the South.

However, unlike the stories of the "sons" that follow, Solomon's story begins officially *before* his father's death and not after his father is buried. Solomon is first made king in 1 Chronicles 23:1, and then again in 1 Chronicles 29:22b, this time by "all the assembly":

וְדָוִיד זָקֵן וְשָׂבַע יָמִים וַיַּמְלֵךְ אֶת־שְׁלֹמֹה בְנוֹ עַל־יִשְׂרָאֵל:

David was old and full of days and he made Solomon his son king over Israel (1 Chron. 23:1).

...וַיַּמְלִיכוּ שֵׁנִית לִשְׁלֹמֹה בֶן־דָּוִיד וַיִּמְשְׁחוּ לַיהוָה לְנָגִיד וּלְצָדוֹק לְכֹהֵן:

...and they made Solomon the son of David king a second time, and they anointed Yahweh as prince (!)[15] and Zadok as priest (1 Chron. 29:22).

Between these two occasions are nearly seven long chapters of cultic organization (including genealogy-like lists), substantially slowing down the rate of narrative movement. Immediately following Solomon's first coronation, you launch into the details of the Levitical duties of temple administration, judges and officers of the court, gatekeepers, and musicians (מִשְׁמָרוֹת, "service" or lit. "watches"; 1 Chron. 23:3-32; 24:20-31), the duties of the Aaronic כֹּהֲנִים (24:1-19), the further division of the Levites as choristers (ch. 25), gatekeepers (26:1-19), temple duties (26:20-32) and finally, the king's functionaries (ch. 27). After the descriptions of David's temple and court preparations, he gives a long speech to his "brothers" and his "people" concerning Solomon's future as king and temple builder (28:2-10). This oration is followed by more details of the written plans David hands over to Solomon (28:11-18), another speech to Solomon (28:19-21), a speech to the whole congregation (29:1-5), notice of the donations by the officials (29:6-9), David's praise[16] of Yahweh (29:10-19), some praise and cultic worship by the congregation (29:20-22a), until *finally* Solomon is made king by the assembly. After his initial coronation by David, Solomon must wait until all of this detail about cultic organization is narrated before he can occupy "the throne of Yahweh as king in place of his father" (1 Chron. 29:23a). The effect of all this descriptive detail (and genealogy-like lists) is the *delay* of the son's story.

Might this be the first chink in the golden armour of the ideal dyad that underwrites your narrative movement? Are you reluctant to let the son's story unfold, delaying it as much as possible with a pedant's eye for the details and the intricacies of your cult (of the father)? Is this tension around the succession of the son, despite the harmony between father and son, caused by your awareness that the son's fate is the same as the father's, the necessary conclusion to your story to enable the next son's tale to be told and for time to move forward? While there is no narrative tyranny concerning Solomon's succession, no wars, no fratricide, no plotting or scheming, and so forth, this formal delay suggests the desire of the father for the continuation of his own story despite the fact that his son's story has begun. Indeed, even though you tell us that Solomon is crowned, is successful and is obeyed by all Israel (29:23b), that he has the fealty of all the men of importance in Israel (29:24), that he is greatly exalted by Yahweh, and that he receives royal splendour which surpasses any that has preceded him (29:25), David's story is *still* yet to end. In the next verse you state that "David, the son of Jesse, reigned over all Israel" (29:26). This piece of information about the father is followed by the regnal summary of his rule, and a reminder that all of David's story may be found in the writings (כְּתוּבִים) of Samuel the seer, in the words of (בְדִּבְרֵי) the prophet Nathan and in the words of (וּבְדִבְרֵי) Gad the seer (29:29). Even though Solomon's story has (finally!) begun, you remain reluctant to let go of the father and his great story.

*

11. *Greedy from birth,*
    undernourished,
    the destruction of love's daughters
    who bleed to save the streets
    their order, their rightness of direction.
    With no place of our own.

*

Solomon's story, like his father's, is one of great political success and even greater prosperity. However, unlike his father, Solomon's reign is marked by peace, by Yahweh's granting him wisdom, and by building the temple for (the name of) Yahweh. David tells his son that he (the father) cannot build the temple because Yahweh has told him "you are a man of war" (אִישׁ מִלְחָמוֹת אַתָּה) and "you have shed blood" (דָּמִים שָׁפַכְתָּ; 1 Chron. 28:3 and 1 Chron. 22:8). And yet, in chapter 17, the prophet Nathan is instructed by Yahweh (1 Chron. 17:3) to inform David of Yahweh's words about a future son who will build a house for Yahweh. Yahweh, speaking in the first person, says that he will raise up one of David's offspring (זֶרַע, 17:11), and "I will be a father to him and he will be a son to me" (אֲנִי אֶהְיֶה־לּוֹ לְאָב וְהוּא יִהְיֶה־לִּי לְבֵן; 1 Chron. 17:13). Yahweh says that it will be his (Yahweh's son) who will build Yahweh's house, and that the throne of Yahweh's son will be established for ever:

הוּא יִבְנֶה־לִּי בַיִת וְכֹנַנְתִּי אֶת־כִּסְאוֹ עַד־עוֹלָם:
אֲנִי אֶהְיֶה־לּוֹ לְאָב וְהוּא יִהְיֶה־לִּי לְבֵן וְחַסְדִּי לֹא־אָסִיר
מֵעִמּוֹ כַּאֲשֶׁר הֲסִירוֹתִי מֵאֲשֶׁר הָיָה לְפָנֶיךָ: וְהַעֲמַדְתִּיהוּ
בְּבֵיתִי וּבְמַלְכוּתִי עַד־הָעוֹלָם וְכִסְאוֹ יִהְיֶה נָכוֹן עַד־עוֹלָם:

He shall build for me [Yahweh] a house and I will maintain his throne forever. I will be a father to him and he shall be a son to me and I will not remove my benevolence from him as I removed it from the one who was before you [i.e. Saul]. And I will install him in my house and in my kingdom forever, and his throne shall be established forever (1 Chron. 17:12-14).

Curiously, it is Solomon's throne that is established forever, not David's. Furthermore, Yahweh, who usurps the place of the father in relation to the son, Solomon, symbolically removes David's status as "father." In your ideal world, where the father and son are united, and history progresses ostensibly without struggle between the two, Yahweh also holds absolute power over the successes of the son and replaces the father. However, the father's end is here also the *deification* of his symbolic place in relation to the son, for it is now Yahweh, the god of Israel, who is father to Solomon. Is this perhaps a guilt-ridden compromise on the part of the son who must rid himself of the father so his own story can take place? And all of this hinges on the building of a house for the father, or rather, for his name, though this too is rather ambiguous. The temple is referred to as both בֵּית־יהוה (the house of Yahweh; e.g. 2 Chron. 3:1) and בַּיִת לַיהוה (a house for Yahweh; e.g. 2 Chron. 2:11), while also being known as בֵּית הָאֱלֹהִים (the house of the 'Elohim, or the god; e.g. 2 Chron. 3:3). But it is also בַּיִת לְשֵׁם יהוה (a house for the name of Yahweh; e.g. 2 Chron. 1:18). Given that Yahweh seems problematically present in your narrative world (anointed as a prince, and perhaps even blessed by David), we could be forgiven for thinking that this character is going to dwell in the house that you have built for him. Indeed, at the beginning of Solomon's dedication speech, 2 Chronicles 6:2, he states explicitly that he built "a lofty house" (בֵּית זְבֻל)[17] for Yahweh, a place for him "to dwell forever" (עוֹלָמִים לְשִׁבְתְּךָ, "for you to dwell forever"). And yet, as Solomon's speech continues, including his relaying of Yahweh's words to David (2 Chron. 6:5-6, 8-9), he repeatedly refers to the house built for Yahweh's name (2 Chron. 6:5, 7, 8, 9, 10, 20, 26, 33, 34, 38) and of Yahweh's dwelling in the sky (2 Chron. 6:23, 25, 27, 30, 33, 35, 39). The uncertainty of all this is made explicit in Solomon's words to Yahweh:

כִּי הַאֻמְנָם יֵשֵׁב אֱלֹהִים אֶת־הָאָדָם עַל־הָאָרֶץ הִנֵּה שָׁמַיִם
וּשְׁמֵי הַשָּׁמַיִם לֹא יְכַלְכְּלוּךָ אַף כִּי־הַבַּיִת הַזֶּה אֲשֶׁר בָּנִיתִי:

For can it be true that god ('Elohim) would dwell with man upon the earth? Behold the highest sky cannot contain you, how much less this house which I have built? (2 Chron. 6:18).

Ultimately, the great father-god is located in the sky. The temple becomes the site of the sacrificial cult, the place of prayers to Yahweh, and the house of his name (for all to fear).[18] Solomon's work is done.

I want to dwell a while longer in this sacred architectural space. Given that you spend a substantial amount of narrative space (2 Chron. 1:18–4:22) providing explicit details concerning the appearance of this monument, I now want to listen closely to your description of the temple. Furthermore, given that the institution of the blessed Davidic monarchy (the crowning achievement of which is, arguably, Solomon's building of this temple) came about through the murder of the bodies of Saul and his sons – male bodies that evoke an empty, container-like *maternal* space – there are a number of descriptions concerning this sacred, architectural space that I think now warrant close attention, for reasons we shall soon see.[19]

5. *Double-Sexing Sacred Space: The Temple in Chronicles*

The first feature that interests me about this sacred building is the temple vestibule or hall (הָאוּלָם) located at one end of the temple building:

וְהָאוּלָם אֲשֶׁר עַל־פְּנֵי הָאֹרֶךְ עַל־פְּנֵי רְחַב־הַבַּיִת אַמּוֹת
עֶשְׂרִים וְהַגֹּבַהּ מֵאָה וְעֶשְׂרִים וַיְצַפֵּהוּ מִפְּנִימָה זָהָב טָהוֹר:

The vestibule [or porch] in front of the nave of the house was twenty cubits long, equal to the width of the house; and its height was a hundred and twenty cubits. He overlaid it on the inside with pure gold (2 Chron. 3:4).

This vestibule as you describe it is twenty cubits wide and one hundred and twenty cubits high. Given that the entire length of the temple is sixty cubits, and its width twenty cubits, this enormous vertical structure at the entrance is architecturally improbable, though perhaps not impossible.[20] Still, it is rather a precious "thing," something you have overlaid inside with gold. And the second intriguing feature is that your temple seems utterly devoid of windows,[21] and you make only brief mention of doors to the great court (2 Chron. 3:9), and "the entrance of the house, the innermost doors to the Holy of Holies, and the doors of the house for the Temple..." (4:22). Is there only one entrance to this house, with all other doors being internal, or leading to the courtyards? In trying to imagine this internal space without windows, with one door leading outside, and a series of internal doors, I find myself in darkness. Without any details of the windows, and with only one main entrance, the building as you describe it is a cave-like space, with all its internal chambers.

The third interesting feature is your description of the curtain that separates the Holy of Holies from the main section of the temple:

וַיַּעַשׂ אֶת־הַפָּרֹכֶת תְּכֵלֶת וְאַרְגָּמָן וְכַרְמִיל וּבוּץ וַיַּעַשׂ עָלָיו כְּרוּבִים:

And he made the curtain of blue and purple and crimson (fabrics?) and linen, and he worked cherubim upon it (2 Chron. 3:14).

A delicate piece of fabric separates the holiest place of your construction, not a wall or a door. Something tear-able, though untorn, decorated with cherubim similar to the ones you locate within the inner sanctum, the holiest place for you, where you will locate the Father's law and contain (restrain?) his name and presence. Within this cave-like architectural space, with one principal entrance, no windows, and what appears to be a number of internal rooms or chambers, we arrive at this intricate curtain, beyond which is the Holy of Holies.

I want to suggest that this temple, with its curious vestibule and internal structure, is testimony to the repressed status of the maternal body, for it reveals, symptomatically, the phantasy of the mono-productive male body: a male (phallic) body with a womb. It exposes the repressed status of the maternal body in this discourse. First of all, the vaginal and cave/womb-like interiority of the maternal body is useful to your representation. The maternal body, repressed from the beginning of the narrative, returns here in your imaginary service as a prop, even a stage, for your sacred drama. But even more striking is that this architectural construct reveals, symptomatically, the phantasy of the mono-productive body that sustains this discourse. The temple consists of both an enormous, almost unsupportable erection along with a vaginal and womb-like internal space. In other words, this temple, as you describe it, is a doubly-sexed body: a male (phallic) body with a womb.[22] Furthermore, the curtain separating the Holy of Holies from the rest of the temple is untorn, signifying your preference, if you like, for the *virginal* maternal body. The Father will be both honored and contained by the son in this maternal space: no sexual alliance for these two.

*

12.   *We never faint like wounded men.*
      Our bodies fall differently
      more like turfed sparrows
      out a train window on Central Station.
      Thud.
      Nothing gentle, nothing heroic,
      Thank-you anyway
      Men's bodies fall one way,
      Women's another.
      But if you're offering bread and wine
      in a carb-free tea-totalling time
      I'll have some of that
      some of you
      and a little bit of rest
      on my mother's breast.
      I've nothing else to do.

*

And what of the word that you use repeatedly in your description, the word that counts out space for you: אַמּוֹת (plural of אַמָּה), meaning "cubits?" The first two consonants of this useful word (and concept) give us another word, אַם, meaning "mother."[23] "Mother" is here present as a unit of measurement, measuring out both the phallic and vaginal/womb structures of your sacred space for the father. She serves to help you standardize your measurements, enabling you to convert space into place. [24] But, if she is (for you) a unit of measurement of space, how can her own spatial aspects, her own womb-space, even her self *in space* be taken into account? I suggest that what this Hebrew word (אַמָּה) unwittingly reveals is that, for you, the maternal body as a spatial entity (from which, incidentally, you came) is repressed to the point that it becomes something that *measures* space, rather than *being* space or even *being in* space. In other words, the repression of the maternal body enables you not only to appropriate the feminine-maternal body in the service of your phantasy of masculine, mono-sexual production (the male body capable of birth), but also to silence her (re)productive corporeal power through abstraction. Maternal womb-space is reducible to a *standardized concept of measurement* that further enables you (man) to imagine yourself (himself) responsible for all social, political, religious, and economic (re)production.

And within your holiest (womb) space, the place where the Ark of the Covenant will rest, you position two cherubim. The description of these statues is fascinating. First of all, the words used to describe these two cherubim are ambiguous:

וַיַּעַשׂ בְּבֵית־קֹדֶשׁ הַקֳּדָשִׁים כְּרוּבִים שְׁנַיִם מַעֲשֵׂה צַעֲצֻעִים
וַיְצַפּוּ אֹתָם זָהָב:

He made, in the house of the Holy of Holies, two cherubim, a work of צַעֲצֻעִים (meaning unknown), and they overlaid them with gold (2 Chron. 3:10).

You say that the two cherubim are a work of something, but the word you use, צַעֲצֻעִים, is not a known word. Actually, with all those consonants it doesn't even seem to be a Hebrew word. Is it perhaps a transliteration of a word from a culture different to your own? You seem to be struggling to describe these figures.

These cherubim are, nevertheless, described as standing next to each other, facing the house, with their wings outstretched (five cubits per wing):

וְכַנְפֵי הַכְּרוּבִים אָרְכָּם אַמּוֹת עֶשְׂרִים כְּנַף הָאֶחָד לְאַמּוֹת
חָמֵשׁ מַגַּעַת לְקִיר הַבַּיִת וְהַכָּנָף הָאַחֶרֶת אַמּוֹת חָמֵשׁ מַגִּיעַ
לִכְנַף הַכְּרוּב הָאַחֵר: וּכְנַף הַכְּרוּב הָאֶחָד אַמּוֹת חָמֵשׁ מַגִּיעַ לְקִיר
הַבַּיִת וְהַכָּנָף הָאַחֶרֶת אַמּוֹת חָמֵשׁ דְּבֵקָה לִכְנַף הַכְּרוּב הָאַחֵר:

The wings of the cherubim were twenty cubits long; the wing of the one, for five cubits reached (מַגַּעַת ; 3fs Hiph`il participial form of נגע) to the wall of the house and the other five cubit wing reached (מַגִּיעַ; 3ms Hiph`il participial form of נגע) to (or for?) the wing of the other cherub. And the wing of the one cherub, five cubits, reached (מַגִּיעַ; 3ms Hiph`il participial form of נגע) toward the wall of the house and the other five cubit wing cleaved (דְּבֵקָה)[25] to the wing of the other cherub (2 Chron. 3:11-12).

What seems rather curious about these statuary creatures is that each of their wings (which, according to your standard form of measurement, are the same) has a specific gender associated with the verbs of reaching and cleaving.[26] According to the verbs, the inner wings of the cherubim – the ones that touch each other – are masculine in the case of the first cherub, and feminine in the second case. Indeed, they are not described as simply reaching each other in the sense of measured extension. Rather, the feminine wing cleaves to her partner's masculine wing, with this masculine wing reaching to (or for?) this cleaving feminine wing. Each cherub here in the temple of Chronicles reiterates the double-sexing of the temple structure itself, with its enormous phallic erection, and its vaginal- and womb-like internal structure. In other words, each cherub reiterates the temple, which itself figures the governing phantasy of the monoproductive male body: that is, double-sexing equates to an appropriation of maternal productivity by the masculine subject. It seems as if your repression of the maternal body has well and truly enabled your reconstruction of the past as thoroughly ideal.

Furthermore, in 2 Chronicles 8:11, following Solomon's completion of the temple and his other building projects,[27] you tell us that Solomon removes Pharaoh's daughter from the city of David:

וְאֶת־בַּת־פַּרְעֹה הֶעֱלָה שְׁלֹמֹה מֵעִיר דָּוִיד לַבַּיִת אֲשֶׁר בָּנָה־לָהּ
כִּי אָמַר לֹא־תֵשֵׁב אִשָּׁה לִי בְּבֵית דָּוִיד מֶלֶךְ־יִשְׂרָאֵל כִּי־קֹדֶשׁ
הֵמָּה אֲשֶׁר־בָּאָה אֲלֵיהֶם אֲרוֹן יְהוָה׃

> Solomon brought up the daughter of Pharaoh from the city of David to the house which he had built for her, for he said, "No woman shall dwell for me in the house of David, king of Israel, for these things are holy which came to them (אֲלֵיהֶם ; m. pl.), the ark of Yahweh (2 Chron. 8:11).

I am once again struggling to understand you here, particularly this final clause concerning holy things and the ark of Yahweh. This effort to comprehend you is occasioned by the introduction of a woman into the narrative – only one of two women who appear in Solomon's story. What is apparent, however, is the need to distance Solomon's woman from the house of David.[28] The house of David is, of course, the king's palace, not the temple. The mention of holy things which have come to them, and the ark of Yahweh, certainly invokes the cultus, and the removal of a woman from that scene implies the issue of purity. But cultic distancing is invoked alongside a *political* distancing. The two are inextricably related for you. What you seem to be saying here is that these are not places in which women may live. Perhaps more importantly, however, is your statement that "no woman shall dwell *for me.*" These words imply something other than a place for a woman to dwell. For, as we have heard numerous times in the genealogies, women *bear sons for their men.* Are the two activities of birthing sons and the unmentionable sexual act itself banned from the centre of your world because they are a threat to purity and order? If women are present here, in the forefront of your story, are you forced to acknowledge the importance of their bodies for the production of your story?[29] Are those bodies in excess of the symbolic space within which you have interred them as abstracted producers for you? You are the one who has carefully constructed this symbolic universe upon the denial of such bodies and their productive value outside of your own symbolic frameworks. We can hear your anxiety when your own laws of language and meaning production break down towards the end of your sentence where you try to tell us about the things that are holy for you. This is, after all, a house to honour the father, not the mother.

6. *"Silencing" the Father?*

However, not long after the construction of this sacred space built for the father's name, things start to fall apart. The separation of the happy "father-son" union (the united lands of Judah and Israel under one monarchy) and the return of wars and cultic promiscuities follow the end of Solomon's reign. And, if we persist with the familial metaphor, I note that your story of the post-Solomonic past is overwhelmingly the story of the son, "Judah." The father, "Israel," reappears only briefly every now and then, but only in relation to the son's story. The name "Israel," however, will also be the name given to your people as a whole, once again symbolically elevating the name of the father. Broadly speaking, for you, in this idealized recounting of the past, the golden era ends and the son's story (Judah) takes place through the absence of the father (Israel, in the north) and his story. Likewise, within the narrative itself, the stories of actual sons generally only take place upon the deaths of the fathers. Once the son dies, he is buried with his "fathers," thus becoming one of the noble silent, enabling the succession and the story of the next son to then unfold.

On the surface, then, it would seem that the mechanics of this historical discourse – the "son's story" – is one of patrilineal succession enabled by the silencing of the father. In other words, the death of the father generates the "birth" of the son's story "proper." This father-son progression is consistent with the genealogical discourse of 1 Chronicles 1–9, as I have argued in the previous chapter. However, unlike the genealogies, the narrative of Chronicles makes little use of birthing verbs or birth reports. Actually, in your entire narrative history, a masculine form of the birthing verb ילד is used only eight times (1 Chron. 14:3; 20:6, 8; 22:9; 26:6; 2 Chron. 11:21; 13:21; 24:3). Of these eight masculine verbs, only four are active verbs in the Hiph'il (all וַיּוֹלֶד), and each are associated with David,

Reheboam, Abijah, and Joash. In the remaining four cases, the Niph'al passive verb (נוֹלַד) is used.

*

13. *What can I say for you,*
     to what compare you?
     A summer's day or
     some other manly whim?
     But what if I wish nothing more
     than for you to say for you,
     your own, before you die?
     All this description, so impotent.
     Words relaxing to await a flesh,
     a non-sacrifice, a breath?
     And will the word-virgin spring up
     from your garden mouth
     as restorative attempt to love up
     the daughters from their death?

*

Even more remarkably, however, is that within the entire narrative of Chronicles, including the genealogies and lists that interrupt the narrative, the use of a feminine form of the verb ילד ("to bear") appears only with Abihail and Maacah, two of Reheboam's women included in a genealogy-like summary (2 Chron. 11:19, 20).

וַיִּקַּח־לוֹ רְחַבְעָם אִשָּׁה אֶת־מָחֲלַת (בֶּן) [בַּת־]יְרִימוֹת בֶּן־דָּוִיד
אֲבִיהַיִל בַּת־אֱלִיאָב בֶּן־יִשָׁי: וַתֵּלֶד לוֹ בָּנִים אֶת־יְעוּשׁ
וְאֶת־שְׁמַרְיָה וְאֶת־זָהַם: וְאַחֲרֶיהָ לָקַח אֶת־מַעֲכָה בַּת־אַבְשָׁלוֹם
וַתֵּלֶד לוֹ אֶת־אֲבִיָּה וְאֶת־עַתַּי וְאֶת־זִיזָא וְאֶת־שְׁלֹמִית:
וַיֶּאֱהַב רְחַבְעָם אֶת־מַעֲכָה בַת־אַבְשָׁלוֹם מִכָּל־נָשָׁיו וּפִילַגְשָׁיו
כִּי נָשִׁים שְׁמוֹנֶה־עֶשְׂרֵה נָשָׂא וּפִילַגְשִׁים שִׁשִּׁים וַיּוֹלֶד עֶשְׂרִים
וּשְׁמוֹנָה בָּנִים וְשִׁשִּׁים בָּנוֹת: וַיַּעֲמֵד לָרֹאשׁ רְחַבְעָם אֶת־אֲבִיָּה
בֶן־מַעֲכָה לְנָגִיד בְּאֶחָיו כִּי לְהַמְלִיכוֹ:

Reheboam took for himself a woman: Mahalath, the daughter of Jerimoth, son of David and Abihail, the daughter of Eliab, son of Jesse. She bore (וַתֵּלֶד) sons for him: Jeush, Shemariah and Zaham. And after her he took Maacah, the daughter of Absalom, son of David, and she bore (וַתֵּלֶד) for him Abijah, Attai, Ziza and Shelomith. Reheboam loved Maacah, the daughter of Absalom above all his women and his *pilagshim* – for he married eighteen women and sixty *pilagshim* and he begat (bore?)

twenty-eight sons and sixty daughters. Reheboam appointed Abijah, son
of Maacah, to be leader among his brothers so as to make him king
(2 Chron. 11:18-22).

The greatness of Reheboam, the grandson of David, the son of Solomon,
and the first king of Judah, is apparent in this geneaological account of
his offspring. This importance is evident not only through the number of
women he takes, but also through the qualification of all his women as
belonging to the family of David. The exceptions to this link with David
are presumably the פְּלַגְשִׁים. Reheboam's grandeur is also apparent in that
he, like David,[30] is the subject of the verb, וַיּוֹלֶד ("and he begot/bore").[31]
The result of Reheboam's miraculous productivity is twenty-eight sons
and sixty daughters. But what about the mention of love here? Significantly, this is the only time in your version of the past that you mention
the love of a man for a woman. There must have been a story to tell about
this relationship. Instead, it seems even the love of a man for a woman
is silenced for what is of central importance to you, the continuation
of the (patrilineal) monarchic line. The only consequence you mention
about Rheboam's love for Maacah is that her son is chosen from among
all Reheboam's sons to be king. I can only imagine the effects such a love
could have on this small group of women.

In the two cases where the feminine form of the verb ילד ("to bear")
is used, the familiar וַתֵּלֶד לוֹ ("and she bore for him") appears. While the
appearance of women with birthing verbs in the genealogies of Chronicles (1 Chronicles 1–9) presents us with enormous struggles concerning meaning production and understanding, this genealogical intrusion
into the narrative which includes women and birthing verbs seems to
flow rather smoothly. However, by the time we come to the introductory regnal formula for Abijah in 2 Chronicles 13:2, genealogical sense
and continuity are once again disconcerted by the presence of a female
name:

בִּשְׁנַת שְׁמוֹנֶה עֶשְׂרֵה לַמֶּלֶךְ יָרָבְעָם וַיִּמְלֹךְ אֲבִיָּה עַל־יְהוּדָה׃
שָׁלוֹשׁ שָׁנִים מָלַךְ בִּירוּשָׁלִַם וְשֵׁם אִמּוֹ מִיכָיָהוּ בַת־אוּרִיאֵל
מִן־גִּבְעָה וּמִלְחָמָה הָיְתָה בֵּין אֲבִיָּה וּבֵין יָרָבְעָם׃

In the eighteenth year of King Jeroboam's reign, Abijah began to rule over
Judah. He ruled for three years in Jerusalem, and the name of his mother
was Micaiah, daughter of Uriel from Gibea. There was war between Abijah
and Jeroboam (2 Chron. 13:1-2).

While in 11:20 and 11:22 Reheboam's favourite wife, Maacah, daughter
of Absalom, is named as Abijah's mother, his mother in 13:2 is listed as

Micaiah, daughter of Uriel. This later account directly contradicts the earlier story about Abijah's father, Reheboam, and his favourite woman, the one that he loves. Indeed, Abijah is destined for the throne because of this love. Is that debt too much for the son to bear so that a new mother is procured for the formal preface to Abijah's story? And, perhaps not surprisingly, you suddenly bring up the war between Abijah, king of Judah, and Jeroboam, king of Israel: "son" and "father" at war.

*

14. *Led for so long by those who*
     care little for us and
     our ways, those false seers
     who are paid to produce us differently
     each time the seasons change.
     We salute you, we really do,
     But don't introduce yourselves to our children.
     They now know how to hate you.

*

Returning to my earlier point concerning the dearth of birthing verbs in the narrative, while the production of sons is crucial to the forward movement of your story (indeed, without at least one son for each father there is no story), narratives of the production of children are almost entirely absent from your narrative discourse. This absence means that there are no stories about a woman's sexual act with a man, her pregnancy, and her birthing of a child (son). Significantly, sex and birth are not features of your idealized narrative account of your past. In the narrative of Chronicles, not even the masculine forms of the verb ילד ("to bear") seem particularly necessary. Since birthing verbs are certainly not integral to each story, your story of the past progresses without any sense of corporeal origins (except, perhaps, the corpse of the father).

In the genealogies, as I argued in the previous chapter, the logic of temporal movement is patrilineal. Likewise, narrative temporal movement is constituted by the progression from father to son. However, I have also argued in the previous chapter that patrilineal succession generates a tension between father and son. Here in the narrative, this tension remains. For narrative time to move forward, the father must produce a son. It is generally (though not always) the case that the death of the father is required so that the story of the son can take place. And yet, the son himself must become a father of a son and eventually suffer the same fate as the father: silence.[32] This silencing of the father is replicated on a broader narrative scale: Chronicles is the son's (Judah's) story. The father

("Israel," and his own monarchic line, in the north) and his story generally remain unheard. How is this tension resolved?

Your dominant re-presentation of origins and history is that of the (male) subject who is debt-free with respect to nature in general and the maternal body specifically. "His" birth is symbolic; "he" is born through the word. Indeed, he is even without debt to the sexual acts of male and female bodies, rendering those corporeal acts inaudible, if you like. However, unlike the mother, your father is *compensated* for your insistence on his silence in a number of ways:

1. Yahweh usurps the place of David, the father of Solomon (1 Chron. 17:13), thus deifying the place of the father in the process (the father is now god himself);
2. The name "Israel" is given to Jacob, the father of the twelve eponymous tribes of Israel. As I suggested earlier, the father and his son(s) are symbolically identical (the father is "Israel" and the sons are "Israel"), suggesting that the phantasy of mono-sexual production is also a phantasy of self-generation; man is able to give birth to himself;
3. The father's name, "Israel," comes to represent the entire people of Yahweh; and
4. The son builds a monumental, sacred house for the father's *name*.

I suggest that while the father is compensated quite generously for his silence (it is in your best interests after all, for, it is your fate as well), it is maternal silence that is necessary to sustain this compensation: the symbolic deification of the father and his name.

*

15. *Now your little dolly-whores circle her*
    knowing they know where you hide
    the Jerusalem pit's trap door
    out of there, away from her,
    from the burden of her time,
    from the nausea of her emanations,
    from the wisdom of her silent words
    that speak only of the possibility
    of a beauty that's as rare and
    perfect as an in-can-tā-tion.

*

Curiously, though, your narrated story of monarchic origins (1 Chronicles 10) is a dramatically violent story about the penetration, death, and beheading of a male body (a father), and the murder of the bodies of his sons. As I have argued earlier, the word used in this text, גּוּפָה, with its semantic range that includes a hollowed out space and enclosed-ness, evokes both the maternal body, and also the body as clean and proper. The corpses of Saul and his sons do not seem to be problematic, defiling objects in 1 Chronicles 10:11-12. Narratively speaking, they rapidly proceed from being fresh corpses to being bones:

וַיִּשְׁמְעוּ כֹּל יָבֵישׁ גִּלְעָד אֵת כָּל־אֲשֶׁר־עָשׂוּ פְלִשְׁתִּים
לְשָׁאוּל: וַיָּקוּמוּ כָּל־אִישׁ חַיִל וַיִּשְׂאוּ אֶת־גּוּפַת שָׁאוּל וְאֵת
גּוּפֹת בָּנָיו וַיְבִיאוּם יָבֵישָׁה וַיִּקְבְּרוּ אֶת־עַצְמוֹתֵיהֶם תַּחַת
הָאֵלָה בְּיָבֵשׁ וַיָּצוּמוּ שִׁבְעַת יָמִים:

> And all the men of Jabesh Gilead heard what the Philistines had done to Saul. All the valiant men arose and they took the body (גּוּפַת) of Saul and the bodies (גּוּפֹת) of his sons and they brought them to Jabesh. They buried their bones under the oak in Jabesh and they fasted seven days (1 Chron. 10:11-12).

The process of decay here is swift indeed. And it is interesting that the valiant men must deny their bodies food at this point. I suspect that this rapid transformation from corpse to bones, along with the mention of fasting, betrays your (masculine) denial of the body as a natural entity on which you depend for your existence. The (masculine) body is not imagined to be under the temporal laws of nature at all. And this denial of the (masculine) body is commensurate with the repression of the maternal body. Indeed, without the repression of that body you could not sustain your phantasy of mono-sexual production, the Imaginary male body capable of birth.

Now, in direct contradiction to this image of the (masculine) body as clean and proper, beyond nature (it is capable of birthing, after all, in your Imaginary universe), I want, now, for us to focus on three kings whose stories conclude with very messy bodies indeed. These three kings – Jehoram, Asa, and Uzziah – are kings who are struck with horrid bodily diseases that inflict long and painful deaths. I am interested in these three kings because of the diseases inflicted upon them as punishment: their diseases render their bodies as *abject*. In a story that makes very little reference to bodies, these diseased bodies "bear" interrogation.

7. Return of the Repressed: The Three Diseased Kings of Chronicles[33]

Jehoram, son of Jehoshaphat, becomes king of Judah in 2 Chronicles 21:1 when his father dies. His succession is fairly typical in that there is no dispute between brothers, or usurpation of the place of power:

וַיִּשְׁכַּב יְהוֹשָׁפָט עִם־אֲבֹתָיו וַיִּקָּבֵר
עִם־אֲבֹתָיו בְּעִיר דָּוִיד וַיִּמְלֹךְ יְהוֹרָם בְּנוֹ תַּחְתָּיו׃

And Jehoshaphat lay with his fathers and was buried with his fathers in the
city of David. Jehoram his son became king in his place (2 Chron. 21:1).

However, soon after this, Jehoram murders all of his brothers, presumably so his reign will have no internal, familial competition:

וַיָּקָם יְהוֹרָם עַל־מַמְלֶכֶת אָבִיו וַיִּתְחַזַּק וַיַּהֲרֹג אֶת־כָּל־אֶחָיו
בֶּחָרֶב וְגַם מִשָּׂרֵי יִשְׂרָאֵל׃

When Jehoram had ascended to his father's throne and was established,
he slew all of his brothers by the sword, and also some of the princes of
Israel (2 Chron. 21: 4).

Jehoram is one of the kings whose reign is marked by gross disregard for
the law. He murders his brothers and some princes, builds high places in
the hill country of Judah, and he leads the people of Judah astray:

גַּם־הוּא עָשָׂה־בָמוֹת בְּהָרֵי יְהוּדָה וַיֶּזֶן אֶת־יֹשְׁבֵי יְרוּשָׁלַם
וַיַּדַּח אֶת־יְהוּדָה׃

And also he made high places in the hill country of Judah and he caused
the dwellers in Jerusalem to commit fornication (religious? sexual?) and he
thrust Judah into idolatry (2 Chron. 21:11).

In a letter sent to Jehoram from Elijah the prophet, Jehoram is told that
he will be punished for the following reasons (which reiterate the narrative that you have just given to us):

כֹּה ׀ אָמַר יְהוָה אֱלֹהֵי דָּוִיד אָבִיךָ תַּחַת אֲשֶׁר לֹא־הָלַכְתָּ
בְּדַרְכֵי יְהוֹשָׁפָט אָבִיךָ וּבְדַרְכֵי אָסָא מֶלֶךְ־יְהוּדָה׃
וַתֵּלֶךְ בְּדֶרֶךְ מַלְכֵי יִשְׂרָאֵל וַתַּזְנֶה אֶת־יְהוּדָה וְאֶת־יֹשְׁבֵי
יְרוּשָׁלַם כְּהַזְנוֹת בֵּית אַחְאָב וְגַם אֶת־אַחֶיךָ בֵית־אָבִיךָ
הַטּוֹבִים מִמְּךָ הָרָגְתָּ׃

Thus says Yahweh, god of David your father, "Because you have not walked
in the ways of Jehoshaphat your father, and in the ways of Asa king of
Judah, but have walked in the way of the kings of Israel and have caused
Judah and the dwellers of Jerusalem to commit fornication (religious?
sexual?) like the house of Ahab caused fornication (religious? sexual?), and
also you have killed your brothers of your father's house, who were better
than yourself (2 Chron. 21:12-13).

It seems that Jehoram's evil lies in his similarity with the kings of Israel, especially Ahab, who is the father of Athaliah, Jehoram's wife. The behaviour of those kings in Israel (Judah's "father") is explicitly described as fornication (וַתַּזְנֶה: "and he caused to fornicate"), both in verse 11 and verse 13. It is ambiguous as to whether the fornication is literal (i.e. sexual) or metaphorical (i.e. religious).[34] Nevertheless, according to Elijah these acts (which are either literally sexual or metaphorically sexual) warrant the punishment that is to come upon Jehoram, king of Judah. The punishment, Elijah writes, is this:

הִנֵּה יְהֹוָה נֹגֵף מַגֵּפָה גְדוֹלָה בְּעַמֶּךָ וּבְבָנֶיךָ וּבְנָשֶׁיךָ וּבְכָל־רְכוּשֶׁךָ:
וְאַתָּה בָּחֳלָיִים רַבִּים בְּמַחֲלֵה מֵעֶיךָ עַד־יֵצְאוּ מֵעֶיךָ
מִן־הַחֹלִי יָמִים עַל־יָמִים:

> Yahweh will smite your people with a great plague, your sons, your women/wives, and all your property. And you will have a very great sickness in your bowels (מֵעֶיךָ) until your bowels come out because of the sickness, day after day (2 Chron. 21:14-15)

Immediately following Elijah's letter, you tell us that Yahweh organizes these punishments, with the great plague (מַגֵּפָה גְדוֹלָה; 2 Chron. 21:14) taking the form of the Philistines' spirit/breath (רוּחַ הַפְּלִשְׁתִּים; 2 Chron. 21:16) and the Arabs who are near the Chushites. Both invade Judah, taking all the possessions from the king's house, including his women and his sons (except Jehoahaz). Then Yahweh strikes Jehoram in the bowels with a disease without cure (vv. 16-18). After about two years Jehoram's bowels indeed come out and he dies a terrible death (v. 19).

Jehoram's punishments see him stripped of his possessions, including his women and his sons. But worst of all, perhaps, is the very painful extraction of his bowels. Rather a drastic form of punishment, don't you think? But this word you give us which means "bowels" (מֵעֶה) is very interesting, for it is also a word that means "womb."[35] Generally, the word refers to the internal organs of the body, especially the bowels or intestines. And of course, it makes sense to translate "bowels" here, because, after all, we are talking about a male character. However, by now it should come as no surprise to you that I will insist on highlighting its other meaning, given that so far your genealogical and narrative discourses of the past manifest an overwhelming use of the image of masculine monoproduction through the use of the masculine forms of the יָלַד verb ("he bore"). Indeed, your narrative discourse begins with the murder of a man whose body itself is highly feminized and maternalized. Surely a man with a womb should not overly alarm you.

16. *Hard to get the fashions right down here,*
    though once, she knew it all.
    The head turning was a pleasure
    when the man himself was elegantly quiet.
    But when he gave her a whistle
    dressed in last year's strides,
    she knew he was beneath her
    in her pretty pink twin-set.
    Now the twins-sets have all unravelled
    and she couldn't give a damn
    for a bounty is the thing she knows
    of men and their love-blocked women.

    > *They cannot stand you like this –*
    > *they hiss, they gnash their teeth,*

    > *they cry: "We have destroyed her!*
    > *Ah, this is the day we longed for;*

    > *now we have it; we see it!"*
    > *Of course, they missed the wordiness subliminal.*

*

Yahweh's punishment of Jehoram for his wrong doing is consistent with your image of immediate divine retribution in the rest of the narrative.[36] When a king follows the laws of Yahweh, he is rewarded accordingly, and for each of his sins he is punished accordingly. Many of the kings, in fact, suffer physical punishment leading to death as a consequence of their wrong doings.[37] But only three of these kings suffer explicit bodily afflictions (Jehoram, Asa, Uzziah). Before Jehoram, Asa is punished with a disease of the feet.

וַיֶּחֱלֶא אָסָא בִּשְׁנַת שְׁלוֹשִׁים וָתֵשַׁע לְמַלְכוּתוֹ בְּרַגְלָיו
עַד־לְמַעְלָה חָלְיוֹ וְגַם־בְּחָלְיוֹ לֹא־דָרַשׁ אֶת־יְהוָה כִּי בָּרֹפְאִים:

In the thirty-ninth year of his reign, Asa was diseased in his feet; his disease was exceedingly great. Moreover, in his disease he did not inquire of Yahweh, but of physicians (2 Chron. 16:12).

Although he is a model king for most of his reign, ridding the land of all kinds of abominations (2 Chron. 14:2-7; 15:8-19), Asa witlessly punishes Hanani the seer for informing him of Yahweh's intention to inflict wars upon Judah because of Asa's alliance with Ben-hadad, king of Aram. Out of anger (כָּעַס), Asa puts Hanani in the stocks, or some other uncomfortable instrument of punishment that makes the body crouch (16:10).

Asa's foot disease is implicitly his own punishment for such a cruel act against Hanani, and for his oppression of some other people at that time (16:10). However, even once afflicted, Asa continues to sin by consulting healers instead of Yahweh. Yahweh clearly is not fond of those who inquire elsewhere. And, it seems, either Asa's disobedient inquiring or his skin disease (or perhaps both) prevent him from the standard burial of a king in the tombs of the kings:

וַיִּקְבְּרֻהוּ בְקִבְרֹתָיו אֲשֶׁר כָּרָה־לוֹ בְּעִיר דָּוִיד וַיַּשְׁכִּיבֻהוּ
בַּמִּשְׁכָּב אֲשֶׁר מִלֵּא בְּשָׂמִים וּזְנִים מְרֻקָּחִים בְּמִרְקַחַת מַעֲשֶׂה
וַיִּשְׂרְפוּ־לוֹ שְׂרֵפָה גְּדוֹלָה עַד־לִמְאֹד:

> And they buried him in his grave which he dug for himself in the city of
> David. And they laid him in the bed which was full of all kinds of spices
> prepared by the perfumers' art. And they burnt for him an exceedingly
> large fire (2 Chron. 16:14)

While Asa is honoured with a great fire, his burial in a grave that he has dug for himself (literally?) – and not in the graves/tombs of the kings or upon the graves/tombs of the sons of David (as is Hezekiah; 2 Chron. 32:33) – indicates that his honour or greatness as a king has diminished because of his actions and/or his skin disease. Might you be concerned with infection here?

The nature of this illness in his feet is not entirely clear.[38] It is apparently very painful: עַד־לְמַעְלָה חָלְיוֹ, which, idiomatically can be rendered as "his disease was exceedingly great." This clause, though, may also be translated as "his disease spreading upwards" (Eisemann, 1992: 115). According to Levitical law, there is, of course, an issue with purity and defilement here.[39] Asa's body is not the clean and proper body that you imagine is required so as to maintain order. Like Jehoram's illness, his disease reminds you too much of the unseen, the hidden interior of the masculine body (which, remember, you imagine to be empty and womb-like – an image that sustains your social order – not disordered, messy, and beyond your control). Asa's foot illness, in other words, forces what is supposed to remain hidden (and silent) onto the stage of the visible (and audible). We can "hear" your need for nature in general and the maternal body specifically to remain unheard because it threatens your image of yourself as self-made (and thus pure?)

There are many kings who similarly suffer the dishonour of not being buried with their fathers or kings. You tell us explicitly that Jehoram, Joash, and Ahaz, while buried in "the city of David" in the case of Jehoram and Joash and "in Jerusalem" in Ahaz's case, are not buried in the graves/tombs of the kings (2 Chron. 21:20; 24:25; 28:27). However, like Asa, Uzziah and Manasseh are buried in alternative sites:

וַיִּשְׁכַּב עֻזִּיָּהוּ עִם־אֲבֹתָיו וַיִּקְבְּרוּ אֹתוֹ עִם־אֲבֹתָיו בִּשְׂדֵה

הַקְּבוּרָה אֲשֶׁר לַמְּלָכִים כִּי אָמְרוּ מְצוֹרָע הוּא וַיִּמְלֹךְ יוֹתָם

בְּנוֹ תַּחְתָּיו:

And Uzziah slept with his fathers but they buried him with his fathers (ancestors, perhaps) in the field of graves which were for the kings, because, they said, he was a leper. And Jotham his son succeeded him as king (2 Chron. 26:23)

וַיִּשְׁכַּב מְנַשֶּׁה עִם־אֲבֹתָיו וַיִּקְבְּרֻהוּ בֵיתוֹ וַיִּמְלֹךְ אָמוֹן בְּנוֹ

תַּחְתָּיו:

And Manasseh slept with his fathers but they buried him in his house. And Amon his son succeeded him as king (2 Chron. 33:20)

Manasseh perpetrates all kinds of atrocities during his reign (rebuilds the high places which his father, Hezekiah, had broken down, erects altars to the Ba'als, makes Asherahs, worships and serves all the hosts of heaven, builds altars in Yahweh's house for them, burns his sons in the valley of Ben-Hinnom as an offering, practices soothsaying, divination, and sorcery, and works with a necromancer and a familiar spirit (2 Chron. 33:3-6). We might expect, given Yahweh's response to Saul's affiliation with the feminine-otherworld that Manasseh might suffer extraordinary physical suffering. However, his repentance in 33:12-13 sees his punishment restricted to his less than honourable burial site.

*

17. *You know, it seems like forever that*
    I've told this simple tale,
    almost as if ordained from on high, yet
    he is not smiling, and speaks only of damnations.
    Did I tell it wrong?
    Did I lament too long?
    But are these not the Lamentations?

    Does the poet truly love his muse,
    Or is she his unfarmed meadow?
    I think she is his thinking enemy,
    created, not born,
    to live darkly as his shadow.

*

Uzziah, on the other hand, is generally a very good king whose only crime is his attempt to burn incense in the temple, an act that transgresses the law that only the consecrated Aaronite priests are allowed to burn the incense upon the altar (2 Chron. 26:16-18). Yahweh punishes him by afflicting him with leprosy on his forehead (26:19-20).

וַיִּזְעַף עֻזִּיָּהוּ וּבְיָדוֹ מִקְטֶרֶת לְהַקְטִיר וּבְזַעְפּוֹ עִם־הַכֹּהֲנִים וְהַצָּרַעַת זָרְחָה בְמִצְחוֹ לִפְנֵי הַכֹּהֲנִים בְּבֵית יְהוָה מֵעַל לְמִזְבַּח הַקְּטֹרֶת:

And Uzziah was angry and the censer for burning incense was in his hand. But he got angry at the priests, and leprosy rose up on his forehead before the priests in the house of Yahweh above the altar of the incense (2 Chron. 26:19)

וַיִּפֶן אֵלָיו עֲזַרְיָהוּ כֹהֵן הָרֹאשׁ וְכָל־הַכֹּהֲנִים וְהִנֵּה־הוּא מְצֹרָע בְּמִצְחוֹ וַיַּבְהִלוּהוּ מִשָּׁם וְגַם־הוּא נִדְחַף לָצֵאת כִּי נִגְּעוֹ יְהוָה:

Azariah, the chief priest, and all the priests turned to him and behold he was leprous on his forehead and in terror they hastened him[40] from there. He also hastened himself to go out for Yahweh had struck him (2 Chron. 26:20)

Of all the kings who are punished for their transgressions, be it bodily punishment and/or dishonourable burial, Asa, Jehoram, and Uzziah suffer the most punishing bodily treatment. Initially, there appears to be no consistent reason for the extent and type of punishment that these kings suffer in relation to the crimes committed. For instance, neither Ahaz nor Manasseh are dealt this kind of bodily punishment, even though they both commit cultic atrocities, including human sacrifice (2 Chron. 28:2-4, 22-25; 33:2-9). While Manasseh may escape such extreme punishment because of his repentance, the unrepentant Ahaz simply endures wars with no mention made of the cause of his death. And, while the bodies of Ahaziah, Joash, Amaziah, Amon, and Josiah are fatally wounded in some way (2 Chron. 22:9; 24:25; 25:27-28; 33:24; 35:23-24), there is certainly no sense of disease such as is the case with Asa, Jehoram, and Uzziah.

Yet, while they are not the only kings who are punished bodily (Ahaziah, Joash, Amaziah, Amon, and Josiah are all murdered), I think there is indeed a striking degree of consistency in the punishments of Jehoram, Asa, and Uzziah. Each of these kings is struck with a disease, and each of their diseases occurs for long periods of time. That is, while the other kings may be murdered, their deaths are fairly swift. But Asa's foot disease lasts for approximately two years, as does Jehoram's bowel disease, and leprosy is a disease that slowly kills off the human body, bit by bit. Furthermore, the bodies of these kings are transformed in ways that connote serious pollution of cultic purity laws.

*

18. *Oh, she's cried, let me tell you,*
    to a god long beatified
    by a theological life and
    a philosophical death.
    He's as deaf as a post, as we say.
    But let's listen a little more carefully.
    There may be more than one quiet word,
    More than one quiet breath.

*

These bodies are struck with illnesses that make visible what is supposed to remain invisible. Jehoram's and Uzziah's diseases are explicitly *excretory*, anal in the case of Jehoram and dermatological in the case of Uzziah (and perhaps even Asa, though we cannot be sure). Jehoram's insides literally come out, and Uzziah suffers a disease that pollutes the skin, that secure barrier between the inside and outside of the body. Asa's illness renders his body as defiled, according to your priestly laws, because of the strict taboo against the defective body.[41] Whether or not his illness is explicitly excretory, you do not tell us. However, we can say that Asa's disease, like Jehoram's and Uzziah's diseases, renders his body as abject. In other words, the boundary between inside and out breaks down with the bodies of these three kings.[42] Given that your cultic identity depends upon the strict adherence to laws concerning the inside and outside (especially of the temple, as the priests remind Uzziah), the bodies of these kings literally mark them as thorough contradictions of your law and order, your social and political order that takes place after the murder of Saul.

Indeed, these bodies return me to Saul and *his* strange body. As I have suggested earlier, what generates the story of Israel's monarchic and cultic past, what functions as narrative "origin" for you, is the murder of the feminized and maternalized bodies of Saul and of his sons: the murder/silencing of the feminine constitutes the generative origin of socio-political hi(story). Furthermore, Saul consults with the (feminine) underworld, the world of the dead. As such, he transgresses the boundary between proper and improper, between purity and impurity, between life and death, between masculine and feminine. This is the principal crime you cite as the reason for Yahweh's punishment of Saul (his penetration by the sword, and the humiliation of his broken body by the Philistines, who take and parade his severed head and his armour, leaving his [presumably] naked body behind: 1 Chron. 10:9-10). But is not Saul himself a contradiction of your logic of purity – a male character with a feminized, penetrable, container-like body? Indeed, we might say that Saul, Asa, Jehoram, and Uzziah are more than just contradictions of your social order; they *figure* the breakdown of the (fragile) boundary necessary to keep your (Symbolic, social) order in place, the order required to maintain masculine identity. The bodies of these male characters dangerously merge inside and outside; they blur the boundary.

Clearly, I am fascinated by your male bodies. In the genealogies, the masculine forms of the verb root ילד ("to bear") imply that the act of birthing – reproduction – is appropriable by the masculine subject. Indeed, we heard of how, despite the overwhelmingly reductive association of women with the maternal *function*, the genealogical discourse functions according to the denial or disavowal of maternal-corporeal origins, a silencing of corporeal origins which generates and sustains the phantasy of masculine mono-production. And, at the very beginning of the narrative account of the past, Saul is given a penetrable feminine-maternal body, as are his sons. The murder of Saul and his sons is readable as a further silencing of the feminine through the murder of the maternal(ized) body and its line (the mother-daughter line). This story functions, then, as a narrative account of the primary *repression* required to sustain the particular masculine identity in relation to narrative history: the repression of the maternal body and the mother-daughter genealogy institutes the *properly masculine* subject of history. This masculine subject has no debts to maternal matter, no debts to nature. Actually, if we consider that in Chronicles Jacob/Israel produces the twelve sons who constitute the twelve tribes (Israel produces Israel), then the phantasy of mono-sexual production is also, in Chronicles, a phantasy of masculine *auto-production*, of the (male) self able to give birth to himself.[43]

In the previous chapter, I have argued that the phantasy of masculine mono-sexual production sustains the genealogical construction of your past in Chronicles. This phantasy is dependent upon your *disavowal* of the maternal body as origin. Patrilineal, mono-sexual logic continues with the narrative of Chronicles. However, here in analysis I have determined the *necessarily repressed* status of the maternal body. More than a simple disavowal of maternal origins ("I know I am born of woman, but all the same...") that enables "man" to appropriate the act of birthing as his own – to become the *subject* of the birthing verb – in the narrative of Chronicles we find that the maternal body as origin of the masculine subject is what must be repressed so that "he" may see himself as the sole, productive, clean and proper subject of history. Your story of the murder of Saul and his sons is readable as a narrative of this original repression that generates the properly patrilineal succession narratives. Thus murdered, "she" enables you to tell your story without acknowledging "her" role in your origins. You are able to repress any debt to nature and function as a purely symbolic (and thus immortal?) entity. Very problematic, however, is "her" insistent return at certain points in the narrative, threatening your cultic and socio-political order.

Jehoram is punished by giving "birth" to his bowels/womb. This punishment can be read symptomatically as a return of the repressed maternal body, of material-maternal origins. Jehoram, a man, is capable of something akin to birth: anal birthing if you like.[44] That this "birth" constitutes a punishment means that not only are Jehoram's women and children taken from him but he has also lost the capacity to produce by himself. When your identity hinges on the phantasy of mono-sexual production, such a bowel disease is also the death of Symbolic subjectivity/productivity for you. Furthermore, Uzziah's and Asa's punished bodies are also diseased, with the skin in Uzziah's case breaking open to let the inside out. Asa's abject body is too much of a reminder of the body's debt to nature. Thus, their bodies suffer the breakdown of the stable barrier separating inside (the invisible, unknowable, maternal-feminine) from the outside (the visible, knowable, paternal-masculine). In other words, their diseases allow the unrepresentable, (dis)order of maternal nature to leak into the realm of the representable order of paternal culture. Their punishment consists of a defiling *return of the maternal-feminine*.[45] This bodily seepage makes visible what is supposed to remain invisible: the debts to nature in general and to the maternal body specifically that every bodily subject of culture owes.[46]

In other words, when your principal and necessary phantasy of mono-sexual production – the auto-productive male body – reveals itself by letting slip the necessary repression of the maternal body required to sustain that phantasy, the masculine subject becomes very unstable, as does your monarchy. The long periods of time when the kings are diseased imply that the kings are unable to rule and they certainly would not be allowed entry into the temple. But, why these three kings? What is it about their stories that causes you to let your guard down, let the mother's body slip past the censor and onto the stage, thus rendering her silence as audible and readable? Let us now take a closer look at their stories. First of all, two of these kings are associated with problematic women. Jehoram is married to Athaliah, daughter of Ahab, king of Israel. She murders all of the royal children (except for one) and reigns for six years in Judah. Asa's mother, Maacah, commits the serious crime of making an idol for Asherah. Most importantly, however, is the fact that these are also the only two mothers in the narrative that are engaged in representational activity in some way: verbal speech in Athaliah's case and creative, imagistic production (visual speech) of the feminine as divine, in the case of Maacah. We have heard how problematic Jabez's mother's speech was for you in 1 Chronicles 4:9, so an attentive listening to the stories of these two mothers in the narrative now seems in order. Following this, I shall return to Uzziah, who is not associated with a mother who speaks or creates. We shall have to delve a little deeper, I suspect, in his particular case.

*

19.　*How we've come to depend upon you!*
　　We are not totally innocent
　　And yet you know no other way beyond
　　A loathing of any other voice
　　That might quench your dust-dry thirst
　　So you stick your fingers in your ears
　　And place your tongue in places known
　　Only to your very special kind
　　While she and I
　　Stare vacantly
　　Into a then, a now, even a perhaps
　　And can only feel ourselves on loan.

*

8. The Problematic Representation of the Mother

In your narrative, there are a number of mothers, most of whom are simply named, usually as part of the regnal formulae. They apparently have no story, let alone speech.[47] Actually, while there are far less women mentioned and/or named in the narrative than the genealogies, just as with the genealogical chapters (1 Chronicles 1–9), when they are present in the narrative they are generally associated with maternity.[48] There are, however, only seven female figures that we can really deem to be characters (figures who are integral to the narrative in some way) in this story. They are Pharaoh's daughter, Michal, Maacah (Asa's mother), Jehoshebeath, the Queen of Sheba, Athaliah, and Huldah. It is only the last three who are provided with verbal speech in their stories. Only two of these seven characters, Athaliah and Maacah, are mothers. While I would dearly love to listen to the words of Huldah, and the Queen of Sheba especially, I am going to limit my listening here to the two mothers in this re-telling of the past because, firstly, as I have mentioned, they are both mothers in close association with kings whose bodies suffer diseases that I have argued are instances of the return of the repressed maternal body. And secondly, because the speech of Jabez's mother in 1 Chronicles 4:9 was so problematic for you that I want to persist with the question of why the mother's speech is so threatening to you. Athaliah is the only other mother given verbal speech in Chronicles, and her speech is murderous. Asa's mother doesn't speak verbally. However, her creative production, I shall argue, speaks volumes.

8.1. *The Mother's Murderous Words (2 Chronicles 22:10)*

We are first introduced to Athaliah in 2 Chronicles 21:6, where you inform us that Jehoram "walked in the way of the kings of Israel, as the house of Ahab had done; for the daughter of Ahab was his wife. And he did what was evil in the sight of Yahweh." This daughter of Ahab is Athaliah. Though she is not named as such, we know this to be the case because you eventually reveal, in 2 Chronicles 22:2, that Ahaziah's mother is Athaliah, the granddaughter of Omri,[49] who is the father of Ahab. Furthermore, it seems Athaliah has considerable influence over her husband, and their son after him. Ahaziah also "walked in the ways of the house of Ahab, for his mother was his counselor in doing wickedly. He did what was evil in the sight of Yahweh, as the house of Ahab had done; for after the death of his father they were his counselors, to his undoing" (2 Chron. 22:3-4). Athaliah's influence is responsible for the wrong doings of both her husband and her son. We know, then, from the beginning of her story, that she is a treacherous figure in your eyes.

Importantly, she is also the only mother that speaks in your narrative. Jabez's un-named mother (1 Chron. 4:9) and Athaliah are the only two mothers in Chronicles who are given verbal speech, the former in the genealogies, the latter in the narrative. Eventually, Athaliah becomes a queen who reigns for six years in Judah, though she is never referred to as "queen" (מַלְכָּה) but only as a "mother":

וַעֲתַלְיָהוּ֙ אֵ֣ם אֲחַזְיָ֔הוּ רָאֲתָ֖ה כִּ֣י מֵ֣ת
בְּנָ֑הּ וַתָּ֗קָם וַתְּדַבֵּ֛ר אֶת־כָּל־זֶ֥רַע הַמַּמְלָכָ֖ה לְבֵ֥ית יְהוּדָֽה׃

And Athaliah, the mother of Ahaziah, saw that her son had died, and she arose (וַתָּקָם) and she spoke (וַתְּדַבֵּר) with all the progeny (כָּל־זֶרַע lit. "all the seed") of the kingdom in the house of Judah (2 Chron. 22:10).

While we are not told what her spoken words are, it seems that Athaliah's speech is murderous. The following verse tells us that Joash's sister, Jehoshabeath, saves him from the fate of the other young princes, who are murdered by Athaliah:

וַתִּקַּח֩ יְהוֹשַׁבְעַ֨ת בַּת־הַמֶּ֜לֶךְ אֶת־יוֹאָ֣שׁ

בֶּן־אֲחַזְיָ֗הוּ וַתִּגְנֹ֤ב אֹתוֹ֙ מִתּ֣וֹךְ בְּנֵֽי־הַמֶּ֙לֶךְ֙ הַמּ֣וּמָתִ֔ים וַתִּתֵּ֨ן

אֹת֤וֹ וְאֶת־מֵינִקְתּוֹ֙ בַּחֲדַ֣ר הַמִּטּ֔וֹת וַתַּסְתִּירֵ֜הוּ יְהוֹשַׁבְעַ֣ת

בַּת־הַמֶּ֣לֶךְ יְהוֹרָ֗ם אֵ֨שֶׁת יְהוֹיָדָ֤ע הַכֹּהֵן֙ כִּ֣י הִ֗יא הָיְתָה֙ אֲח֣וֹת

אֲחַזְיָ֔הוּ מִפְּנֵ֥י עֲתַלְיָ֖הוּ וְלֹ֥א הֱמִיתָֽתְהוּ׃

> Jehoshabeath, the daughter of the king, stealthily took Joash, the son of Ahaziah, from among the sons of the king being killed, and she put him and his nurse in the room of couches. Jehoshabeath, daughter of king Jehoram, wife of Jehoiada the priest, hid him from Athaliah because she was the sister of Ahaziah. And she did not kill him (2 Chron. 22:11).

So, Athaliah hears of her son's murder, kills the rest of the king's sons (her grandsons), and rules "over the land" for six years (22:12). However, instead of simply saying that Athaliah murders the royal sons, you mention that she speaks with them, all the offspring of the royal family of Judah (וַתְּדַבֵּר֙ אֶת־כָּל־זֶ֣רַע הַמַּמְלָכָ֔ה לְבֵ֖ית יְהוּדָֽה). This way of describing her actions seems curious indeed. The use of the verb root דבר "to speak" may seem odd given that the effects of Athaliah's actions in 22:11 are the murder of the king's sons.[50] However, I wish to point out that just as with your account of Jabez's mother, here a mother's speech threatens the coherence and continuity of the male line. You are consistent in this respect in both the genealogy and the narrative. Here, however, in the narrative concerning Athaliah, this threat of maternal speech is made explicit. Her speech effectively murders the sons and threatens both the Davidic line and patriliny itself. Dramatically, male-only rule and male succession – the fundamental mechanics of your narrative machinery – have ceased for the moment, as a consequence of a mother's words.

 Jehoshabeath (who may be Athaliah's daughter, though you do not tell us explicitly whether this is so, only that she is Jehoram's daughter and Ahaziah's sister; the mother-daugter relationship is, after all, of no concern to you) hides Joash, the now fatherless son whose story prematurely arises with the murder of his brothers by his father's mother. Importantly, she hides him in the room of couches (or bedchamber) in the temple. We find ourselves in the intimate heart of the symbolic father's house (the temple) protected from the murderous (grand)mother who speaks. Is it possible that we are in the Holy of Holies, the womb of the temple?[51] Jehoshebeath (Athaliah's own daughter?) protects the Davidic line, the blessed line of patrilineal succession, by hiding the only surviving son in the house that glorifies the father and his name; such a dutiful father's daughter. Even her name bears allegiance to the father, for in Hebrew Jehoshabeath means "Yahweh is an oath." The speech act, oath, and its synonymity with the symbolic father Yahweh, is almost in contradiction to Athaliah's murderous speech act, which threatens to bring down the system of patriliny and patriarchal rule itself. The daughter is branded with a name that bears witness to her allegiance to the father (and his form as/of speech).

Interestingly, the issue of cultic purity arises within this story of a ruling mother. In the seventh year of Athaliah's reign, Jehoiada (priest and husband of Jehoshabeath) gathers the army together (23:1) and plots to depose Athaliah and return the Davidic king to the throne. As part of his plan, he instructs the men he has garnered – the Captains of the Hundreds, the Levites from all the cities of Judah, and the heads of the father's (houses) in Israel – to protect the king's house and the house of Yahweh. Furthermore, he says,

וְאַל־יָבֹוא בֵית־יְהֹוָה כִּי אִם־הַכֹּהֲנִים

וְהַמְשָׁרְתִים לַלְוִיִּם הֵמָּה יָבֹאוּ כִּי־קֹדֶשׁ הֵמָּה וְכָל־הָעָם

יִשְׁמְרוּ מִשְׁמֶרֶת יְהוָה:

Let no one into the house of Yahweh, except the priests and the Levites who minister. They may come in, for they are holy. And all the people will keep a watchful guard of Yahweh (2 Chron. 23:6).

The final sentence in this verse is rather strange. Is Yahweh present, and indeed, guard-able by people? Apart from that odd comment, has the father (Yahweh) literally returned with the presence of Athaliah, of "Israel," ruling Judah? I note that the issues of holiness and the threat of impurity have arisen. Also, when Athaliah reappears in the story, she comes towards the people and the house of Yahweh (23:12). At that moment she realizes that they have made Joash king and she tears her garments and says קֶשֶׁר קָשֶׁר ("Greatest of conspiracies!"; 23:13). At this point Jehoiada instructs the captains of the hundreds to

הֹוצִיאוּהָ אֶל־מִבֵּית הַשְּׂדֵרֹות וְהַבָּא אַחֲרֶיהָ יוּמַת בֶּחָרֶב

כִּי אָמַר הַכֹּהֵן לֹא תְמִיתוּהָ בֵּית יְהוָה:

"Bring her out from between the ranks and anyone who follows her will be killed by the sword," for the priest said, "You will not kill her (in?) the house of Yahweh" (23:14).

So, they bring her to the gate of horses (שַׁעַר הַסוּסִים) and kill her there (23:15). To depose a woman and return to your preferred system of patrilineal succession (which I have shown in both this and the previous chapter depends upon the disavowal and repression of the maternal body) requires careful consideration and protection of the holiest space that houses the symbolic father, the name of Yahweh and his law. When Athaliah cries out קֶשֶׁר קָשֶׁר ("Greatest of conspiracies!") it seems obvious that she is referring to Jehoiada's conspiracy. However, I think another reading is also possible. Her expression is *hyperbolic*. Through the hyperbole of the spoken words of this ruling woman/mother, can we not hear "woman" straining to charge you with a violent crime against her: the conspiratorial binding of men together against "woman" for the use of her (silenced) body as foundation and guarantee of their holy order. I think this is why Athaliah must be killed twice (23:15, 21): firstly, and simply, because she is a mother who speaks, and her speech has undone patrilineal patriarchy for six years, and secondly, because she literally figures the return of the repressed (silenced) maternal body.

8.2. *"A Horrid Thing," a "Thing to Shudder at" (2 Chronicles 15:16)*

Maacah, Asa's mother, is also a mother engaged in representational activity, though her speech is visual not verbal. Before Asa is punished with his foot disease, we encounter a strange moment in 2 Chronicles 15. This event occurs after the words of warning from the prophet Azaria son of Oded concerning Yahweh's willingness to be with his people so long as they are with him (15:2-7), and follows Asa's reforms (vv. 8-15). Asa removes his mother Maacah from her position as גְּבִירָה ("powerful woman," usually poorly translated as "queen mother") "because she made for Asherah a מִפְלֶצֶת (a "horrid thing" or "thing to shudder at"):

וְגַם־מַעֲכָה אֵם׀ אָסָא הַמֶּלֶךְ הֱסִירָהּ מִגְּבִירָה אֲשֶׁר־עָשְׂתָה
לַאֲשֵׁרָה מִפְלָצֶת וַיִּכְרֹת אָסָא אֶת־מִפְלַצְתָּהּ וַיָּדֶק וַיִּשְׂרֹף בְּנַחַל
קִדְרוֹן׃

And also, he deposed Maacah, the mother of King Asa, from her position of power (גְּבִירָה), for she had made a horrid thing (מִפְלֶצֶת; "a thing to shudder at") for Asherah. And Asa cut down (וַיִּכְרֹת) her horrid thing, pulverized (it) into dust (וַיָּדֶק), and he burnt (וַיִּשְׂרֹף) (it) in the Wadi Kidron (2 Chron. 15:16).

It would seem that the mother practices a different religion from her son, one that is not to be tolerated. Here the king's mother is worshipping Asherah, a Canaanite goddess of happiness, while her son has entered

into a covenant with Yahweh, "the god of their fathers" (אֱלֹהֵי אֲבוֹתֵיהֶם;
2 Chron. 15:12). In fact, Asa has spent quite a bit of his reign ridding
the land of the foreign altars (מִזְבְּחוֹת הַנֵּכָר), the high places (הַבָּמוֹת),
the sun pillars (הַחַמָּנִים; 14:2; 4), shattering the sacred pillars (הַמַּצֵּבוֹת),
hewing down the asherim (הָאֲשֵׁרִים; 14:2), and taking away the detested
things (הַשִּׁקֻּצִים) from the land of Judah, Benjamin, and the cities he had
taken from the hill country of Ephraim (15:8). This act of his, destroying
an idol, is consistent with his dedication to destroying anything that is
against the laws of Yahweh.

It is worth noting that there is some ambiguity as to what exactly
Maacah has made for the goddess. The word here is מִפְלָצֶת – "a horrid
thing" or "a thing to shudder at." This word appears only in relation to
Maacah's story.[52] What she makes for Asherah is not a sacred pillar or
אֲשֵׁרָה (tree or pole). This מִפְלָצֶת is no simple idol, but something worse,
something that could make one fear for one's life, indeed something that
causes one's *body* to be affected, something that must be utterly ground
down to dust and (somewhat redundantly, even impotently) burnt in the
dry Wadi Kidron. Actually, Asa does not just grind it into dust. וַיָּדֶק is
the (causative) Hiph'il form of דקק (which means to crush, pulverize,
thresh, or to be fine). This stronger form of the verb expresses greater
subjective agency on the part of Asa. He doesn't just pulverize the horrid
thing, he pounds it and pounds it until it is dust.[53]

Is it simply that Maacah makes an image of a divinity that troubles you,
or is it that she makes an image of the feminine as divine? Wouldn't this
make you shudder, bring your body very viscerally to the surface? Not
only would the feminine be divinized, but there would be an exchange
taking place between two female figures, Maacah, the king's mother,
and Asherah, the goddess of happiness. The image would be feminine
and the exchange would be between two women, one human, the other
divine.[54] Furthermore, by offering an image of the female form, the distance between the material and the transcendent would be traversed
and brought into proximity. This feminine imagery would challenge the
very ground of material existence, the unacknowledged building block
of sacred space that guarantees the *containment* of the divine as *masculine* (as we heard earlier with the description of your temple). Does this
exchange *of* the feminine and *between* the feminine bring materiality and
divinity into a sensuate embrace, so much so that the mediating thing is,
in this instance, something to shudder at, something to cause the gravest
fears? Is this proximity of the human with the divine the reason for Asa
seeking (somewhat hysterically) to destroy the מִפְלָצֶת? There are indeed,

many possibilities. Let me, nevertheless, suggest that whatever the case, the pressing threat, here, is an exchange between women – a symbolic exchange between women of language and speech. An exchange, if you like, between mother and daughter. Perhaps what Maacah really represents for you is the threat of a woman-to-woman sociality.[55] This would, of course, be significant as up until this point you've been successful in silencing the possibility of such a thing. There are no words expressed between mother and daughter. Maacah, herself is given no words. And yet, it is clear from your account that she disturbs you.

Furthermore, if we return to 1 Chronicles 4:9, Jabez's mother's poetic naming speech, we can recall that she plays with the word for pain (עֶצֶב). Jabez's name (יַעְבֵּץ) comes about through his mother's rearrangement of consonants, taking poetic licence to give his name something of an etymology:

וְאִמּוֹ קָרְאָה שְׁמוֹ יַעְבֵּץ לֵאמֹר כִּי יָלַדְתִּי בְּעֹצֶב

But his mother called his name Jabez, saying "for I bore in pain."

But importantly for our discussion here, consonantally this word עצב can also mean "to shape or fashion." Furthermore, related to this verb root is the noun, עָצָב, "idol." I have suggested in the previous chapter that Jabez's mother's creative play with words, which speaks to the productive maternal body in pain, also evokes a mediating figure between the human and the divine, perhaps even one created by her. Her speech act not only refers directly to her birthing body in pain but also evokes the creativity of fashioning an object of divinity. Remember that Jabez has no paternal line; he has no discernible paternal ancestry, no line of sons issuing forth from him, and thus no story at all. I have argued that Jabez is frozen in history with a mother who dared to play poetically with words, dared to speak about her birthing experience, dared to bring her maternal body into language, and dared even to equate this maternal body with the divine and her representation.

I think when we bring Jabez's mother speech, Athaliah's murderous speech, her hyperbolic declaration of conspiracy, and Maacah's creative act together, we can understand why Asa and Jehoram are inflicted with these specific illnesses. These are diseases that break down the boundary between inside and outside, purity and impurity, etcetera, illnesses that reveal both the phantasy of mono-sexual production required to sustain patriarchal social order, and the necessary disavowal and repression of the maternal body required to maintain that phantasy, as I argued earlier. Both Jehoram and Asa are associated with mothers engaged in symbolic, representational activity, or – simply – speech (verbal and visual). According to you, all production (speaking, writing, creating, even reproduction) belongs to the masculine. The feminine, but especially the maternal-feminine, is situated at the site of silence *within* your representational framework. Thus, when a mother actually speaks, your patriarchal social order and patrilineal succession is threatened not only with disorder, but the end of the son's story in relation to the father. When a mother speaks (verbally or through images) the phantasy of masculine, mono-sexual production breaks down in your particular account of the past and of Israel's origins.

But what about Uzziah? He is not associated with a mother who "speaks." Only her name, Jecoliah of Jerusalem, is provided (2 Chron. 26:3). Furthermore, there is no mention in Uzziah's story of women or wives. Why is Uzziah struck with a similar, excretory illness? There is a curious statement about Uzziah in 2 Chronicles 26:10 that, I think, provides us with an answer:

וַיִּבֶן מִגְדָּלִים בַּמִּדְבָּר וַיַּחְצֹב בֹּרוֹת רַבִּים כִּי מִקְנֶה־רַּב
הָיָה לֹו וּבַשְּׁפֵלָה וּבַמִּישׁוֹר אִכָּרִים וְכֹרְמִים בֶּהָרִים וּבַכַּרְמֶל
כִּי־אֹהֵב אֲדָמָה הָיָה:

And he built towers in the wilderness (בַּמִּדְבָּר). He dug many wells because he had many cattle in the lowland and in the plain, and he had farmers tending the vineyards in the hill country and in the fertile garden lands, for he loved the earth (2 Chron. 26:10).

Uzziah *loves the earth or soil* (כִּי־אֹהֵב אֲדָמָה הָיָה). In fact, this verse tells us quite a lot about Uzziah. He is a lover of nature, and he looks after it. He loves the soil. Uzziah has a lot of respect for *natural* productivity, something your entire discourse struggles against. But that first sentence is also very interesting. Uzziah builds towers in the wilderness (בַּמִּדְבָּר). This word, wilderness (מִדְבָּר), however, also means "mouth, as an organ of speech." Furthermore, the preposition בּ can mean "in," "with," "at," "by," but it can also mean "against." We can actually translate the sentence as "And he built towers against the mouth, as an organ of speech," though that seems to make little sense.

*

20. *Your problems with him are audible now?*
And he senses something of a leak in us
That clogs our hearts
In a yearning for him,
For us, for we.

But instead you consume your little ones
The ones you love like rare, cool fabric
For only in a known, sweaty fibre-
Voice you speak
Of you, of he.
Of me?

But listen. He is so angry. His anger flares
And we're alight.
He burns just the same.

*

And yet, a word relating to speech arising in this verse, which is largely about Uzziah's love for nature, may not be as nonsensical as it at first seems. A *nature-loving* king who builds monuments *against* the mouth as an organ of speech – that is, against what, in your discourse, is the means by which the male subject is symbolically "born" – is logically consistent. You prefer the image of yourself as self-made without debts to nature, especially without debts to your original enclave in nature – the maternal body. Your debts are purely symbolic. Uzziah's love for nature points, unbearably for you, to your debt to nature. This must be too close to acknowledging that other material source: the maternal body. I think that there is definitely a consistency here. Loving the earth (אֲדָמָה) requires punishment by a disease that signifies a debt to nature and thus destitutes Uzziah as clean and proper (masculine) subject of the Symbolic.

Arguably, all of these three kings, Jehoram, Asa, and Uzziah, allow the debt to nature, and to the maternal body, on to your stage. Your social, political, and cultic order depends upon the silence (the denial and repression) of that debt; the silence of the mother is thus not only the absence of her speech (though her speech is terribly problematic for you). You most effectively silence her through the disavowal and repression of the maternal body.

9. Conclusion

In this chapter, I have argued that the narrative of Chronicles represses the debt of the masculine subject to nature, but more specifically to the maternal body. I have suggested that the curious "beginning" of the Chronicles narrative – the murder of Saul and his sons – can be read symptomatically as a narrative of this *original repression of the maternal body*, the repression that generates the properly patrilineal succession narratives that follow. I have also pointed out that this story of the origins of this particular patrilineal, patriarchal history has *already* silenced the maternal. The "beginning" of Israel's political and cultic order is the murder of a man and his sons. But these are *male* bodies that also "bear" the traces of the maternal body. Already, the mother is absent from the story; she is already silenced. Her body is repressed to allow the mirage of masculine-only production. The maternal body (even a genealogy of maternalized bodies) serves as a prop, at the beginning, for the retelling of this masculine past concerning the institution of patriarchal, socio-political and religious history. Woman and her reproductive body has been reduced to a useful prop, and even further reduced to a useful abstraction (a unit of spatial measurement).

The temporal logic of the Chronicles narrative, like the genealogies, is patrilineal. Time and story move forward through the production of sons. And just as with the genealogies, in the narrative this patrilineal logic effects a tension between father and son. The father must produce a son so that the patrilineal machinery keeps moving. However, in producing a son, he guarantees the eventual ending of his own story, his own eventual silence. I have argued, however, that the father is compensated in many ways for this silence, while the mother is not compensated in any way at all. The "place" of the father is literally made divine when Yahweh becomes the "father" of Solomon (1 Chron. 17:13). The name "Israel" is given to Jacob, the father of the twelve eponymous tribes of Israel. The father's name, "Israel," comes to represent the entire people of Yahweh. And finally, and most importantly, I think, the son builds a monumental, sacred house for the father's *name*.

In Chronicles, however, this temple is portrayed as doubly-sexed. This sacred space for the father and his worship is both phallic (represented by the impossibly enormous erection of the vestibule) and maternal (represented by the enclosed space of the internal chambers, especially by the particular enclosure of the Holy of Holies as described in Chronicles). This double-sexing of the temple figures the phantasy of mono-sexual production, the phantasy of the male body with a womb – the "phallic-womb" – the phantasy that, I have argued, undergirds the "reality of history" according to Chronicles. The description of the temple in Chronicles is thus also a testimony to the necessary status of the maternal body as repressed. This sacred house, built for the "father" and his name, reveals the necessary phantasy needed to sustain the deified name and place of the father: it is a phallic body with a (virgin) womb. The father is contained and, importantly, restrained within the virgin mother. No threat of any sexual activity between these two, activity that might allow that unbearable body to assert its necessity and remind us of our debts to her. Indeed, it is the virgin status of this maternalized space that thus enables the phantasy of the auto-productive (male) body. This displaced appearance of the virgin-mother points to the other necessary repression: sexual difference. Repressing the idea of corporeal pleasure between the father and the mother as distinct sexuate beings enables "man" to believe himself to be the product of paternal labour only, or even self-generated (Israel, the father, and Israel, the sons, are symbolically equivalent in Chronicles, "bearing" the same name).

I also have listened carefully, in this chapter, for the return of that repressed body throughout the narrative. I have argued that the repressed maternal body returns in the form of strange bodily disease. Jehoram, Asa, and Uzziah are the three kings whose bodies signify the breakdown of the barrier separating inside (the invisible, unknowable, maternal-feminine) from the outside (the visible, knowable, paternal-masculine). In other words, their diseases indicate the unrepresentable, (dis)order of maternal nature, with the repressed thus leaking into the realm of the representable order of paternal culture. I have suggested that their pun-ishment by disease consists of a defiling *return of the maternal-feminine*, making visible and audible what is supposed to remain invisible and inau-dible: the debts to nature in general and to the maternal body specifically that every bodily subject of culture owes. The repression of these debts thus sustains both the logic of mono-sexual masculine production *and* the social, political, and cultic order structured by the strict imposition of a distinction between inside and outside.

*

21.   *It's difficult,*
      But, I'll not speak for her
      Because I am the one
      that got away
      from the carnivalé terror
      To the land of questions
      and curious answers
      Offered full of breath
      That sways the hips
      Of words in dance
      In love and health all
      Fibrously in splendour.

*

I was curious as to what these kings had done to deserve such punish-ment. Of course, Asa, like Saul, breaches the law, apparently, by going to a source of knowledge other than Yahweh (the necromancer, in Saul's case, and the physicians in Asa's case. Asa also punishes one of Yahweh's seers). Both Saul and Asa cross over the boundary line, if you like, to a different source not acknowledged as "within" the law (that is, they go to sources of knowledge that are not Yahweh). So, too, Uzziah and Jehoram behave in ways deemed to be in transgression of Yahweh's law.[56] Uzziah breaches the boundary of cultic law and order by lighting the incense in the temple. Jehoram follows the ways of the kings of Israel, causing fornication (either literal or religious). However, the similarities between the three diseased kings and the abject body of Saul have led me to another feature that they share.

I have demonstrated that these three kings are too closely associated with what constitutes "silence" in this discourse: the maternal body as subject (and not simply an appropriable object) of representation, and nature. Jehoram's wife is Athaliah, the mother whose speech eventually, *literally* succeeds in ending patriarchal rule for a period of time, and almost succeeds in destroying the system of patrilineal succession. Asa's mother, Maacah, produces a figure of the feminine as divine. I have suggested that what is really threatening about Maacah's creative act, within the context of Chronicles, is the idea of symbolic exchange between women – an exchange of language and speech, produced by and for women, by and for the mother and her daughter. It is the threat of a woman-to-woman sociality. Finally, Uzziah loves and respects nature. In this particular retelling of the past, natural-corporeal/material-maternal origins have been repressed to enable the masculine subject to perceive himself as debt-free. The type of punishment inflicted upon these kings (diseases that render the inside visible, blurring the boundary in the process) reveals both the logic of patriarchal order, and what must remain unheard (unrepresentable) in order to sustain that order. Through the bodies of these kings who are too closely associated with the maternal subject and with nature, natural, corporeal-maternal origins become readable as what must remain silenced. This necessary silence of the maternal body in this masculine discourse becomes audible.

*

22. *Remember, dear, what has*
    Happened to us.
    I saw you recently with your memory unlaced
    And food for you is nothing but disgrace
    But how I loved you, still
    Remembering your worker hands

That skimmed the pretty things
In lunchtime department stores;
Your style inherited from somewhere
(your mum?)
and passed down to us who've
been schooled in the question
enough to know its elegance,
its charms, its arts, its flaws.

*

9.1. *Figuring Sexual Difference?*

But something about the cherubim in the temple intrigues me. I have argued that the doubly-sexed cherub replicates the doubly-sexed structure of the temple itself. However, I now want to ask if there is not another way we might read these strange cherubim figures in Chronicles. Returning to my earlier discussion in Chapter 2, I am basing this question on Irigaray's insistence that, when it comes to reading the foundational texts of our culture, the critical or analytical reading, while utterly necessary, is, on its own, inadequate:

> The myths and stories, the sacred texts are analyzed, sometimes with nostalgia but rarely with a mind to change the social order. The texts are merely consumed or reconsumed, in a way. The darkness of our imaginary or symbolic horizon is analyzed more or less adequately, but not with the goal of founding a new ethics. The techniques of reading, translating, and explaining take over the domain of the sacred, the religious, the mythical, but they fail to reveal a world that measures up to the material they are consuming or consummating (Irigaray, 1993: 86).

Clearly Irigaray advocates a particular reading strategy, especially with respect to our "sacred" texts, and it is a strategy that is less concerned with knowing the past than it is with rethinking our present and future. For Irigaray, when we read the texts of our past we need to search for "what remains to be discovered, especially the forgotten future in the past."

And so, I ask the following: each cherub is given both sexes, but together, do they long for each other as distinct sexual beings, a longing for sexual difference despite the imposed double-sexing of their own being? Why not have unambiguously feminine cherubim? How are we to understand this desperate verbal instance where a feminine wing cleaves to a masculine wing? If she simply wanted the masculine, could "she" not have turned inwards towards her bi-gendered self, cleaving to the masculine wing on this/her doubly-sexed body? Instead, "she" reaches out beyond to a different "being," or rather, to the masculine wing of the *other* cherub. And let's not forget that these curiously double-sexed cherubim have been placed in the holiest space in the building, that womb-like space sealed only by a curtain, not a door or a wall.[57] Do these angels protest such a structure, portents of a yet-to-be sacrality, which we can recognize, but ultimately must conceal (and yet, alas, cannot)? Do they protest the asexual status of the mother and father (indeed, anticipatorially, do they reject Freud)? This desperate feminine act, reaching out for, holding on to, but more strongly *cleaving* to that masculine wing that belongs to the other begs us, I think, to consider the possibility of a sexual and sexuated difference. In other words, these strange, ancient, doubly-sexed cherubim ask us to consider the possibility of a yet-to-exist, genuinely heterosexual economy (a radical heterosexuality: the love that dares not speak its name?), one that refuses the phantasy of mono-sexual, masculine production. This cleaving feminine wing belongs to a doubly-sexed entity as do Saul and Jehoram explicitly, and Asa and Uzziah more implicitly through the seepage of the maternal that their bodies betray, in Chronicles. But does "she," who is housed and protected (why?) in that most holy space, not ask us, even perhaps (silently, yet, now *audibly*) beg us, to set her free? Perhaps her rejection of this imposed foreign gender will be painful, like Jehoram's, Asa's, and Uzziah's punishment. Perhaps she is willing to endure that. Perhaps the day will come when the pain will have actual rewards, if it happens at all. But most importantly, I think, she wants us to set her free so she may love the other, the masculine who, here, himself, can only, simply, reach for her. We need to hear this.

Conclusion

In both the genealogical discourse (1 Chronicles 1–9) and the narrative section of Chronicles (1 Chronicles 10–2 Chronicles 36), the "feminine" is understood primarily as the symbolic (re)producer of the masculine *for man*: "she" is the (silent) mother of sons. Overwhelmingly, women are associated with this symbolic function. At the same time, however, the maternal body itself is rarely present in this construction of religio-political origins. Beginning with Adam (1 Chron. 1:1), with no sign of Eve, and beginning again with the murder of Saul (1 Chronicles 10), the one who inquires of the feminine, and his line, our analysand betrays his desire and indeed *need* for the recognition of paternal origins only. I have argued that while the disavowal and repression of corporeal maternal origins, along with the primary association of the "feminine" with the maternal function for men may seem like a contradiction, these two features of the textual discourses of Chronicles are in fact logically co-extensive. "Woman" is interned as the Symbolic site of reproduction (of the son), while her reproductive body represents the un-representable within that Symbolic order: the maternal body constitutes the principal silence of this masculine discursive production of the past. In other words, "woman," as the son's mother, is the *silent* mother.

Importantly, however, in Chronicles "woman" confounds the production of meaning which depends on the logic of patrilineal succession for its consistency. In the genealogies, where most of the female figures appear, they are associated with the production of "sons" for a particular male line. However, "she" disconcerts meaning and sense when "she" appears, more often than not in conjunction with the verb root יָלַד ("to bear"). These so-called birth narratives (De Vries, 1989) within the genealogy section (1 Chronicles 1–9), a form that does not really require a verb, are hardly even narratives. Other than the production of a name, they tell us nothing of the birth act itself. It is this decorporealized, symbolic understanding of "origin" that makes possible an appropriation of the verb, יָלַד, by the men of this story. Men appropriate this verb of giving birth. The masculine forms of the verb root יָלַד ("to bear") appear many more times than the feminine in the genealogies, and with far greater success in terms of the production of meaning and sense. When many of the feminine forms of the verb occur, meaning becomes fragmented.

In the narrative of Chronicles, we can perhaps attribute the virtual silence of women to their relative absence. However, I have shown that there is a more complex strategy of silencing women that is readable in the Chronicles narrative. Women are most radically silenced through the repressed status of the maternal body. I showed that the strangely violent, corporeal "beginning" of the Chronicles narrative – the murder of Saul and his sons – can be read symptomatically as a narrative of the *original repression of the maternal body*. This repression generates the properly patrilineal succession narratives that follow. Furthermore, the repressed status of the maternal body is readable through the diseased bodies of Jehoram, Asa, and Uzziah, whereupon the maternal body "returns." I argued that "her" return occurs at these points in the narrative because these kings are too closely associated with what constitutes "silence" in this discourse: the maternal body as subject (and not simply an appropriable object) of representation, and nature. Ironically, this close association allows us to hear this silence differently, for the return of the repressed maternal body makes the silence of women *audible*: in being reduced to the symbolic maternal function (and thus silenced because of the repressed and disavowed status of their maternal bodies), women have been silenced to enable the phantasy of mono-sexual, masculine production required to sustain this particular (masculine) literary (re)production of Israel's social, political, and cultic past.

In writing this particular book, bringing an Irigarayan mode of reading to the book of Chronicles, I have become aware of two important and related factors. Firstly, there is a constant risk of falling silent, of falling prey to that silenced maternal voice that constitutes my place in "his" discourse, of remaining the *son's* mother, the mother who has no female genealogy: no mother, and no daughter of her own. By this, I mean there is always a risk of "repenting" and rewriting in a traditional (masculine) mode, of remaining the dutiful father's daughter. Such a book would certainly have been easier to write. Secondly, I realize that a stylistic irony is apparent in this book. When I discuss the work of Irigaray in Part I, my own discourse belongs to what, I think, Irigaray would claim is a "masculine" mode of writing: argument through exposition. In Part II, however, while reading a *masculine* text, my mode shifts into something more akin to what, following Irigaray, I claim is a "feminine" mode of critical inquiry and writing, based on her re-theorization of the psychoanalytic setting: argument through psychoanalytic and poetic discourses. I came to realize that I needed to effect a "relation between" these two quite distinct sections. Indeed, I needed to effect this relation as a relation between the sexes, if you like, between the masculine mode of reading and writing (Part I) and the feminine mode (Part II). The endnotes became the first means through which this connection was made. I was able to return to many of the points I had made in that earlier section of the book. Importantly, this "return" was often to that discursive place that functioned as the origin of my own thinking and writing about Chronicles: the "maternal" texts of Irigaray. However, the endnotes also enabled me to cite certain arguments from traditional (masculine) Chronicles scholarship and, I hope, thus emphasized the need for the two to come together. In other words, the endnote discussions effect both the relation between the sections/sexes *and* the production and sustenance of the mother-daughter relationship, on the symbolic level. Crucially, the procedure of "return" to Irigaray at certain points in the latter section provided me with a sense of producing my own relation to symbolic maternal origins, a relation that kept me strong enough to persist, *indeed to insist on speaking*, with this masculine text, "as woman," "as the daughter's mother." Similarly, the poetic text enabled me to maintain a link to the world of women. The poems interrupt the usual flow of academic reading, problematizing, I think the progression of time for "you," my reader, reminding "you" that "I" have my own genealogy, another temporal progress. It is important to remember that, for Irigaray, sexual difference, indeed love between the sexes, is only possible once the mother-daughter relationship becomes Symbolically valuable, even audible. We currently still battle against a destructive lack of Symbolic difference, being interned as the Symbolically silent mother of the son. The mode of reading I have learned from Irigaray and brought to the book of Chronicles begins this process of reading and speaking as both the mother of a daughter, and the daughter of a mother.

As such, this book begins the work of constructing a future of reading that departs radically from the existing/traditional readings of Chronicles. For most of this book, I have been concerned with the question of what it means to read biblical texts "as a woman." My question concerning reading has been, and still is, artfully guided by a number of women writers, but most significantly Luce Irigaray and Michelle Boulous Walker, who is, herself, a reader of Irigaray. What I consider to be the most important contribution of this book is the introduction of what I have called a "mother-daughter" reading practice to biblical studies. All throughout the work of Luce Irigaray, the most exigent question concerns how women can articulate a return to and desire for maternal origins: how to create a genealogy of women. For Irigaray, this question is crucial because until women are able to do so, they remain trapped in a Symbolic system, in a language, that silences them *as women* so that only the masculine can sustain its valuable identity:

> In some way, the vertical dimension is always being taken away from female becoming. The bond between mother and daughter, daughter and mother, has to be broken for the daughter to become a woman. Female genealogy has to be suppressed, on behalf of the son-father relationship, and the idealization of the father and husband as patriarchs. But without a vertical dimension (since verticality has always been confused with erection), a loving ethical order cannot take place among women (Irigaray, 1993b: 108).

In other words, I think my reading of Chronicles demonstrates that when women read and engage with the work of other women, we can and do "undo" the silence of women in the texts of patriarchy. That I read the work of Michelle Boulous Walker and other women (Elizabeth Grosz, Elizabeth Hirsh, Margaret Whitford, etc.), who have also read the work of Luce Irigaray, establishes the strength of maternal verticality, if you like, of the mother-daughter line. And it also establishes a genealogical breadth of intellectual sisters: Irigaray's mode of reading, psychoanalytic in its practice, enables and validates an *intellectual woman-to-woman sociality*. And so, I give the penultimate word to Luce Irigaray, who reminds us that we need this sociality of women:

> If we are not to be accomplices in the murder of the mother we also need to assert that there is a genealogy of women. Each of us has a female family tree: we have a mother, a maternal grandmother and great-grandmothers, we have daughters. Because we have been exiled into the house of our husbands, it is easy to forget the special quality of female genealogy; we might even come to deny it. Let us try to situate ourselves within that female genealogy so that we can win and hold on to our identity (Irigaray, 1993a: 19).

And the final word?

מְהֵיטַבְאֵל בַּת־מַטְרֵד בַּת מֵי זָהָב:

Mehetavel, the daughter of Matred, the daughter of Me Zahab (1 Chron. 1:50).

God benefits the daughter of the continuing one, the daughter of the waters of gold.

Notes

Introduction

1. Of course, women have written on Chronicles (Sara Japhet [1979, 1993, 1997], Alice Laffey [1992], Christine Mitchell [1999], Kirsten Nielsen [1999]). However, they neither identify their readings as feminist readings, nor does the issue of women's absence in Chronicles concern them much. Alice Laffey's entry on Chronicles in the *Women's Bible Commentary* is little more than a role call that notes the present female characters and figures, as well as the omissions from and the additions to Samuel–Kings. As such, she practices the comparative approach that most Chronicles scholars employ.

2. The term is Dyck's (1998).

3. For a detailed discussion of the use of the term "all Israel" in Chronicles, see Japhet (1997: 265-78).

4. The genealogies give us fourteen tribes in total. For a good discussion of the discrepancy between the ideal of twelve and the actual number of tribes mentioned, see Japhet (1997: 278-85).

5. See Eskenazi (1988: 30-33). Mary Douglas (1993) provides an interesting analysis of post-exilic Judah, with regards to Numbers, arguing that we may discern in the final form of Numbers a distinctly inclusive, anti- Ezra/Nehemiah ideology. For an excellent critical discussion of Douglas' thesis, see Camp (2000: 216-26).

6. The most notable proponents of a connection between an anti-Israel and anti-Samaritan theme in Chronicles are Wellhausen (1973), Torrey (1970), and Noth (1987). For an excellent discussion of the inclusivist versus exclusivist debates in Chronicles scholarship, see Dyck (1998: 24-50).

7. See also Welch (1939).

8. 1 Chron. 2:17; 2:34-35; 4:18; 7:14 are all unique to Chronicles. 1 Chron. 2:3 is said to be based on Genesis 38. Japhet's point is that their inclusion indicates the distinct Chronistic tendency to emphasize the "foreign" elements of Israelite identity.

9. See also Japhet (1979: 218), who describes the Chronicler's depiction of the relationship between the people and the land as "autochthonic in its basic features."

10. Braun (1979: 59-61), De Vries (1986), Whitelam (1989), Williamson (1977: 135), and Williamson (1982: 24-26, 134).

11. See Laffey (1992) for a survey of the female characters in Chronicles who also appear elsewhere in the Hebrew Bible, and the female names unique to Chronicles. Laffey also notes the absence of Bathsheba, Abigail, and Jezebel. These absences are

understood by Laffey as simply the effect of the Chronicler's emphasis on Yahweh worship, the temple, and the lack of concern for the history of the Northern Kingdom of Israel (p. 114).

Part 1

1. See Mitchell (1974); Copjec (1994); Grosz (1989, 1990); Gallop (1982, 1985).

2. Irigaray trained as a psychoanalyst, attended Lacan's Seminar, and was famously excommunicated from the *école freudienne* for *Speculum of the Other Woman* (Irigaray, 1985a), a work which was taken to be an intellectually aggressive attack against the modern master of psychoanalysis in France, Lacan himself.

3. For example, see Bach (1990: 43 n. 22; 1993: 341 n. 2); Rashkow (1993: 79, 124 n. 1; 1998: 35); Sherwood (1996: 254-55, 275).

4. Irigaray begins her "Questions to Emmanuel Levinas" by referring briefly to the Song of Solomon (Irigaray, 1991c: 178-79). Her "The Fecundity of the Caress: A Reading of Levinas, *Totality and Infinity*, 'Phenomenology of Eros' " (Irigaray, 1993b: 185-217), while reminiscent of the Song of Songs, is also, as Gibson (2001) suggests, a rethinking in many ways of the fall narrative in Genesis 2–3 (on the fall narrative, see also Irigaray, 1993a: 178-79). She has also engaged critically with the work of Elisabeth Schüssler Fiorenza in "Equal to Whom?" (Irigaray, 1997). "I Announce to You that We are Different" (Irigaray, 2000a: 54-61) is a rethinking of the Annunciation story in the New Testament. However, a longer engagement with the Hebrew Bible appears in "The Crucified One: Epistle to the Last Christians," the final chapter of the final section ("When the Gods Are Born") of *Marine Lover of Frederick Nietzsche* (Irigaray, 1991b: 164-90, esp. 174-75). While *The Postmodern Bible* mentions this latter in its discussion of Irigaray's status as a postmodern feminist, describing her reading as *midrashic* (Bible and Culture Collective, 1995: 259), her later absence in *The Postmodern Bible Reader* (Jobling *et al.*, 2001) is, I think, conspicuous given her consistent, though somewhat sporadic, return to biblical narratives.

5. On the theological aspects of Irigaray's work, see, for example, Joy, O'Grady, and Poxon (2002, 2003); Ward (1996); Stockton (1994); Gross (1986).

6. See Bible and Culture Collective (1995: 187-95, esp. 188).

7. For example, see Freud's famous analysis of Dostoevsky through his reading of *The Gambler* (Freud, 1928a). More significantly, however, is the fact that Freud's analysis of Judge Schreber and the development of his great theory of psychosis takes place through the reading of Schreber's *writing*. Freud never met Schreber, never sat in the analytic setting with him. In other words, his theory came about as a literary analysis of an author.

8. Notable examples of this approach in biblical studies are Zeligs (1988), Sanford (1985), Halperin (1993).

9. There are a number of other biblical scholars who are using psychoanalytic theory in interesting ways (for example, Boer [1999a, 1999b 2002], Moore [1992]), yet the main interpretive approach of these scholars is not psychoanalytic.

10. Peter Brooks is another well-known theorist who brings psychoanalysis and narratology together. Brooks argues that psychoanalysis provides a model that, unlike pure formalism and narratology, can account for the dynamics of texts. By this,

Brooks means that the psychoanalytic model he develops can account for the desire of and for meaning not only in the production of narrative, but also in the practice of reading narrative, the movement through and towards meaning: "In the attempt to go beyond pure formalism – while never discarding its lessons – psychoanalysis promises, and requires, that in addition to such usual narratological preoccupations as function, sequence, and paradigm, we engage the dynamic of memory and the history of desire as they work to shape the recovery of meaning within time. Beyond formalism, Susan Sontag argued some years ago, we need an erotics of art. What follows may be conceived as a contribution to that erotics, or, more soberly, a reading of our compulsions to read" (Brooks, 1984: 36).

   11. See especially Jobling (1997).

Chapter 1

   1. This quote comes from an interview with Irigaray, conducted by Thérèse Dumouchel and Marie-Madeleine Raoult, that was published as "Les Femmes-mères, ce sous-sol muet de l'ordre social," in *Le corps-à-corps avec la mere* (Montreal: Editions de la pleine lune, 1981). The translation here is David Macey's.

   2. See Grosz (1986: 190-91).

   3. Ironically, Irigaray opens this final section of her book by stating that "(t)he myth of the cave, for example, or as an example, is a good place to start" (p. 243). As I explain, later in this chapter, this backward movement from Freud to Plato is characteristic of what Irigaray considers to be the psychoanalytic process.

   4. For a detailed summary of Irigaray's "Plato's *Hystera*," see Whitford (1991: 103-13). See also Vasseleu (1998: 3-18), who discusses Irigaray's essay along with Derrida's thesis that metaphors of light are constitutive of the language of philosophy (Derrida, 1982), and Boulous Walker (1998: 11-30).

   5. It is interesting to note that Boulous Walker argues that the body plays an ambiguous role in the parable of the cave, and is not entirely denied or disavowed (Boulous Walker, 1998: 13ff.).

   6. On the difference between Freud's narcissistic and realist models of the ego, see Grosz (1990: 24-31). The narcissistic ego is able to "take itself, its own image, parts of its own body as an 'object', and invest them as if they were external or 'other'. It is constituted as an ego only through alienation, through the creation of a necessary rift between lived immediacy of perception/sensation, and mediated reflection or self-distance. Its identity is bound to relations with others. It is a sedimentation, a locus, of images of others which form its self-image" (Grosz, 1990: 30).

   7. Lacan relies on Wolfgang Köhler's *The Mentality of Apes* (1951).

   8. On this issue, see Lacan (1998: 65-119), Copjec (1989), and my own discussion in Kelso (2002: 165-71).

   9. Ultimately, for Lacan, this sexual differentiation according to a relation to the phallus means that woman is not entirely trapped by the substitutive logic of the phallus. When Lacan says, in Seminar XX that woman is "not whole" (Lacan, 1999), he means that there is something of woman that escapes the logic of man. Man, who misperceives himself as an exception to the rule of lack (represented by the mother who does not have the phallus), can never access the Other because the Other is that

which is beyond the limit of masculine knowledge, i.e., beyond the phallus. And in sexual terms, this means that man can never enjoy the body of the woman without dismantling or fetishizing her in parts. Woman, however, being "not whole," can know something of jouissance beyond phallic jouissance. But, alas, she can never know what she knows.

10. See esp. Gallop (1981), Hogan (1990: 108-10).

11. In this book, I am using *"ph*antasy" when referring to unconscious and Imaginary scenarios or images, and not *"f*antasy." However, the use of f-antasy as equivalent to ph-antasy is rather common (as is seen in the quote from Žižek below). In psychoanalytic terms, phantasy is not simply the avoidance of reality through the conscious construction of alternative realities (as in fantasy fiction) but is the very means (albeit unconscious) by which a subject makes sense of the Real within the Symbolic. Phantasy is not the hallucinatory realization of desire, but the very constitutive feature of desire: "a fantasy constitutes our desire, provides its co-ordinates; that is, it literally 'teaches us how to desire'...fantasy mediates between the formal symbolic structure and the positivity of the objects we encounter in reality – that is to say, it provides a 'schema' according to which certain positive objects in reality can function as objects of desire, filling in the empty places opened up by the formal symbolic structure" (Žižek, 1997: 7).

12. I keep the masculine pronoun used consistently by Lacan because, for Irigaray, it is *only* a masculine relation to origins that Lacan is elaborating.

13. In his essay, "The Mirror Stage as Formative of the Function of the I as Revealed in Psychoanalytic Experience," Lacan (1977: 1-7) states explicitly that the formation of the subject that psychoanalysis is able to experience or witness through analytic technique is directly opposed to philosophical idealism: "It is an experience that leads us to oppose any philosophy directly issuing from the *Cogito*" (p. 1).

14. While the phallic phase is "contemporaneous with the Oedipus complex" (Freud, 1924: 174) and therefore not, strictly speaking, pre-Oedipal, the female genital (i.e. vagina) is undiscovered in the phallic phase. Definitive genital organization (a sexual polarity of male-penis female-vagina) is only "realized" at puberty (Freud, 1923: 145; 1924: 174).

15. In *Speculum*, Irigaray claims that Freud is trapped within both the phallic and anal stages. As Gallop points out, while this may seem contradictory, it is rather necessary to consider Irigaray's claims in light of Freud's insistence that the stages of development are not strictly diachronic or distinct (Gallop, 1982: 69).

16. As Irigaray points out, Freud states explicitly that the boy's ideal love object throughout his entire life is his mother. If the husband and his sons have the same (type of) love object, how can the Oedipal complex and its resolution take place? For Irigaray, this is one of the crucial internal contradictions of Freud's theory of sexual difference. The Oedipal complex does not serve to articulate sexual difference, as Freud would have it. Rather, Freud's Oedipal theory ensures the successful passage of the (socio-symbolic) law of the father (Irigaray, 1985a: 31; 1985b: 70).

17. The first quote is from Freud (1917b: 128). The second is from Freud (1932b: 101).

18. "Her love was directed to her *phallic* mother; with the discovery that her mother is castrated it becomes possible for her to drop her as an object, so that the

motives for hostility, which have long been accumulating, gain the upper hand. This means, therefore, that as a result of the discovery of women's lack of a penis they are debased in value for girls just as they are for boys and later perhaps for men" (Freud, 1932a: 126-27).

19. Irigaray is not suggesting that all women are melancholics. In fact, she suggests that "the little girl probably does not have a capacity for narcissism great enough to allow her to fall back on melancholia, and that capacity is too depleted to build up such a complex defense against anxiety and the 'catastrophe' brought upon her by the 'accomplished fact' of castration." What she is suggesting is that the sexuality of "woman" manifests a certain number of the symptoms of melancholia, though in a scattered rather than organized or coherent manner (Irigaray, 1985a: 71).

20. Again, it is important to realize that Irigaray is drawing parallels between melancholia and Freud's theory of feminine sexuality. She is not making an assertion about *all* women.

21. A number of Irigaray's earlier readers, especially materialist feminists, rejected her work on the basis of essentialism, metaphysical idealism, positivism, ahistoricism and apoliticism (notably Plaza, 1978; Fauré, 1981; Moi, 1985). Toril Moi (1985) famously claims that Irigaray, while criticizing the "logic of the Same" that creates and sustains conceptualization in Western thinking, falls prey to the very same logic when she seeks to produce her own definition of femininity. Moi states that "to define 'woman' is necessarily to essentialize her" (Moi, 1985: 139). In other words, for Moi, Irigaray cannot avoid the temptation to invent a new concept of "woman." Indeed, for Moi, Irigaray's project involves "a basic assumption of analogy between women's psychology and her 'morphology'…which she rather obscurely takes to be different from her anatomy" (Moi, 1985: 143). In other words, Irigaray is rejected because her work, especially her writing on the female body and its desires, is perceived as simply reflecting a given status of the body. However, other early readers such as Jane Gallop (1983) and Margaret Whitford (1986) insisted that Irigaray's understanding of the body was manifestly materialist in that, for Irigaray, the body is only ever understood as the effect of its environment, "knowable" only through language. For Irigaray, language is the means by which we can *construct* the body. See Fuss (1989: 56-57) and Schor (1994) for more in-depth discussions of Irigaray's reception.

22. This is something Freud admits in "Female Sexuality" near the end of his life, when he returns to the perplexing question of the "pre-Oedipal" mother-daughter relation. Freud likens this "discovery" of the importance of the pre-Oedipal phase in girls to "the discovery, in another field, of the Minoan-Mycenaean civilization behind the civilization of Greece" (Freud, 1931: 226), and questions the universality of his own thesis "that the Oedipus Complex is the nucleus of the neuroses" (Freud, 1931: 226).

23. See Kristeva (1989).

24. It is not enough, in other words, to diagnose the problem without criticizing the problem in its broader context. As Margaret Whitford (1991: 80-84) points out, for Irigaray it is crucial to attend to the *logic* of women's symbolic destitution or *déréliction* (abandonment), to expose that logic as profitable for some and devasting for others, to enable the relationship between women (and their status as differentiated) to be articulable: "…there is no possibility whatsoever, within the current logic of

sociocultural operations, for a daughter to situate herself with respect to her mother: because, strictly speaking, they make neither one nor two, neither has a name, meaning, sex of her own, neither can be 'identified' with respect to the other… How can the relationship between these two women be articulated? Here 'for example' is one place where the need for another 'syntax,' another 'grammar' of culture is crucial" (Irigaray, 1985b: 143).

25. Translated as "Body against Body: In Relation to the Mother" (Irigaray, 1993a: 9-21), and "The Bodily Encounter with the Mother" (Irigaray, 1991d: 34-46).

26. At this point in his argument Freud reduces "the senses" to just one of them: vision. The shift away from the mother/sensible toward the father/intellectual is, in actual fact, a shift away from the visible as limit to knowledge. The Jewish ban on images (ban on the mother?) is the major mark of this successful shift forward in human civilization.

27. "Matriarchy," though not defined by Freud, appears briefly in *Totem and Taboo*, and is discussed in more detail in *Moses and Monotheism*. Freud's postulated murder of the primal father as cultural, religious, and moral origin appears consistently throughout his works on social psychology (esp. *Group Psychology and the Analysis of the Ego* (Freud, 1921), *The Future of an Illusion* (Freud, 1928b), and *Civilization and its Discontents* (Freud, 1930).

28. Aeschylus (1959: 92).

29. Zeus, having eaten the mother, Metis, out of fear that her maternal cunning might be his downfall like the father gods who preceded him, Ouranos and Kronos, not only remains uncastrated and in power, but accomplishes birth himself.

30. See esp. "Women on the Market" (Irigaray, 1985b: 170-91).

31. On the mother-daughter relationship in the Hebrew Bible, see Bronner (1999).

32. On this, in relation to Genesis 34, see Kelso (2003).

Chapter 2

1. Irigaray's more recent work, from the early 1990s onwards, seems less interested in discussing psychoanalysis. However, as Penelope Deutsche (2002) has shown, even the more accessible and politically pragmatic concerns of works such as *je, tu, nous* (1993c) and *Thinking the Difference* (1994) are integrated with Irigaray's concern for psychoanalysis and language. As Deutsche argues (and Whitford before her), Irigaray's concern with sexual difference, whether in philosophy or in the current political environments in the West, is guided by psychoanalytic theory and practice: "I am trained as a psychoanalyst and that's important (in spite of current practices and theories) for theorizing identity as sexual. I also have a background in philosophy, in which psychoanalysis takes its place as a stage in the understanding of the development of consciousness and History, particularly with reference to the sexed determinations of them. Being educated in both of these fields has meant that my thought on women's liberation has gone beyond simply a quest for equality between the sexes" (Irigaray, 1993c: 11).

2. Irigaray's general critique of psychoanalysis is developed in her essay "The Poverty of Psychoanalysis," Irigaray (2002a: 205-26); for a different translation, see Whitford (1991: 79-104). This essay is directed at Lacanian psychoanalytic practice

specifically. Irigaray indicts the psychoanalytic practice of Lacan's followers on three theoretical grounds. First, psychoanalysts refuse to acknowledge any historical determination behind psychoanalysis and its theories, especially its attitudes to women and female sexuality, thereby naturalizing and eternalizing its own theories. Second, the particular social order out of which psychoanalysis arises – Western "civilization" – is, according to Irigaray, founded upon an unacknowledged matricide. Within such an order there can be no acknowledgment of debt to woman and her body. Third, while psychoanalytic theory claims to uncover the various phantasies supporting the subjectivities of its analysands, it fails to acknowledge and analyse its own phantasmatic structure, a structure that according to Irigaray supports and sustains male identity. As I discussed in detail in the last chapter, psychoanalysis thus perpetuates the dominant cultural phantasies that position women in the place of lack, of the "nothing to see."

3. See esp. "Plato's Hysteria," in Irigaray (1985a: 241-364). On the exclusion and silence of women in philosophy, see Whitford (1991: 101-22), Le Doeuff (1989: 100-28), and Boulous Walker (1998: 9-26).

4. Or rather, the site of the production of a discourse by two subject positions effected through the blurring of the subject-object relation in the analytic scene of representation.

5. Gail Schwab translates this as "nothing more than a dead-end, knowledge from a bygone era" (Irigaray, 2002a: 208).

6 See also, for example, Brooks (1984), Gallop (1985: 22-30), and Eagleton (1983: 151-93). For a discussion of the notion of transferential reading in biblical studies, see Jobling (1997).

7. A discussion of the relationship between Irigaray and deconstruction, or more explicitly Irigaray and Derrida, is beyond the boundaries of this book, which is concerned mainly with Irigaray and psychoanalysis. On the relationship between Irigaray and Derrida, see Burke (1981), Whitford (1990: 123-39), Chanter (1995: 225-54).

8. I hesitate to use the term deconstruction at all, with respect to Irigaray's work. There has been a tendency of certain commentators to think of Irigaray's work in terms of deconstruction, however, this tendency covers over too many of the subtle differences that Irigaray's project works toward.

9. See especially "The Setting in Psychoanalysis," Irigaray (2002a: 193-204).

10. On the use of utopian topoi in Irigaray's work see Whitford (1994). See also Muraro (1994), who expresses her dissatisfaction with Irigaray's image of the mother and daughter sharing the eucharist together (Irigaray, 1993a: 21). Muraro finds the image "artificial" (Muraro, 1994: 322).

11. See also "Divine Women," (Irigaray, 1993a: 55-72), "Letting Be Transcendence," (Irigaray, 2002b: 65-75), "Sorcerer Love: A Reading of Plato, *Symposium*, Diotima's Speech," (Irigaray, 1993: 20-33).

12. See Žižek (2000: 107-108). Žižek criticizes John Gray who, on a series of Oprah Winfrey shows, proposed "a vulgarized version of narrativist-deconstructivist psychoanalysis: since we ultimately 'are' the stories we are telling ourselves about ourselves, the solution to a psychic deadlock lies in a 'positive' creative rewriting of the narrative past" (p. 107). While Gray accepts the radical Freudian notion of a

traumatic kernel, he perceives his role as therapist to enable the analysand to rewrite the scene as a positive, even banal experience. Instead of confronting the traumatic scene head on, the analysand simply denies it through an optimistic mind over matter approach that simply changes the content of representation, rather than the framework itself. This is where psychoanalysis and American ego psychology part ways most dramatically.

13. For critical questions concerning the function and efficacy of the hysterical voice in Irigaray, see Plaza (1978) and Chisholm (1994).

14. In her criticisms of contemporary practitioners of Lacanian analysis, Irigaray chastises the prescriptive Lacanian theory brought to the analytic scene as an "imperialism of the Unconscious" that effectively protects those analysts from "the risk that *your own* death might ensue" (Irigaray, 2002a: 206). The "death" here is, of course, the death of the subject of the Symbolic, not the biological death.

15. See Boulous Walker (1998) for a fascinating discussion of the appropriative gesture by which "man" is able to write. Boulous Walker's thesis is that the psychotic appropriation of the maternal body, paradigmatically in the case of Schreber, is a feature of "normal" masculine writing.

16. See the Bible and Culture Collective (1995: 247-51).

17. For a detailed discussion of this aspect of Irigaray's work, see Whitford (1991: 156-65).

18. See esp. Kristeva (1984). See also Grosz (1989: 39-98) and Boulous Walker (1998: 103-33) for critical discussions of Kristeva's poetic subject and the maternal.

19. See Boulous Walker (1993).

20. See Ostriker (1997) for a discussion of revisionist biblical poetry.

Part II

1. For example, see Johnson (1969: 80); De Vries (1989: 27); Coggins (1976: 6); Williamson (1982: 2).

Chapter 3

1. When Hebrew words appear in different brackets throughout this book, both (Qere) and [Ketiv] are supplied.

2. The standard form of the biblical genealogy is defined by De Vries as "a special type of oral or written LIST that enumerates individual and tribal descent from an originating ancestor through intermediate persons down to the last. It is built on a system of enumeration rather than narration, though brief narrative items may be included" (De Vries, 1989: 32). Not *two* ancestors but *one*. Any doubt as to which ancestor, paternal or maternal, is dispelled when De Vries goes on to define the two types of this form: "It may be linear, tracing descent *from father to son*, and so on for several generations...or it may be segmented, identifying siblings and from them tracing collateral branches" (De Vries, 1989: 32; italics mine). The point that needs to be made from the very beginning of a study of biblical genealogies is that the form itself (and its particular variations) sets a particular standard of male-male, father-son descent, a standard that pre(de)scribes all subsequent definitions.

It is not my intention to challenge the definition of genealogy. But patrilineage has remained so under-analysed in biblical genealogical studies that it has become naturalized. Furthermore, the absence of critique when it comes to patrilineage has effected a universalizing of what is very much a gendered construct. For example, Roddy Braun defines segmented genealogies as the "tracing of all the descendants of a given family" (Braun 1997: 95). If segmented genealogies trace *all the descendants*, then are we to presume that there was an enormous production of male children in the ancient world, and a relative dearth of daughters? And the descendants of whom? As stated above, the definitions of "genealogy" make it clear that *all the descendants* are given one ancestral line, one ancestor. And all lines lead back to Adam, not Eve.

3. In biblical studies, the first nine chapters are said to designate the pre-history of the kingdom of Judah. See Braun (1986: 6-7); Johnson (1969: 47-57). For a rhetorical critical approach, see Duke (1999: 119-20).

4. 1 Chron. 1:19 has the third, masculine singular of the verb in Pu'al (יֻלַּד): "And to Eber two sons were born."

5. We can only be sure of the gender of Hebrew names when there is an associated verb or substantive such as "sister" because the gender of Hebrew names does not necessarily indicate the gender of the character. In other words, we can only presume that all names in the genealogies, unless specified as feminine through the use of a verb or substantive, are male names. This, of course, is not an outrageous presumption, given the overwhelmingly masculine nature of this genealogical discourse and the narratives that follow.

6. This temporal priority needs to be understood in terms of a constructed, diegetic temporality.

7. 1 Chron. 2:10-13 (7 times), 18(1), 20 (2), 22 (1), 36-41 (12), 44 (2), 46 (1); 4:2 (2), 8(1), 11(1), 12 (1), 14 (2); 5:30-40 (20); 7:32 (1); 8:1 (1), 7 (1), 8 (1), 11 (1), 32(1), 33 (3), 34 (1), 36 (3), 37 (1); 9:38 (1), 39 (3), 40 (1), 42 (3), 43 (1).

8. I am using De Vries' formal category here. According to De Vries, the birth report is a "recording of a birth in narrative style, with special notice of the mother" (De Vries, 1989: 428).

9. In Aggadic literature, there is a dominant tradition which holds that Eglah is another name for Michal, the daughter of Saul given to David by the king for his defeat of the Philistines (1 Sam. 18:20ff.). See Eisemann (1987: 40).

10. Chananiah's sons are four "generations" after the time of the Babylonian exile.

11. The Hebrew reads וְאֵלֶּה אֲבִי עֵיטָם: "And these were the father of Etam" (1 Chron. 4:3).

12. Indeed, this anxiety about Jabez and his story continues with the Rabbinic interpreters (see Eisemann, 1987: 396-401), who connect the Jabez of 4:9 with the Jabez of 2:55 ("And families of scribes, dwellers in Jabez..."). The Jabez of 2:55 often is interpreted either as a place named after the Jabez of 4:9 (he being more honourable because of his skill with Torah), or more literally as the same figure in 4:9, who becomes a teacher. For example, R' Nosson interprets Jabez's prayer in the following way: "*If you will surely bless me* – with Torah (that is, that I will know much Torah); *and enlarge my boundaries* – with students; *and Your hand will be with me* – that I will not forget my learning; *and You will avert evil* – that I will meet friends who complement

my nature (a play on the word הרעם, as though it derived from רע, *friend*); *that I not* – that my evil inclination will not prevent me from learning Torah; *be saddened* – If You do all this for me – good; if not I will go to my grave in sorrow. And from R' Yehudah HaNassi: "*If you will surely bless me* – by allowing me to be fruitful; *and enlarge my boundaries* – with sons and daughters; *and Your hand will be with me* – in my business affairs; *and You will avert evil* – that neither my head, ears nor eyes will trouble me; *that I not* – that my evil inclination will not prevent me from learning Torah; *be saddened* – If You do that for me – good; if not I will go to my grave in sorrow" (*Temurah*, 16a). It is as if the Rabbis feel they must continue Jabez's story by giving him a line of descendents, either sons and daughters, or students.

13. For example, Japhet (1993: 114) follows Curtis' textual manipulations whereby 4:18b is transposed to after 4:17a (Curtis, 1910: 111), thus enabling Mered to have his two wives who each produce sons for him.

14. As I shall discuss in the next chapter, birthing verbs are rare in the narrative of Chronicles (1 Chronicles 10—2 Chronicles 36). Furthermore, narratives of sexual activity, pregnancy and birth (apart from 1 Chron. 4:9) are absent from both the genealogies, as we have just heard, and from the narratives, where we might expect at least the possibility of such stories.

15. For De Vries, this "other story" is the Pentateuch. In answer to the question concerning the extensive use of genealogies in Chronicles, he argues that "ChrH does not need to retell the pentateuchal narrative, for that has already been told. Rather it gathers together the names of tribes and families to show that *Israel is now and ever will be complete*" (De Vries, 1989: 18). I am not interested in dismissing De Vries' argument. Nor am I concerned with arguing for some kind of authorial intention. I am speaking specifically about unconscious mechanisms, that is, unconscious strategies for silencing women.

Chapter 4

1. This inquiring of the feminine is made explicit in 1 Samuel 28, where Saul seeks out a female necromancer, usually known as the "witch" (אֵשֶׁת בַּעֲלַת־אוֹב בְּעֵיר דוֹר; lit. the mistress of necromancy in 1 Sam. 28:7) of Ein Dor.

2. The strangeness of this narrative beginning is also reflected in the later (male) readership. For some commentators, for example, this narrative beginning is something of a shock for the reader. Curtis (1910: 180) states that the "narrative of the battle of Mt. Gilboa is introduced abruptly, the Chronicler taking for granted that the events which led to it were well known to the reader." Coggins (1976: 64), too, remarks that the opening of the narrative account "seems very abrupt." According to Ackroyd (1973: 49) the "reader is brought suddenly out of the lists of names," although Ackroyd's alleged reader, like Coggins' and Curtis', is thrown into a story that is familiar. "The Chronicler," they all argue, assumes that his reader is familiar with this material in its more "original," and lengthier, literary context (i.e. 1 Sam. 31:1-13). And so the abruptness of the narrative beginning is in some sense softened by the presumed awareness on the part of the reader of this story's "other" existence in Samuel. This is not a first instance, an original appearance, a story thrown out at a reader who is unprepared, according to these contemporary critics. However, that

these contemporary readers *need* to alleviate the violence of this story indicates to me the importance of this violent corporeal origin for my own purposes here.

3. Note that in the parallel story from 1 Sam. 31:10 Saul's armour is hung in the "house of Ashtaroth" (בֵּית עַשְׁתָּרוֹת). Ashtaroth is the plural of Ashtoreth, a goddess associated with war. Does our analysand struggle even to mention a feminine form of divinity, just as he "forgot" to mention that the necromancer was, in 1 Samuel 28, a woman with connections to the underworld?

4. For example, the RSV translates this verse as "The battle pressed hard upon Saul, and the archers found him; and he was wounded by the archers."

5. Where וַיָּחֶל is read as the Qal waw consecutive imperfect 3ms of חיל (to whirl, dance, writhe).

6. Nor is this word found anywhere else in the entire Hebrew canon, for that matter.

7. גְּוִיָּה is the word used in the parallel text of 1 Sam. 31:12.

8. Generally, this word is understood by scholars to be "later" Hebrew.

9. According to Koehler Baumgartner, the supposed root of this word is גּוּף. While this supposed root form does not appear anywhere in the Hebrew canon, it is believed to be the root because of its meanings in other Semitic languages. In Arabic, this word means "corpse," but it also can mean "to be hollow," "inner," or "belly." Furthermore, another related word is גַּף. This word, which also means "body," "self," "height," or "elevation," is supposedly derived from the root נָפַף. Again, while this root does not appear in the Hebrew canon, its meanings in another Semitic language are what I find interesting, and important for my argument above. In Syriac, גנפ means "curved," and "convex." Thus, the semantic range of the word used, גּוּפָה, for the bodies of Saul and his sons is, I believe, undeniably evocative of the (masculine Imaginary) hollowed out, curved belly-space of the maternal womb. Thanks to Professor Michael Lattke (University of Queensland) for his assistance here with the Aramaic and Syriac forms (private communication).

10. In the hiphil 3ms, the verb יָפִיפוּ means "to shut or close" (Neh. 7:3).

11. For example, *Enuma Elish* proffers the murder and halving of the mother goddess Tiamat's body as the origin of the sea and the sky. And in the *Oresteia*, Clytemnstra's murder gives us, according to Irigaray, the "murder of the mother" as origin of patriarchal law and order (Irigaray, 1991d).

12. Returning to Chapter 1 and my discussion of Irigaray's reading of Plato's cave, I am making a claim here that is similar to Irigaray's insight that maternal matter has already been repressed to enable this myth of the cave, for the men are trapped in a cave, not a womb. In other words, the maternal body serves as a stage or prop for masculine discourses, without women being present except for their function as the mute foundation of masculine discourses.

13. In other words, while on the surface the murder of Saul appears to be reminiscent of Freud's thesis concerning the murder of the primal father, I argue that this symptomatic reading reveals the hidden sacrifice beneath the body of the sacrificial male. This is consistent with Irigaray's thesis that the murder of the mother constitutes the origin of patriarchal history, and her insistence that this other sacrificial body must be brought out of the crypt: "It would seem to me to be more appropriate to inquire whether, under the sacrificed victim, another victim is often hidden" (Irigaray,

1993a: 76). The necessity of such an interpretive exhumation relates not simply to our reinterpretation of foundational myths, but to social and religious practice in the past, present, and future: "Therefore, could it not be argued that the hidden sacrifice is in fact this *extradition*, this ban on women's participation in religious practice, and their consequent exile from the ultimate sources of social decision making" (Irigaray, 1993a: 78).

14. Jacob is referred to by the name of "Israel" twelve times in Chronicles (1 Chron. 1:34; 2:1; 5:1[2], 3; 6:23; 7:29; 16:13, 17; 29:10, 18; 2 Chron. 30:6), while the name "Jacob" is only used twice (1 Chron. 16:13, 17). As Williamson points out, in 1 Chron. 16:13, which is part of David's psalm of thanksgiving to Yahweh (1 Chron. 16:7-36), the name "Israel" is used to refer to Jacob, while the parallel text of Ps. 105:6 refers to Abraham:

$$\text{זֶרַע אַבְרָהָם עַבְדּוֹ בְּנֵי יַעֲקֹב בְּחִירָיו:}$$

(O) seed of Abraham his servant, sons of Jacob, his chosen ones (Ps. 105:6).

$$\text{זֶרַע יִשְׂרָאֵל עַבְדּוֹ בְּנֵי יַעֲקֹב בְּחִירָיו:}$$

(O) seed of Israel his servant, sons of Jacob, his chosen ones (1 Chron. 16:13).

Here, according to Chronicles, Jacob displaces Abraham as the founding father of Israel. Williamson notes that this verse in Chronicles is the only place in which the verb root בחר ("he chose") is used in conjunction with the people of Israel as a whole (Williamson, 1977: 64), further emphasizing the importance of Jacob/Israel as founder of the people of Yahweh.

15. Most English Bibles translate this clause with Solomon as the one anointed as Yahweh's prince or leader, no doubt because of the problematic suggestion that Yahweh is somehow beneath Solomon, and also because of the close, corporeal proximity implied by anointing. However, the Hebrew clearly has Yahweh anointed as prince just as Zadok is anointed as priest.

16. Or does David "bless" Yahweh, as ברך tends to mean?

17. בֵּית זְבֻל can be translated as "a lofty/elevated house" or "an exalted house." Given the height of the temple vestibule, I have preferred the former here in my translation.

18. See Yahweh's speech to Solomon in 2 Chron. 7:11-22.

19. My own fascination with these architectural descriptions is guided by Elizabeth Grosz's work on architecture and the body, especially her "Women, *Chora*, Dwelling" (Grosz, 1995: 111-24) where she argues that there are "theoretical issues that link the very *concept* of architecture with the phallocentric effacement of women and femininity, the cultural refusal of women's specificity or corporeal and conceptual autonomy and social value" (Grosz, 1995: 112). In biblical studies, Mieke Bal's work on Judges (Bal, 1988) is perhaps better known, and her analysis of the architectural spaces in Judges, especially the house, is also inspirational for my work here. Bal argues that in the Book of Judges that the maternal body has been repressed. Using Freud's explication of the *unheimlich*, the uncanny, and playing with the literal

translation of "unhomeliness," Bal reads the "house" in Judges as the figuration of this problematic original site within the *male* Imaginary – the maternal body. The "house" in Judges is the threshold of violence, made uncanny because of the repressed status of the maternal body. That which was once known, once familiar, but now repressed, is also now the uncanny. Her argument is that this repressed maternal origin returns in the form of "traces that are displaced and disfigured" (Bal, 1988: 197).

20. For most scholars, this figure of 120 cubits must be an error on the part of the ancient writer or copyist. For a more interesting reading of this feature of the temple as it appears in Chronicles, see Boer (1997: 146, 161) who introduces the argument from utopian studies that descriptive language breaks down within utopian writing.

21. Windows with recessed frames (חַלּוֹנֵי שְׁקֻפִים אֲטֻמִים) are a feature of the temple as described in 1 Kings (6:4).

22. Instead of dismissing this description of the temple vestibule in Chronicles as an error, my Irigarayan-inspired psychoanalytic reading of the temple description as a whole enables me to build upon Irigaray's thesis that the phallus monopolizes conceptual (masculine) thought, and that the maternal body is the mute foundation of that thought: "The phallus erected where once there was the umbilical cord? It becomes the organizer of the world of and through the man-father, in the place where the umbilical cord, the first bond with the mother, gave birth to the body of both man and woman" (Irigaray, 1991d: 38). "This is how men gather together in the mystery of the here and now present of a body and a blood that have not figured on the stage and thus allow that stage to be set. Many, many years ago, in our tradition, the pick was driven into the earth-mother's womb in order to build the sacred enclosure of the tribe, the temple, finally the house" (Irigaray, 1993a: 47).

The temple in Chronicles reveals, if you like, the phallocentric logic underwriting the very *concept* of sacred architectural space. As Grosz puts it (with respect to Irigaray's thesis on the masculine appropriation of the maternal body): "Irigaray claims that masculine modes of thought have performed a devastating sleight-of-hand: they have obliterated the debt they owe to the most primordial of all spaces, the maternal space from which all subjects emerge, and which they ceaselessly attempt to usurp... The production of a (male) world – the construction of an 'artificial' or cultural environment, the production of an intelligible universe, religion, philosophy, the creation of true knowledges and valid practices of and in that universe – is implicated in the systematic and violent erasure of the contributions of women, femininity, and the maternal" (Grosz, 1995: 121).

23. In the traditional, though problematic understanding of Hebrew grammar and philology, the words אֵם (mother) and אַמָּה (cubit) derive from the same root – אמם – a word which suggests width and roominess, denoting a container-like space. Other words said to derive from this root are "mother-city" (אַמָּה), "foundation" (אַמָּה), and one of the words for "tribe" or "people" (אַמָּה).

24. Martha Nussbaum (1986) argues that in ancient Greek philosophy, particularly around the time of Plato, the importance of exact or standardized measurement and counting came to be crucially linked to knowledge: "Evidently, then, a science of deliberative measurement would be an enormous advantage in human social life. And this is an idea for which the tradition of Greek reflection about *techne* and human understanding has by Plato's time prepared the way. The connection between numbering

and knowing, the ability to count or measure and the ability to grasp, comprehend or control, runs very deep in Greek thought about human cognition... The denumerable is the definite, the graspable, therefore also the potentially tellable, controllable; what cannot be numbered remains vague and unbounded, evading human grasp" (Nussbaum, 1986: 107; quoted in Whitford, 1990: 209).

It is Nussbaum's point that measurement, particularly *standardized* measurement becomes crucial to masculine (Greek) thinking at a certain point that interests me, though here I am concerned with a Hebrew word that represents a standardized measurement of space.

25. Consonantally, we may read this word דבקה as the 3fs Qal form of דבק, "she cleaved," though with qere (as it is pointed/spoken), the word is a feminine adjective. Given the repeated verbal forms of נגע in 3:11-12, and the gender pattern that emerges here with the verbs, the pointing may be an interesting example of Masoretic interpretation. That is, while the masculine wing only reaches to (or for?) the feminine wing, the latter cleaves, which is considered a more forceful verb according to Jewish tradition (Eisemann, 1992: 21). Perhaps our medieval scribes could not consider the possibility of a stronger feminine verbal act?

26. It is important to note that this bi-gendering of the cherubim is absent from the parallel description in 1 Kgs 6:27, where only feminine forms of the verb נגע are used. In other words, there is no bi-gendering of the cherubim because all of the verbal acts associated with the wings are feminine. Furthermore, the feminine cleaving wing in Chronicles is not present in 1 Kgs 6:27. There, the two middle feminine wings are described as touching (נֹגְעֹת; the Qal, feminine plural participle of נגע).

27. One of these projects is the building of Upper Beth Horon and Lower Beth Horon (2 Chron. 8:5). This information directly contradicts 1 Chron. 7:24, which tells us that Sheerah, the daughter of Beriah, built these cities, yet another instance of "masculine" appropriation of "feminine" labour.

28. This is the only mention of Solomon's alliance with Pharaoh's daughter in Chronicles, which is mentioned four other times in Kings (1 Kgs 3:1; 7:8; 9:16; 11:1). However, the reason for her removal from the city of David is somewhat different in Kings:

אַךְ בַּת־פַּרְעֹה עָלְתָה מֵעִיר דָּוִד אֶל־בֵּיתָהּ אֲשֶׁר בָּנָה־לָהּ
אָז בָּנָה אֶת־הַמִּלּוֹא׃

However, the daughter of Pharaoh went up from the city of David to her house which he had built for her; then he built the Millo (1 Kgs 9:24).

First of all, in Kings it is Pharaoh's daughter who is the subject of the verb in the sentence. Here, she "went up from the city of David" (עָלְתָה מֵעִיר דָּוִד), whereas in Chronicles, Solomon is the subject of the sentence, making Solomon responsible for her relocation: וְאֶת־בַּת־פַּרְעֹה הֶעֱלָה שְׁלֹמֹה מֵעִיר דָּוִיד ("Solomon brought up the daughter of Pharaoh from the city of David"). There is no indication in Kings that Pharaoh's daughter must be relocated because of her status as Solomon's woman in close contact with the holy ark. She simply has a new house. Thus, in Chronicles, "woman" becomes a problematic object in relation to sacred space, an object that must be removed by "man."

29. For most scholars, the issue in 2 Chron. 8:11 is with gender, not with ethnicity. That is, it is because Pharaoh's daughter is a woman that Solomon removes her from the city of David where the ark of the covenant of Yahweh is located, not because she is an Egyptian (for example, Dillard [1987]: 65, Japhet [1993]: 626, and Myers [1965]: 49). However, Armin Siedlecki (1999) argues that there is no evidence in Chronicles, or elsewhere in the Hebrew Bible, which suggests that women must be kept away from what has been consecrated to the god of Israel. Essentially, Siedlecki rejects the argument of Dillard (1987) that the phrase לֹא־תֵשֵׁב אִשָּׁה לִי (which Dillard translates as "no wife of mine") emphasizes gender rather than ethnicity. Siedlecki argues that foreigners are, however, kept apart from the holy things of god, both in Chronicles (notably 1 Chron. 11:4—18:20: David's wars with the Philistines, Edomites, Moabites, Ammonites, and Arameans set around the ark narrative) and elsewhere in the Hebrew Bible (e.g. Ezek. 44:9; Siedlecki, 1999: 251-52). I think the concept of gender is too broad here, for it is a specific concept of the feminine that is being excluded, or rather, *silenced*, even here: maternal reproductive capacity.

30. וַיִּקַּח דָּוִיד עוֹד נָשִׁים בִּירוּשָׁלָ͏ִם וַיּוֹלֶד דָּוִיד עוֹד בָּנִים וּבָנוֹת:

> And David took more women in Jerusalem, and David begat (bore?) more sons and daughters (1 Chron. 14:3).

Interestingly, in contrast to the genealogy of David given in 1 Chron. 3:5-8, where sons are born for David (נוּלְּדוּ־לוֹ) by women who are often named, here in the narrative of David's rule, David himself begets (וַיּוֹלֶד) more sons and daughters. Not only do the wives remain unnamed but David has become the subject of the active verb ילד in the Hiph'il ("to cause to bear," "to beget"), which is surely more fitting for the great king.

31. Reheboam's son, Abijah, is also given many women and children as a mark of his success:

וַיִּשָּׂא־לוֹ נָשִׁים אַרְבַּע עֶשְׂרֵה וַיּוֹלֶד עֶשְׂרִים וּשְׁנַיִם בָּנִים וְשֵׁשׁ עֶשְׂרֵה
וַיִּתְחַזֵּק אֲבִיָּהוּ
בָּנוֹת:

> Abijah established himself and he took for himself fourteen women and he bore twenty-two sons and sixteen daughters (2 Chron. 13:21).

Unlike his father's women, Abijah's remain nameless and are given no status as reproducers. Abijah, it seems, is capable of all production here.

32. I think this tension is most evident with David and Solomon, as I suggested above. Even though there is no war, or struggle between father and son, or between Solomon and his brothers, there is a definite stalling of the son's story.

33. Of all three kings, only Jehoram's disease is unique to Chronicles. However, while Asa and Uzziah are struck with their diseases in Kings (1 Kgs 15:23 and 2 Kgs 15:5 respectively), Chronicles goes to great lengths to give reasons for their illnesses. I am interested in exploring these diseases in the context of Chronicles, especially with respect to my argument that the maternal body is repressed in the Chronicles narrative.

34. In the Hiphil, זנה can mean either "to cause to commit sexual fornication" or "to cause to commit religious fornication." I am not concerned as to which meaning is here relevant, but only that sexual language has come into play.

35. For example, Gen. 25:23, where Yahweh tells Rebecca that two peoples are in her womb (בְּ), and that two peoples shall come from her womb (מֵעֶה) divided. Note that two words for womb are used here, with מֵעֶה associated with the birth itself; see also Isa. 48:19; Ps. 71:6; Ruth 1:11.

36. Scholars have noted that "immediate divine retribution" is one of the most obvious features that distinguish the Chronicler's version of Israel's history from the Deuteronomist's. See Wellhausen (1973: 203-10).

37. 2 Chron. 16:12-13 (Asa); 21:18-19 (Jehoram); 22:9 (Ahaziah); 24:25 (Joash); 25:29 (Amaziah); 26:19-21 (Uzziah); 33:24 (Amon); 35:23-24 (Josiah).

38. Diseases such as gout, dropsy, and especially gangrene have all been suggested by various scholars (e.g. Coggins, 1976: 207; Myers, 1965: 95). Furthermore, the reference to "feet" may even be a euphemism for Asa's genitals (Coggins, 1976: 207).

39. According to Levitical law, Asa's illness, whether it be in his foot or in his genitals, is problematic for cultic purity reasons: "Say to Aaron, None of your descendants throughout their generations who has a blemish may approach to offer the bread of his God. For no one who has a blemish shall draw near, a man blind or lame, or one who has a mutilated face or a limb too long, or a man who has an injured foot or an injured hand, or a hunchback, or a dwarf, or a man with a defect in his sight or an itching disease or scabs or crushed testicles" (Lev. 21:17-20; RSV).

According to Kristeva (1982), biblical abominations, such as these examples of the abject male body, "aim at cutting back or resorbing" the phantasy of the devouring mother (see below, n. 28): "The body must bear no trace of its debt to nature: it must be clean and proper in order to be fully symbolic. In order to confirm that, it should endure no gash other than that of circumcision, equivalent to sexual separation and/or separation from the mother. Any other mark would be the sign of belonging to the impure, the non-separate, the non-symbolic, the non-holy" (Kristeva, 1982: 102).

40. By translating וַיְּבְהֲלוּהוּ as "and in terror they hastened him," I am employing both senses of בהל in the Hiphil: "to dismay or terrify" and "to hasten or hurry."

41. See Douglas (1966) and Kristeva (1982) for their discussions of "clean and proper" boundary production in the Hebrew Bible. Essentially, Kristeva builds upon Douglas' ground-breaking work on taxonomies of purity and impurity in the Hebrew Bible by suggesting that the taxonomy that orders the Symbolic relations between proper and improper, pure and defiled, sacred and profane etc., especially in Leviticus, depends upon the distinction between the speaking subject and a phatasmatic maternal body from which it came: "Would the dispositions *place-body* and the more elaborate one *speech-logic of differences* be an attempt to keep a being who speaks to his God separated from the fecund mother? In that case, it would be a matter of separating oneself from the phantasmatic power of the mother, that archaic Mother Goddess who actually haunted the imagination of a nation at war with the surrounding polytheism. A phantasmatic mother who also constitutes, in the specific history of each person, the abyss that must be established as an autonomous (and not encroaching)

place and *distinct* object, meaning a *signifiable* one, so that such a person might learn to speak" (Kristeva, 1982: 100).

42. See, again, Kristeva (1982: 101-103; 108-10). For Kristeva, a disease such as leprosy, which affects the skin ("the essential if not initial boundary of biological and psychic individuation," p. 101) is intolerable because it presents the speaking subject of "civilization" with the unbearable reminder of its maternal-corporeal origins. Within the biblical logic of cultic and social order, the maternal body is understood as defiled because of menses and childbirth itself, both of which blur the necessary distinction of self and other, subject and object, inside and outside. Diseases such as Uzziah's, Jehoram's and Asa's, then, can be understood as threatening social and cultic order, on the one hand, and threatening the stability and identity of the masculine subject himself.

43. Here is Irigaray's initial pithy response to a question concerning Marx's suggestion that "humanity assigns itself only those tasks that it can accomplish": "If I am not mistaken, Marx also says that History is the process by which man gives birth to himself" (Irigaray, 1985b: 126).

In renaming Jacob "Israel" in its reconstruction of Israel's monarchic past, Chronicles betrays this phantasy of male self-birth through History. See also Boulous Walker's discussion of Althusser's argument that Freud gives birth to himself through his conception of psychoanalysis (Boulous Walker, 1998: 38-42). As Boulous Walker puts it "Freud is depicted as the original father, the self-generating origin from which all others flow" (Boulous Walker, 1998: 39).

44. The spectre of Freud's (male) body capable of birthing through the anus arises every time I read this passage. See Kelso (2004). I refer my reader back to Chapter 1 and my discussion of Irigaray's thesis that it is precisely the phantasy of the body capable of anal birth that sustains Freud's theories of sexuality.

45. Here, I am suggesting something different to Kristeva who insists that the fantasies of male birthing of the bowels and the obsession with the leprous and decaying body are the effect of a failed introjection of the mother by the speaking (male) subject, instead incorporated as all-consuming, devouring, and intolerable: "The obsession of the leprous and decaying body would thus be the fantasy of a self-birth on the part of a subject who has not introjected his mother but has incorporated a devouring mother. Phantasmatically, he is the solidary obverse of a cult of the Great Mother: a negative and demanding identification with her imaginary power. Aside from sanitary effectiveness, that is the fantasy that Levitical abominations aim at cutting back or resorbing" (Kristeva, 1982: 102). In other words, for Kristeva, subjective destitution occurs because of a failed psychic process, a failure that generates these particular fantasies of self-birth by the masculine subject. What I am suggesting here is that in Chronicles, the masculine subject *depends upon this phantasy* for the stability of his symbolic existence. Subjective destitution occurs because the appropriative power of the mother by the masculine subject has been removed.

46. In other words, the grotesque leakage of the internal body is consistent with masculine fear, if you like, of all that belongs to the feminine: "And once the man-god-father kills the mother so as to take power, he is assailed by ghosts and anxieties. He will always feel a panic fear of she who is the substitute for what he has killed. And the things they threaten us with. We are going to swallow them up, devour them,

castrate them... That's no more than an age-old gesture that has not been analyses or interpreted, returning to haunt them" (Irigaray, in Whitford, 1991: 49-50).

47. Mothers' names included in the regnal formulae and not given any story (unlike Athaliah, who appears in her son Ahaziah's regnal formula in 2 Chron. 22:2) are Naamah (2 Chron. 12:13), Micaiah (2 Chron. 13:2), Azubah (2 Chron. 20:31), Zibiah (2 Chron. 24:1), Jehoaddan (2 Chron. 25:1), and Jecoliah (2 Chron. 26:3).

48. The women in 1 Chronicles 10—2 Chronicles 36, in addition to the mothers named in the regnal formulae, are *David's women* (1 Chron. 14:3), Michal (1 Chron. 15:29), Eleazer's daughters (1 Chron. 23:22), Herman's daughters (1 Chron. 25:5b), a *nameless woman* from Dan, whose son is the artisan given to Solomon by the king of Tyre (2 Chron. 2:14), Pharaoh's daughter (2 Chron. 8:11), the Queen of Sheba (2 Chron. 9:1-12), Mahalah, *Abihail*, and *Maachah*, the wives of Reheboam (2 Chron. 11: 18-22), *Abijah's women* (2 Chron. 13:21), *Maacah* (2 Chron. 15), *Athaliah* (2 Chron. 22:10 – 23:21), Jehoshabeath (2 Chron. 22:11), *Shimoth the Ammonitess* and *Shimrith the Moabitess*, the mothers of the two men who kill Joash (2 Chron. 24:26), and Huldah (2 Chron. 34:22-28) (All italicized words in this paragraph refer to mothers).

There are also the brief references to females in 1 Chron. 16:3; 2 Chron. 15:13; 28:10a; 20:13; 21:14, 17; 28:8a, 10a; 29:9; 31:18; 35:25; 36:17b. In these general references to (un-named) females, their presence is coupled with an emphasis on the negativity of certain situations, especially Yahweh's wrath. Furthermore, they are often included in a line-up of the least powerful (the little ones, the sons, the daughters) and are often associated with the spoils of battle. Their removal by certain enemies serves to heighten the punishment of your men. All in all, if there is an implied dialogue between two parties in these moments of gender inclusiveness, it is always a dialogue between masculine subjects. The presence of women is always in relation to the religio-political concerns of men.

49. The Hebrew has the word "daughter." There is no Hebrew word for "granddaughter."

50. The story from Kings opens the following way:

וַעֲתַלְיָה֙ אֵ֣ם אֲחַזְיָ֔הוּ (וּרָאֲתָה֙) [רָאֲתָ֖ה] כִּ֣י מֵ֣ת בְּנָ֑הּ וַתָּ֨קָם֙
וַתְּאַבֵּ֔ד אֵ֖ת כָּל־זֶ֥רַע הַמַּמְלָכָֽה׃

Athaliah (was) the mother of Ahaziah, and she saw that her son had died. She arose and she put to death (וַתְּאַבֵּד, Pi'el of אבד: "she made perish") all the progeny of the kingdom (2 Kgs 11:1).

51. In the tradition of the Jewish Sages, the bedchamber here in Chronicles refers to the Holy of Holies in the Temple (Eisemann, 1992: 164).

52. See the parallel text of 1 Kgs 15:13.

53. We can see how desperate Asa's actions are when we compare the verbs here in 2 Chron. 15:16 with those from the parallel verse in 1 Kgs 15:13. In 1 Kgs 15:13, Asa "cut down her horrid thing and burned [it] in the Wadi Kidron" (אֵת־ אָסָ֤א וַיִּכְרֹת֙ מִפְלַצְתָּ֔הּ וַיִּשְׂרֹ֖ף בְּנַ֥חַל קִדְרֽוֹן).

54. Importantly, according to Irigaray, women need a notion of the feminine as divine to enable the distinction between mother and daughter, and between women themselves: "If women have no God, they are unable either to communicate or

commune with one another. They need, we need, an infinite if they are to share *a little*. Otherwise sharing implies fusion-confusion, division, and dislocation within themselves, among themselves. If I am unable to form a relationship with some horizon of accomplishment for my gender, I am unable to share while protecting my becoming. Our theological tradition presents some difficulty as far as God in the feminine gender is concerned. There is no *woman* God, no female trinity: mother, daughter, spirit. This paralyzes the infinite of becoming woman since she is fixed in the role of mother through whom the *son* of God is made flesh" (Irigaray, 1993a: 62).

55. Returning to Chapter 1, I argued that, for Irigaray, a non-destructive sociality of women (mothers and daughters amongst themselves) is indeed a threatening idea for patriarchal societies. The mother-daughter relationship constitutes a real threat to this social order that requires both the separation of the mother and the daughter, and their lack of subjective distinction as prisoners of the maternal site within the symbolic: "In our societies, the mother/daughter, daughter/mother relationship constitutes a highly explosive nucleus. Thinking it, and changing it, is equivalent to shaking the foundations of the patriarchal order" (Irigaray 1991a: 50). For patriarchal, hom(m)o-sexual order to sustain itself, it is necessary to ensure that woman remains imprisoned in her maternal function, the site of her silence (cf. Boulous Walker, 1998). This ensures that all relationships among women – the vertical mother-daughter relationship and the horizontal axis of women-amongst-themselves – are excluded from the symbolic and are marked by a poverty of existence that Irigaray calls *déréliction*.

56. Having restricted my topic to the representational production of maternal characters in Chronicles, I have been unable to approach and listen to the words of Huldah. It is, however, most interesting that when the book of the Torah (lit. "the book of the law of Yahweh by the hand of Moses") is found in 2 Chron. 34:14ff., it is Huldah, a woman prophet, who is consulted. I think it will be interesting to read this employment of a woman prophet, within the context of Chronicles, now that we understand the silencing strategies at work in Chronicles.

57. Curiously, though not surprisingly, a Jewish tradition (*Malbim*) holds that the configuration of the cherubim in Chronicles maintains the sexual distinction of masculine and feminine (representing the source and recipient of Divine favour respectively), indicating that there is a barrier between Yahweh and Israel. Only when the two angels face each other, constituting one unit (i.e. the removal of any notion of sexual difference) is the relationship between God and Israel as it should be (Eisemann, 1992: 20).

BIBLIOGRAPHY

Ackroyd, P. R. 1973. *I & II Chronicles, Ezra, Nehemiah*. London: SCM Press.

Adam, A. K. A. 2000. *Handbook of Postmodern Biblical Interpretation*. St Louis, MO: Chalice Press.

Aeschylus. 1959. *The Oresteian Trilogy*. Trans. Philip Vellacott. London: Penguin Books.

Angelou, M. 1988. *I Know Why the Caged Bird Sings*. London: Hutchinson/Virago.

Atkinson, J. J. 1903. *Primal Law*. London.

Atwood, M. 1986. *The Handmaid's Tale*. London: J. Cape.

Bach, A. 1990. "The Pleasure of Her Text." In Alice Bach, ed., *The Pleasure of Her Text: Feminist Readings of Biblical and Historical Texts*: 25-44. Philadelphia: Trinity Press.

—1993. "Breaking Free of the Biblical Frame-Up: Uncovering the Woman in Genesis 39." In Athalya Brenner, ed., *A Feminist Companion to Genesis*: 318-42. Sheffield: Sheffield Academic Press.

Bal, M. 1987. *Lethal Love: Feminist Literary Readings of Biblical Love Stories*. Bloomington: Indiana University Press.

—1988. *Death and Dissymmetry: The Politics of Coherence in the Book of Judges*. Chicago and London: University of Chicago Press.

—1989. *Anti-Covenant: Counter-Reading Women's Lives in the Hebrew Bible*. Sheffield: Almond Press.

—1991a. *Reading Rembrandt: Beyond the Word-Image Opposition*. The Northrop Frye Lectures in Literary Theory; Cambridge: Cambridge University Press.

—1991b. *On Story-Telling – Essays in Narratology*. Ed. David Jobling. Sonoma, CA: Polebridge Press.

Bible and Culture Collective. 1995. *The Postmodern Bible*. London and New Haven, CT: Yale University Press.

Boer, R. 1997. *Novel Histories: The Fiction of Biblical Criticism*. Sheffield: Sheffield Academic Press.

—1999a. *Knockin' on Heaven's Door*. London and New York: Routledge.

—1999b. "David Is a Thing." In Fiona C. Black, Roland Boer and Erin Runions, eds, *The Labour of Reading: Desire, Alienation, and Biblical Interpretation*: 163-76. Atlanta, GA: Society of Biblical Literature.

—2002. "Non-Sense: *Total Recall*, Paul, and the Possibility of Psychosis." In George Aichele and Richard Walsh, eds, *Screening Scripture: Intertextual Connections between Scripture and Film*: 120-54. Harrisburg, PA: Trinity Press.

Boulous Walker, M. 1993. "The Aesthetics of Detail." In Wayne Hudsen, ed., *Aesthetics after Historicism*: 79-91 Brisbane, QLD: IMA.

—1998. *Philosophy and the Maternal Body: Reading Silence*. London: Routledge.

Braidotti, R. 1989. "The Politics of Ontological Difference." In Teresa Brennan, ed., *Between Feminism and Psychoanalysis*: 89-105. London: Routledge.

Braun, R. 1979. "Chronicles, Ezra and Nehemiah: Theology and Literary History." In J. A. Emerton, ed., *Studies in the Historical Books of the Old Testament*: 52-64. VTSup, 30; Leiden: E. J. Brill.

—1997. "1 Chronicles 1–9 and the Reconstruction of the History of Israel: Thoughts on the Use of Genealogical Data in Chronicles in the Reconstruction of the History of Israel." In Graham, Hoglund and McKenzie, eds, *Chronicler as Historian*: 92-105.

Braun, R. L. 1986. *1 Chronicles*. WBC, 14; Waco, TX: World Books.

Brenner, A., and C. Fontaine, eds. 1997. *A Feminist Companion to Reading the Bible: Approaches, Methods, and Strategies*. Sheffield: Sheffield Academic Press.

Bronner, L. L. 1999. "The Invisible Relationship Made Visible: Biblical Mothers and Daughters." In A. Brenner, ed., *Ruth and Esther*: 172-91. A Feminist Companion to the Bible, 2nd Series; Sheffield, Sheffield Academic Press.

Brooks, P. 1984. *Reading for the Plot: Design and Intention in Narrative*. Oxford: Clarendon Press.

Burke, C. 1981. "Irigaray through the Looking Glass." *Feminist Studies* 7(2): 288-306.

Burke, C., N. Schor, and M. Whitford, eds. 1994. *Engaging with Irigaray: Feminist Philosophy and Modern European Thought*. New York: Columbia University Press.

Camp, C. V. 2000. *Wise, Strange and Holy: The Strange Woman and the Making of the Bible*. JSOTSup, 320; Sheffield: Sheffield Academic Press.

Chanter, T. 1995. *Ethics of Eros: Irigaray's Re-writing of the Philosophers*. London and New York: Routledge.

Chisholm, D. 1994. "Irigaray's Hysteria." In Burke, Schor and Whitford, eds, *Engaging with Irigaray: Feminist Philosophy and Modern European Thought*: 263-83.

Coggins, R. J. 1976. *The First and Second Books of Chronicles*. Cambridge: Cambridge University Press.

Copjec, J. 1989. "The Orthopsychic Subject: Film Theory and the Reception of Lacan." *October* 49: 53-71.

—1994. *Read my Desire: Lacan Against the Historicists*. Cambridge, MA: MIT Press.

Curtis, E. L., and A. A. Madsen. 1910. *A Critical and Exegetical Commentary on the Book of Chronicles*. Edinburgh: T&T Clark.

Darwin, C. 1871. *The Descent of Man*. 2 vols.; London.

Derrida, J. 1982. *Margins of Philosophy*. Trans. Alan Bass. Brighton, Sussex: The Harvester Press.

Deutsche, P. 2002. *A Politics of Impossible Difference: The Later Works of Luce Irigaray*. Ithaca, NY: Cornell University Press.

De Vries, S. J. 1986. "The Forms of Prophetic Address in Chronicles." *Hebrew Annual Review* 10:15-36.

—1989. *1 and 2 Chronicles*. Forms of the Old Testament Literature. Grand Rapids, MI: Eerdmans.

Dillard, R. B. 1987. *2 Chronicles*. WBC, 15; Waco, TX: World Books.

Douglas, M. 1966. *Purity and Danger: An Analysis of Concepts of Pollution and Taboo*. London: Routledge and Kegan Paul.

—1993. *In the Wilderness: The Doctrine of Defilement in the Book of Numbers*. JSOTSup, 158; Sheffield: Sheffield Academic Press.

Duke, R. 1999. "A Rhetorical Approach to Appreciating the Books of Chronicles." In Graham and McKenzie, eds, *Chronicler as Author*: 100-35.

Dyck, J. 1998. *The Theocratic Ideology of the Chronicler*. Leiden; Boston: E. J. Brill.

Eagleton, T. 1983. *Literary Theory: An Introduction*. Minneapolis, MN: University of Minnesota Press.

Eisemann, M. 1987. *Divrei HayamimI/I Chronicles: A New Translation with a Commentary Anthologized from Talmudic, Midrashic and Rabbinic Sources.* Ed. Y. Danziger. New York: Mesorah Publications.

—1992. *Divrei HayamimII/II Chronicles: A New Translation with a Commentary Anthologized from Talmudic, Midrashic and Rabbinic Sources.* New York: Mesorah Publications.

Eskenazi, T. C. 1988. *In an Age of Prose: A Literary Approach to Ezra–Nehemiah.* Atlanta, GA: Scholars Press.

Ewald, H. 1867. *History of Israel.* Trans. R. Martineau; London: Longmans & Green.

Fauré, C. 1981. "The Twilight of the Goddesses, or the Intellectual Crisis of French Feminism." *Signs* 7(1) (Autumn): 81-86.

Felman, S. 1977. "To Open the Question." *Yale French Studies* 55/56: 5-10.

—1982. *Literature and Psychoanalysis. The Question of Reading: Otherwise.* Baltimore: The Johns Hopkins University Press.

—1987. *Jacques Lacan and the Adventure of Insight: Psychoanalysis in Contemporary Culture.* Cambridge, MA: Harvard University Press.

Freud, S. 1905. *Three Essays on the Theory of Sexuality. The Standard Edition of the Complete Psychological Works of Sigmund Freud.* SE, vol. 7. Ed. and trans. James Strachey. London: Hogarth.

—1911. "Formulations of Two Principles of Mental Functioning." SE, vol. 12.

—1913. *Totem and Taboo.* SE, vol. 13.

—1914. "On Narcissism: an Introduction." SE, vol. 14.

—1917a. "Mourning and Melancholia." SE, vol. 14.

—1917b. "On Transformations of Instinct as Exemplified in Anal Erotism." SE, vol. 17.

—1921. *Group Psychology and the Analysis of the Ego.* SE, vol. 18.

—1923. "The Infantile Genital Organisation. An Interpolation into the Theory of Sexuality." SE, vol. 19.

—1924. "Dissolution of the Oedipus Complex." SE, vol. 19.

—1928a. "Dostoevsky and Patricide." SE, vol. 21.

—1928b. *The Future of an Illusion.* SE, vol. 21.

—1930. *Civilization and Its Discontents.* SE, vol. 21.

—1931. "Female Sexuality." SE, vol. 21.

—1932a. "Femininity." SE, vol. 22.

—1932b. "Anxiety and Instinctual Life." SE, vol. 22.

—1939. *Moses and Monotheism.* SE, vol. 23.

Fuss, D. 1989. *Essentially Speaking: Feminism, Nature and Difference.* New York: Routledge.

Gallop, J. 1981. "Phallus/Penis: Same Difference." In Janet Todd, ed., *Men by Women*: 243-51. New York: Holmes & Meier. Reprinted in Gallop, 1988.

—1982. *Feminism and Psychoanalysis: The Daughter's Seduction.* London: Macmillan.

—1983. "Quand nos lèvres s'écrivent: Irigaray's Body Politic." *Romanic Review* 74:1 (January): 77-83.

—1985. *Reading Lacan.* Ithaca and London: Cornell University Press.

—1988. *Thinking through the Body.* New York: Columbia University Press.

Gatens, M. 1991. *Feminism and Philosophy: Perspectives on Difference and Equality.* Cambridge: Polity Press.

Gibson, M. 2001. "Guiltless Credit and the Moral Economy of Salvation." *Journal of Social and Political Thought.* Online edn 1(3: 1-19; http://yorku.ca/jspot/3/mgibson.htm).

Graham, M. P., K. G. Hoglund, and S. L. McKenzie. eds. 1997. *The Chronicler as Historian.* JSOTSup, 238; Sheffield: Sheffield Academic Press.

Graham, M. P., and S. L. McKenzie. 1999. *The Chronicler as Author: Studies in Text and Texture.* JSOTSup, 263; Sheffield: Sheffield Academic Press.

Gross, E. 1986. *Irigaray and the Divine*. Sydney: Local Consumption.

Grosz, E. 1986. "What is Feminist Theory?'" In Carol Pateman and Elizabeth Grosz, eds, *Feminist Challenges: Social and Political Theory*: 190-204. Sydney: Allen & Unwin.

—1989. *Sexual Subversions: Three French Feminists*. St Leonards, NSW: Allen & Unwin.

—1990. *Jacques Lacan: A Feminist Introduction*. Sydney: Allen & Unwin.

—1995. *Space, Time, and Perversion: The Politics of Bodies*. St Leonards, NSW: Allen & Unwin.

Haigh, S. 1994. "Between Irigaray and Cardinal: Reinventing Maternal Genealogies." *The Modern Language Review* 89(1): 61-70.

Halperin, D. 1993. *Seeking Ezekiel: Text and Psychology*. University Park, PA: Pennsylvania University Press.

Hass, M. 2000. "The Style of the Speaking Subject: Irigaray's Empirical Studies of Language Production." *Hypatia* 15(1): 64-89.

Hirsch, M. 1989. *The Mother/Daughter Plot: Narrative, Psychoanalysis, Feminism*. Bloomington, IN: Indiana University Press.

Hirsh, E. 1994. "Back in Analysis: How to Do Things with Irigaray." In Burke, Schor and Whitford, eds, *Engaging with Irigaray*: 285-315.

Hodge, J. 1994. "Irigaray Reading Heidegger." In Burke, Schor, Whitford, eds, *Engaging with Irigaray*: 191-209.

Hogan, J. 1990. *The Politics of Interpretation*. New York: Oxford University Press.

Irigaray, L. 1977. "Women's Exile." Trans. Couze Venn. *Ideology and Consciousness* 1: 62-76.

—1985a. *Speculum of the Other Woman*. Trans. Gillian C. Gill. Ithaca, NY: Cornell University Press.

—1985b. *This Sex Which Is Not One*. Trans. Catherine Porter. Ithaca, NY: Cornell University Press.

—1991a. "Women-Mothers, the Silent Substratum of the Social Order." Trans. David Macey. In Whitford, ed., *Irigaray Reader*: 47-52.

—1991b. *Marine Lover of Friedrich Nietzsche*. Trans. Gillian C. Gill. New York: Columbia University Press.

—1991c. "Questions to Emmanuel Levinas." Trans. Margaret Whitford. In Whitford, ed., *Irigaray Reader*: 178-89.

—1991d. "The Bodily Encounter with the Mother." Trans. David Macey. In Whitford, ed., *Irigaray Reader*: 34-46.

—1992. *Elemental Passions*. Trans. Joanne Collie and Judith Still. New York: Routledge.

—1993a. *Sexes and Genealogies*. Trans. Gillian C. Gill. New York: Columbia University Press.

—1993b. *An Ethics of Sexual Difference*. Trans. Carolyn Burke and Gillian C. Gill. Ithaca, NY: Cornell University Press.

—1993c. *je, tu, nous: Toward a Culture of Difference*. Trans. Alison Martin. New York: Routledge.

—1994. *Thinking the Difference: For a Peaceful Revolution*. Trans. Karin Mouton. London: Athlone Press.

—1997. "Equal to Whom?" Trans. Robert L. Mazzola. In Graham Ward, ed., *The Postmodern God: A Theological Reader*: 198-213. Oxford: Blackwell.

—1999. *The Forgetting of Air in Martin Heidegger*. Trans. Mary Beth Mader. Austin, TX: University of Texas Press.

—2000a. *To Be Two*. Trans. Monique M. Rhodes and Marco F. Cocito-Monoc. London: Athlone Press.

—2000b. *Why Different? A Culture of Two Subjects. Interviews with Luce Irigaray*. Eds. Luce Irigaray and Sylvère Lotringer; trans. Camille Collins. New York: Semiotexte.

—2002a. *To Speak Is Never Neutral*. Trans. Gail Schwab. New York: Routledge.

—2002b. *The Way of Love*. Trans. Heidi Bostic and Stephen Pluháček. London and New York: Continuum.

Jantzen, G. M. 1997. "Luce Irigaray. b. 1930: Introduction." In Graham Ward, ed., *The Postmodern God: A Theological Reader*: 191-97. Oxford: Blackwell.

Japhet, S. 1979. "Conquest and Settlement in Chronicles." *JBL* 98: 205-18.

—1993. *I & II Chronicles: A Commentary*. London: SCM Press.

—1997. *The Ideology of the Book of Chronicles and its Place in Biblical Thought*. BEATAJ, 9; Bern: Peter Lang.

Jay, N. 1981. "Gender and Dichotomy." *Feminist Studies* 7(1): 38-56.

Jobling, D. 1997. "Transference and Tact in Biblical Studies." In Timothy K. Beal and David M. Gunn, eds, *Reading Bibles, Writing Bodies*: 208-18. Biblical Limits; London and New York: Routledge.

—1998. *1 Samuel*. Berit Olam: Studies in Hebrew Narrative and Poetry. Collegeville, MN: The Liturgical Press.

Jobling, D., T. Pippin, and R. Schleifer, eds. 2001. *The Postmodern Bible Reader*. Oxford: Blackwell.

Johnson, M. D. 1969. *The Purpose of Biblical Genealogies with Special Reference to the Setting of the Genealogy of Jesus*. SNTSMS, 8; New York: Cambridge University Press.

Joy, M., K. O'Grady, J. L. Poxon, eds. 2002. *French Feminists on Religion: A Reader*. London and New York: Routledge.

—2003. *Religion in French Feminist Thought: Critical Perspectives*. London and New York: Routledge.

Kelso, J. 2002. "Gazing at Impotence in Henry King's *David and Bathsheba*." In George Aichele and Richard Walsh, eds, *Screening Scripture: Intertextual Connections Between Scripture and Film*: 155-87. Harrisburg, PA: Trinity Press.

—2003. "Reading the Silence of Women in Genesis 34." In Roland Boer and Edgar W. Conrad, eds, *Redirected Travel: Alternative Journeys and Places in Biblical Studies*: 85-109. JSOTSup, 382; London and New York: T&T Clark.

—2004. "Athaliah to Elijah the Tishbite." In Philip R. Davies, ed., *Yours Faithfully: Virtual Letters from the Bible*: 85-88. London: Equinox.

Kirkham Hawkins, F. 2000. "Irigaray." In Adam, ed., *Handbook of Postmodern Biblical Interpretation*: 131-37.

Köhler, W. 1951. *The Mentality of Apes*. London: Routledge and Kegan Paul.

Kristeva, J. 1982. *Powers of Horror: An Essay on Abjection*. Trans. Leon S. Roudiez. New York: Columbia University Press.

—1984. *The Revolution in Poetic Language*. Trans. Margaret Waller. New York: Columbia University Press.

—1989. *Black Sun: Depression and Melancholia*. Trans. Leon S. Roudiez. New York: Columbia University Press.

Labahn, A., and E. Ben Zvi. 2003. "Observations on Women in the Genealogies of 1 Chronicles 1–9." *Biblica* 84 (2003): 457-78.

Lacan, J. 1977. *Écrits: A Selection*. Trans. Alan Sheridan. London: Routledge.

—1991. *The Seminar of Jacques Lacan. Book One: Freud's Papers on Technique 1953–1954*. Ed. Jacques-Alain Miller; trans. John Forrester. New York: Norton.

—1998. *The Four Fundamental Concepts of Psycho-analysis*. Ed. Jacques-Alain Miller; trans. Alan Sheridan. London: Vintage.

—1999. *On Feminine Sexuality: The Limits of Love and Knowledge, Book XX, Encore 1972–1973*. Ed. and trans. Bruce Fink. New York: Norton.

Laffey, A. 1992. "I and II Chronicles." In Carol A. Newsom and Sharon H. Ringe, eds, *The Women's Bible Commentary*: 110-15. London: SPCK.

Le Doeuff, M. 1989. *The Philosophical Imaginary*. Trans. Colin Gordon. Stanford: Stanford University Press.

McKay, H. A. 1997. "On the Future of Feminist Biblical Criticism." In Brenner and Fontaine, eds, *Feminist Companion to Reading the Bible*: 61-83.

Milne, P. J. 1997. "Toward Feminist Companionship: The Future of Feminist Biblical Studies and Feminism." In Brenner and Fontaine, eds, *Feminist Companion to Reading the Bible*: 39-60.

Mitchell, C. 1999. "The Dialogism of Chronicles." In Graham and McKenzie, eds, *Chronicler as Author*: 311-26.

Mitchell, J. 1974. *Psychoanalysis and Feminism*. London: Allen Lane.

Moi, T. 1985. *Sexual/Textual Politics: Feminist Literary Theory*. London; New York: Methuen.

—1999. *What Is a Woman? And Other Essays*. Oxford: Oxford University Press.

Moore, S. D. 1992. *Mark and Luke in Poststructuralist Perspectives: Jesus Begins to Write*. New Haven, CT: Yale University Press.

Moore, B. E., and B. D. Fine. 1990. *Psychoanalytic Terms and Concepts*. New Haven, CT: Yale University Press.

Muraro, L. 1994. "Female Genealogies." In Burke, Schor and Whitford, eds, *Engaging with Irigaray*: 317-33.

Myers, J. M. 1965. *II Chronicles*. Anchor Bible; New York: Doubleday.

Nielsen, K. 1999. "Whose Song of Praise? Reflections on the Purpose of the Psalm in 1 Chronicles 16." In Graham and McKenzie, eds, *Chronicler as Author*: 327-36.

Noth, M. 1987. *The Chronicler's History*. Trans. H. G. M. Williamson. JSOTSup, 50; Sheffield: Sheffield Academic Press.

Nussbaum, M. 1986. *The Fragility of Goodness: Luck and Ethics in Greek Tragedy and Philosophy*. Cambridge: Cambridge University Press.

Ostriker, A. S. 1997. "A Triple Hermeneutic: Scripture and Revisionist Women's Poetry." In Brenner and Fontaine, eds, *Feminist Companion to Reading the Bible*: 164-89.

Plato. 1974. *The Republic*. Trans. Desmond Lee; Harmondsworth, Middlesex: Penguin Books.

Plaza, M. 1978. " 'Phallomorphic Power' and the Psychology of 'Woman': A Patriarchal Vicious Circle." *Ideology and Consciousness* 4(8): 4-36.

Ragland-Sullivan, E. 1992. "The Imaginary," and "Lacan, Jacques." In E. Wright, ed., *Feminism and Psychoanalysis: A Critical Dictionary*: 173-76, 201-207. Oxford: Blackwell

Rashkow, I. 1993. *The Phallacy of Genesis: A Feminist Psychoanalytic Approach*. Louisville, KY: Westminster/John Knox Press.

—1998. "A Feminist Reading of Genesis 19.1-11." In Athalya Brenner, ed., *Genesis*: 82-107. Feminist Companion to the Bible, 2.1; Sheffield: Sheffield Academic Press.

—2000. *Taboo or Not Taboo: Sexuality and Family in the Hebrew Bible*. Minneapolis, MN: Fortress Press.

Reinhartz, A. 1997. "Feminist Criticism and Biblical Studies on the Verge of the Twenty-First Century." In Brenner and Fontaine, eds, *Feminist Companion to Reading the Bible*: 30-38.

Sandford, J. 1985. *King Saul, the Tragic Hero: A Study in Individualism*. New York and Mahwah, NJ: Paulist Press.

Schor, N. 1994. "Previous Engagements: The Receptions of Irigaray." In Burke, Schor, Whitford, eds, *Engaging with Irigaray*: 3-14.

Sherwood, Y. 1996. *The Prostitute and the Prophet: Hosea's Marriage in Literary-Theoretical Perspective*. JSOTSup, 12; Sheffield: Sheffield Academic Press.

Siedlecki, A. 1999. "Foreigners, Warfare and Judahite Identity in Chronicles." In Graham and McKenzie, eds, *Chronicler as Author*: 229-66.

Slotki, I. W. 1952. *Chronicles*. London: Soncino Press.

Smith, W. Robertson. 1894. *Lectures on the Religion of the Semites*. London, 2nd edn.

Spivak, Gayatri Chakravorty. 1988. *In Other Worlds: Essays in Cultural Politics*. New York: Routledge.

Stockton, K. B. 1994. *God between their Lips: Desire between Women in Irigaray, Brontë, and Eliot*. Stanford, CA: Stanford University Press.

Torrey, C. C. 1970. "The Chronicler as Editor and Independent Narrator." In *idem, Ezra Studies*: 208-51. New York: reprint edition, Ktav.

Vasseleu, C. 1998. *Textures of Light: Vision and Touch in Irigaray, Levinas and Merleau-Ponty*. London: Routledge.

Ward, G. 1996. "Divinity and Sexuality: Luce Irigaray and Christology." *Modern Theology* 12(2): 221-37.

Welch, A. C. 1939. *The Work of the Chronicler: Its Purpose and Date*. London: British Academy.

Wellhausen, J. 1973. *Prolegomena to the History of Israel*. Gloucester, MA: Peter Smith.

Whitelam, K. W. 1989. "Israel's Traditions of Origin: Reclaiming the Land." *Journal for the Study of the Old Testament* 44: 19-42.

Whitford, M. 1986. "Luce Irigaray and the Female Imaginary: Speaking as a Woman." *Radical Philosophy* 43 (Summer): 3-8.

—1990. *Luce Irigaray: Philosophy in the Feminine*. London: Routledge.

—1994. "Irigaray, Utopia, and the Death Drive." In Burke, Schor and Whitford, eds, *Engaging with Irigaray*: 379-400.

Whitford, M., ed. 1991. *The Irigaray Reader*. Oxford: Blackwell.

Williamson, H. G. M. 1977. *Israel in the Books of Chronicles*. Cambridge: Cambridge University Press.

—1982. *1 & 2 Chronicles*. New Century Bible Commentary; Grand Rapids, MI: Eerdmans.

Wright, J. W. 1997. "The Fight for Peace: Narrative and History in the Battle Accounts in Chronicles." In Graham, Hoglund, McKenzie, eds, *Chronicler as Historian*: 150-77.

Zeligs, D. F. 1988. *Psychoanalysis and the Bible: A Study in Depth of Seven Leaders*. New York: Human Sciences Press.

Žižek, S. 1989. *The Sublime Object of Ideology*. London: Verso.

—1997. *The Plague of Fantasies*. London and New York: Verso.

—2000. *The Fragile Absolute – or, Why Is the Christian Legacy Worth Fighting For?* London and New York: Verso.

Indexes

Index of References

Old Testament

INDEX OF AUTHORS

Printed in the United Kingdom
by Lightning Source UK Ltd.
126944UK00001B/151-162/P